No. 2816
$21.95

SUNSPACES

Home Additions For Year~Round Natural Living

By JOHN H. MAULDIN

Photography by JOHN H. MAULDIN and JUAN L. ESPINOSA

TAB TAB BOOKS Inc.

Blue Ridge Summit, PA 17214

LIST OF TRADEMARKS

Beadwall	Zomeworks Corp.
Exolite	CYRO Industries
Filon	Vistron Corp.
Flexigard	3M Co.
Heat Mirror	Southwest Technologies
Heat Motor	Heat Motors Inc.
Insulider	Jaksha Energy Systems Inc.
Lascolite and Crystalite	Lasco Industries
Lexan	General Electric Corp.
Mylar®, Tedlar®, and Teflon®	E.I. Du Pont de Nemours & Co.
Plexiglas	Rohm & Hass Co.
SolarVent	Dalen Products Inc.
Styrofoam®	Dow Chemical USA
Sun-Lite	Kalwall Corp.
Thermax	Celotex Corp.
Velcro®	American Velcro Inc.
Visqueeen	Ethyl Film Products
Window Quilt	Appropriate Technology Corp.

FIRST EDITION
FIRST PRINTING

Copyright © 1987 by John H. Mauldin

Printed in the United States of America

Library of Congress Cataloging in Publication Data

Mauldin, John H.
    Sunspaces : home additions for year-round natural living / John H.
Mauldin ; photography by John H. Mauldin and Juan L. Espinosa.
        p.   cm.
    Bibliography: p.
    Includes index.
    ISBN 0-8306-7816-6 : ISBN 0-8306-2816-9 (pbk.) :
    1. Sunspaces—Design and construction. I. Title.
TH3000.S85M38   1987
643'.55—dc19   87-21913
                                                    CIP

Questions regarding the content of this book should be addressed to:

    Reader Inquiry Branch
    Editorial Department
    TAB BOOKS Inc.
    P.O. Box 40
    Blue Ridge Summit, PA 17214

Edited by Suzanne L. Cheatle   Designed by Jaclyn Saunders   Front and rear cover photographs courtesy of Janco Greenhouses.

CONTENTS

Acknowledgments

SPECIAL APPRECIATION IS DUE Juan Espinosa of Pueblo, Colorado, for much of the photographic work for this book and for many instances of collaboration on the theory and practice of sunspaces/greenhouses.

Appreciation is expressed to the Pueblo Energy Resource Center for its library of information on sunspaces and for the chance to participate in various ways in solar/energy conservation services to the public, to Erwin Young of Alamosa, Colorado, for sharing much practical experience with sunspaces and many nice pictures, to Clint Tawse of Pueblo for providing observations in regard to building construction and building inspection, to Tom Standish for sharing his results with low-cost public-assistance sunspaces, to Robert Cain of the University of Southern Colorado library for assistance in obtaining maps, to Lloyd Romero of Viva Enterprises of Pueblo, Colorado, for some technical production work, to Kim Tabor from TAB BOOKS for instigating this project, and to the many sunspace owners who cooperated in the photography of their sunspaces. Many exciting sunspaces were visited and many ingenious ideas photographed that could not be included in the very difficult final picture selections.

Appreciation is expressed to the American Society of Heating, Refrigerating, and Air-Conditioning Engineers (ASHRAE), 1791 Tullie Circle NE, Atlanta, GA 30329, for permission to adapt and reprint solar radiation table data.

Appreciation is expressed to the National Center for Appropriate Technology, P.O. Box 3838, Butte, MT 59701, for their tireless public efforts on behalf of sunspaces and for permission to reprint solar charts.

Appreciation is expressed to the following companies for supplying photographs, slides, and explanatory literature for their sunspace products:

APPROPRIATE TECHNOLOGY CORP.
P.O. Box 975, Brattleboro, VT 05301

BETTER PRODUCTS INC.
P.O. Box 1052, Alamosa, CO 81101

CREATIVE STRUCTURES INC.
RD 1 Box 173, Quakertown, PA 18951

JAKSHA ENERGY SYSTEMS INC.
1900 Broadway NE, Albuquerque, NM 87102

JANCO GREENHOUSES
9390 Davis Ave., Laurel, MD 20707

SOLAR RESOURCES INC.
P.O. Box 1848, Taos, NM 87571

STURDI-BUILT MFR. CO.
11304 SW Boones Ferry Rd, Portland, OR 97219

SUNPLACE, INC.
6601 Amberton Dr., Rte. 100 Industrial Pk.
Baltimore, MD 21227

SUN ROOM CO.
P.O. Box 301, Leola, PA 17540

VEGETABLE FACTORY INC.
71 Vanderbilt Ave., New York, NY 10169

This book is an expansion of a booklet on sunspaces prepared for the Pueblo Energy Resource Center.

Introduction

THE SUNSPACE OR GREENHOUSE—a room with large south-facing windows—is now one of the most popular features on new houses and is being added to many existing homes. Its popularity comes from its versatility in adding living space, obtaining "free" heat and light from the sun, and providing a new place for recreation. Experience in many climates with various methods of solar heating has shown that the sunspace or solar greenhouse is especially advantageous because of its efficiency coupled with low cost. Although a sunspace can be added to almost any type of building regardless of size, the discussion in this book is limited to residential applications for single- and some multiple-family dwellings.

Sunspaces must be distinguished from greenhouses. The difference is mainly a matter of intended use, but there are differences in design also. The sunspace is intended for obtaining heat, for providing working or recreational space, or for other imaginative uses. The greenhouse is intended for horticulture, which is the growing of plants, whether ornamental, food-bearing, or early-starting. This book assumes that a generally useful sunspace is the reader's principal interest, and occasional reference is made to special aspects of greenhouses. More distinctions between the two are given in later discussions. The term *sunspace* will be used as a general reference for a sunspace or greenhouse unless the discussion is specific to greenhouses. Other terms in common use are *solarium, sunroom, sunporch,* and sometimes *conservatory* or *hothouse.* These terms do not seem to refer as clearly to the wide variety of sunspace uses. Some manufacturers' and builders' literature will not distinguish the types of uses, but this book will show that the uses must be kept in mind.

In addition to describing the features and principles of a sunspace, this book can help you in several practical ways. First, this book describes the possible uses of a sunspace so that you can decide which are most important to your interests and needs. This discussion is useful whether you are adding a sunspace to an existing house or planning a sunspace as part of a new house. Then sunspace principles are covered fully, at a technical level accessible to all. A separate chapter shows in detail how the principles are used to design a real sunspace. Although it is difficult to specify one particular design to serve most purposes and climates, for simplicity a simple generic design is shown in most illustrations. The book emphasizes economical sunspaces and provides information gleaned from practical experience with sunspaces. Some common myths about the use of the sun are dispelled, and some potential mistakes are discussed.

Whether you are planning to build or to buy a sunspace, this book can be helpful. Designing, and possibly building, your own sunspace might at first seem feasible, or it might seem too difficult. You should be aware of options and choices in special materials and assembly methods in order to make wise financial decisions and to obtain a sunspace with long life, reliability, and low maintenance. Being acquainted with how sunspaces are built will aid you in properly maintaining them. It is quite feasible for any homeowner with some skills at construction to do the entire sunspace project—or major parts of it—at substantial savings. This book provides guidance in skills with which you might be unfamiliar but that you will need.

If a sunspace is to be custom-built, there are three general approaches. You can build it personally; you can function as a contractor and supervise work by others; or you can hire a general contractor to execute the plans of the owner or designer. Particularly in the last case, you must know much about sunspaces in case it is difficult to find a contractor familiar with them. The lowest cost for the sunspace will occur if you do all the work. This book provides many of the construction details for several general ways of constructing sunspace structures. Discussion of building codes is also given.

If you do not wish to become involved in the details of design and construction, then three general options remain: you can hire a contractor to install a prepackaged factory-assembled unit; you can hire a contractor to assemble and install a commercial kit; or you can hire a contractor or architect to design a sunspace to your general requirements and supervise its construction. These options, particularly the last, will cost more. This book provides information on choosing and working with companies and contractors, including many practical hints relevant to sunspace construction. Ultimately, responsibility for the sunspace—its appearance, quality, durability, operation, and maintenance—must rest with you, the owner. There is no substitute for having some degree of practical and theoretical knowledge about the sunspace. You should read as much of this book as possible before making any financial or design decisions.

To further aid you, many special topics about sunspaces are provided. They include safety and environmental aspects, problematical sites, auxiliary heating, hot tubs, and legal aspects. Photographs of a wide variety of sunspaces are provided to inspire you as to the possibilities. Some manufacturers' products are shown, but it is impossible to maintain a current list of all manufacturers and to give accurate specifications and pricing. Addresses of some manufacturers are listed in the Acknowledgments. Brand names of products are used occasionally and as examples only, with no implication that such brands are recommended or that omitted brands of similar products might be inferior.

Throughout the book reference is made to other sources for special details and information. When such a reference is made, for example, *see Alward, in the Book Section of the References*, you can find the complete reference to that work in the specified section of the References. Some specialized tables of information are provided in the text where needed. Other maps and tables of general utility are referred to in the Appendix. Any of the information and methods provided might require judicious modification and adaptation to special local conditions and requirements, even if such guidance is not given in this book.

PRELIMINARY DECISIONS

cAS ITS NAME IMPLIES, a sunspace has much to do with the sun. It is an enclosed, sheltered space with ready access to the sun in most or all seasons. Sunlight enters through transparent material called *glazing*, which can be glass or plastic. In our era of generally rising energy prices, obtaining some heat from the sun has become economical and fashionable. Many old solar-heating methods have been revived, and some new ones invented. Solar water-heating systems have remained relatively expensive and involve some dedication to complex plumbing and its maintenance. Water heating, unless done on a large scale, does not get at the heart of the homeowner's energy bills: money spent for space heat. Solar space-heating systems using collectors based on air or water have also proven to be expensive and technically demanding. Although more heat is provided and payback time can be attractively short, a space-heating system installed all over the roof or backyard has not caught the interest of many homeowners.

Even when energy prices are temporarily steady and governmental support of solar systems has diminished, one solar-based product has moved ahead in the market at an increasing rate: the sunspace. The reasons are many. Sunspaces can be made very attractive, with the diligent owner/builder having as good a chance at achieving a beautiful home addition as any manufacturer could. The sunspace can be installed almost anywhere, as long as access to the sun is considered. Sunspaces have been obtained by adding a room, by converting an old enclosed porch, by adding windows to a room, and sometimes by building a separate structure.

The sunspace has been used for working and playing, for incorporating a hot tub or small swimming pool, for growing plants (within limitations), or just for collecting heat. Balanced ecologies have been established in greenhouses combining plants and large fish tanks. Solar energy can be converted to vegetables and food for edible fish while the water tanks moderate heat flow. The light in the sunspace is desirable even when the sun is not shining, giving a feeling of being outdoors while protected from wind, rain, insects, and other vagaries. You might have something new in mind.

There are a few activities that would not work well in sunspaces: for example, displaying or storing materials that would be injured by sunlight or heat (fine furniture, fine arts, photographs, food), getting a good tan (the ultraviolet rays do not penetrate most glazings), or cooking on an open fire (without extremely good ventilation). It also would not be wise to locate the deep-freeze or air conditioner there.

The cost for space and heat can be very reasonable if you have a sunspace. Using general estimates, the structural costs can range between $10 and $50 per square foot (applicable either to floor area or to glazing area). Each square foot of glazing can collect about 200,000 Btus per heating season. This amount of heat costs (as gas or electricity) between $2 and $5. Depending on location and utilities available, the sunspace could pay for itself in as little as 2 years. Elaborate manufactured units might payback in 20 years or more.

At its simplest, the sunspace is a passive solar heater. A beautiful and functional structure replaces solar collectors strewn on stilts across the roof or hanging on the walls of the house. More effectiveness is obtained at a small cost in complexity if active heat storage and transport is used to bring the heat to the house. The sunspace also provides its own place for heat storage.

Some amount of heat storage is easy, almost inevitable. Substantial storage would be needed if the sunspace is to contribute to heating the house at night. The floor of the sunspace could provide storage, or it could be built under the floor or in the walls. When the stored heat is used, it is transported in the form of hot air. Duct and fan arrangements for storage and home heating are particularly simple to set up when a sunspace is the heat collector. If much hot water is needed for the home, hot tub, or pool, the sunspace can be the best way to heat it, too.

You might wonder why you should add a sunspace? Why not just install many big windows on the south side of the house? The partial answer is that, if enough windows are added to gain a useful amount of heat, then there will be substantial overheating in that room during much of the year. The add-on sunspace permits the use of doors and insulation to isolate the sunspace from the house. Letting the sunspace become too hot in daytime (and too cold at night) rather than having these fluctuations in the house is called *buffering*. The sunspace moderates, or buffers, the heat flow from sun to house. Another answer is that it could be more costly to tear apart the walls of the existing house than to add the sunspace. Walls are not simply a place to have windows; they hold up the next floor (if any) and the roof, and they might carry plumbing and wiring.

Although it might seem that the utilization of solar energy in sunspaces is relatively recent, greenhouses glazed with glass have been in use since glass was invented. Before that, early builders arranged stone or adobe buildings to best capture winter sunlight and reject summer heat. The art of using the sun for dwellings seems to have been neglected in recent centuries, however. Porches are common on older houses, but sunporches, sunrooms, and solariums are very rare, regardless of climate or age of house. The ideal might be to integrate the sunspace with the house at the time the house is designed and constructed, but current homeowners must consider "retrofitting" the sunspace to the house.

SUNSPACE vs. GREENHOUSE

One of the most basic choices facing the sunspace owner or builder is whether the sunspace will be used for growing large numbers of plants or for other activities, such as recreation. The two types of uses are somewhat incompatible, and it is very difficult to design a sunspace to fit all possible uses. Probably you already know the general use you want, but you should review the relevant considerations of heat level, light, humidity, and layout.

If you want to grow plants for food or profit on a large scale, a greenhouse is indicated. Small numbers of ornamental plants can survive in a sunspace, provided the temperature is moderate at all times. Another question to consider is whether the plants will be permanently in the greenhouse/sunspace or will be there only in certain seasons. You could use the greenhouse to keep plants over the winter that are placed outdoors in other seasons. If it is too difficult to keep the greenhouse warm in winter, you can use it for plants only in the warmer seasons. Perhaps you will use the greenhouse as a season extender, for starting food or flowering plants for the garden outside or for sale.

Plants need light, heat, and moderately high humidity. Sunlight is inadequate for most plants in winter, particularly those used for food, so light rather than heat becomes the most important factor in greenhouse design. There are ways to augment the light level for greenhouses, most commonly with overhead glazing and reflectors. Overhead glazing usually provides too much heat for plants in greenhouses and must be vented out even in winter. In most climates, overhead glazing gives excessive heating in sunspaces also.

Another need of plants is warmth at night as well as in the daytime. A sunspace can be let to cool down, even freeze, at night, but a greenhouse needs at least 40° F, and more for most food plants. In extreme conditions, all the sun entering the greenhouse in daytime might be needed to maintain the minimum temperature, and there would be no heat to spare for other uses.

Because space is at a premium in an enclosed area, a greenhouse used for growing food is likely to be packed with plants, taking advantage of every level and location. The layout or floor plan of a greenhouse might be different from, and more carefully planned than, a sunspace. A greenhouse might work better if it is taller than a sunspace. A greenhouse could be built unattached, separate from the house, whereas it is much better to attach a sunspace to the house. Finally, using the greenhouse to grow food would require much more attention to the climate conditions in the greenhouse (heat, light, humidity, venting) than would a sunspace. Greenhouses need much daily attention, whereas a sunspace might not need any daily attention.

Commercial greenhouses continue to be built with both sides of the roof glazed, presumably for light. Many have been oriented without regard to the sun's path. Only recently has it been demonstrated that the north wall and roof should be insulated for the best overall heat gain. The *Brace design*, named for the Brace Institute in Montreal, is the first modern design of a greenhouse, developed out of necessity in the Canadian climate. In this freestanding greenhouse, which can be built to any size, the north wall is insulated and sloping, eliminating a north-facing roof (FIG. 1-1). More light is gained than in the old-style greenhouse because the north wall can reflect light toward the ground.

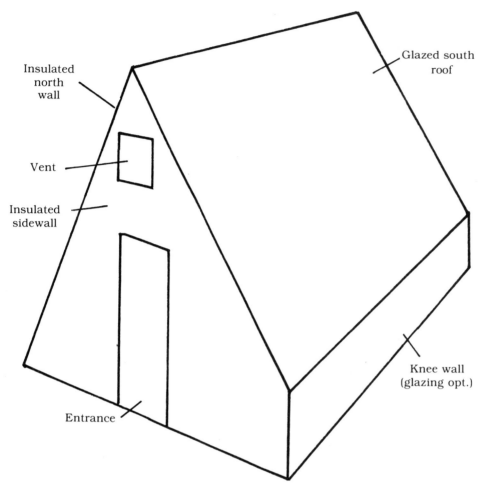

Insulated
north
wall

Glazed south
roof

Vent

Insulated
sidewall

Knee wall
(glazing opt.)

Entrance

Fig. 1-1. *The original Brace design for a free-standing greenhouse, a forerunner of contemporary sunspaces.*

If the sunspace you want to build will generally not be used for plants, you still should make some choices in regard to its use. As mentioned, it makes a difference whether a pool or tub of water is present, particularly if it is uncovered, and especially if the water is warm or hot. Then the sunspace is a high-humidity area. If the sunspace is principally to heat the home and is of small size, it could be permitted to get much hotter than people would find comfortable for relaxing or working. If the sunspace is all that you can afford at the present, but you might add equipment such as a hot tub in the future, then you must make allowances at this time for space for the hot tub, for accessibility to install plumbing and wiring, and for protection of the house from moisture.

In regard to humidity, greenhouses share high humidity in common with sunspaces used to hold hot tubs or pools. For conservation purposes and control of air quality, you should cover tubs and pools when they are not in use. Sunspaces or greenhouses with high humidity must be designed with special materials and construction to avoid moisture damage. Some uses of sunspaces might require low humidity for comfort, in conflict with the moderately high humidity needed by plants. Plants in sunspaces would have to be few, hardy, and frequently watered.

It is difficult to compare the economics of food versus energy production in a greenhouse, but generally, more monetary value would be obtained from the heat. The choice of whether to grow food or produce heat is left to you. It is not difficult to obtain substantial heat from a greenhouse, but the warm air will be humid and there will be difficulty keeping the plants wet because of the air flow. The air cannot be permitted to reach the temperatures needed for efficient heating because the planted regions might become too hot for plants.

GENERAL DESIGN DECISIONS

It is the purpose of Chapters 2 and 3 of this book to provide the basis for making design decisions and adding details of the design. This introductory section provides an overview of the process and sets the stage. Once you have decided the use of the sunspace, the factors of site, size, location, and orientation need attention. It will be assumed henceforth that you are interested in a sunspace. The parts of a simple attached sunspace are shown in FIG. 1-2.

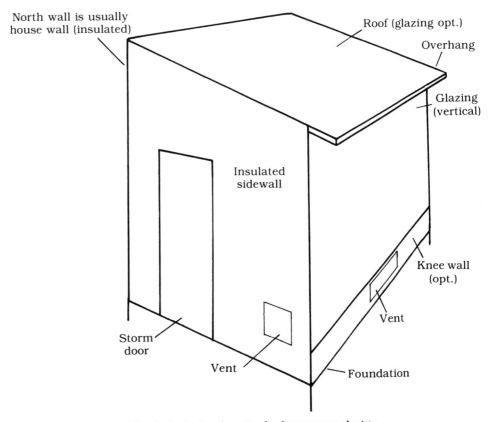

Fig. 1-2. A simple, attached sunspace design.

You must choose the size, in terms of floor area, according to planned uses, affordability, and amount of home heating desired. For efficiency, the shape of the sunspace should not be too long and narrow. For best heat retention, the floor area should be large. The height of the sunspace might be on a level with adjoining rooms of the house or increased to one and a half or two levels. The latter choice is simpler if the house is two stories high.

The orientation of the sunspace should be toward due south if at all possible. The wall that faces southward should be mostly glazed. If the sunspace cannot face due south, then a sidewall would also face partly south and might be glazed as well. Sometimes good southern exposure is prevented by the location or shape of the house, the presence of trees or a wall, or ground that slopes to the north. Ingenuity is needed to find the best place for the sunspace. Occasionally, building code restrictions or neighborhood covenants will affect the siting and size of the sunspace.

Although it is assumed that you have access and rights to the ground for sunspace placement, there is little reason why a sunspace cannot be on a flat roof, on an adjacent garage, or even on an apartment building if reinforcing can be added. Penthouses and lofts with glass roofs have been on buildings for a long time. A roof site must be capable of holding the weight of the sunspace and withstanding any added loads from wind and snow—usually not the case in residential buildings. Even if the roof can hold the weight, a useful element of a sunspace cannot be included: a massive floor to store heat. How to proceed in these unusual cases should be clear later when the strength of the sunspace itself is discussed.

Environmental factors must be considered in siting. You must know the climate of the area. This knowledge might be lacking if you have just moved to a new location. In rare cases, the local climate could be so hostile that the intended sunspace would provide only light and would cost heat to use. In most areas, however, you need only be concerned as to the amount of cloudiness in winter. The amount and direction of wind is also a factor. Since glazing cannot easily be insulated and protected while in use, you need to know if there are high, cold western winds, and provide shelter from them for the sunspace.

OBTAINING A SUNSPACE

Whether to build all parts of the sunspace yourself, to buy a kit, or to engage a contractor will be determined by your level of experience in construction and the amount of money you can spend. As a home addition, the sunspace is likely to qualify for a home improvement loan. Fortunately, the project sounds simple enough that a lender would probably accept you as the builder. The economic benefits of the heat gained for the house could be considered in applying for a loan. Engaging a contractor to build from your plans would raise the total cost to at least three times what you would pay for the materials alone. A factory-built greenhouse could cost as much as ten times what you could build it for, although manufactured ones are likely to involve materials and methods you could not incorporate yourself.

Buying a sunspace rather than building it yourself will not necessarily prevent problems from arising in regard to building code approval, incompetence of the builders or installers, or major flaws in design or materials. General contractors are usually not familiar with sunspace technologies, and a specialist must be sought.

The solar specialist should not be expensive since there are usually more people offering to do solar work than there are customers. If you are certain you cannot do all the work without commercial assistance, it might be best to locate local experts to help with selected portions. You will benefit greatly from having done at least some of the work and from having supervised all of it.

For all but the smallest, most temporary structures, a building permit is probably required. A detached structure in a casual neighborhood or distant location might not need a permit. Before you invest much time and money in planning, you should investigate the local building, zoning, and other requirements.

SOME ENERGY CONSIDERATIONS

If you live deep in the South or desert Southwest, keeping sun out of the sunspace might be your major concern most of the year, and energy collection is wanted only occasionally in winter. If you live anywhere else in the United States, however, choosing a sunspace primarily for heating purposes is a sensible approach. As with any solar installation, the lowest cost approach is to first be sure that the house is as well insulated and weathertight as possible. Even sunspaces do not compete well with caulk and insulation for energy dollars. Then consider what fraction of home heating you want the sunspace to handle. For modest sunspace designs, the payback on heating is good up until more than 80 percent of the home heating bill is eliminated. Sunspaces do not work well on cloudy days, and an extravagant amount of heat storage is needed to cover more than two days without sun.

Perhaps you need an energy audit. Using principles given later in this book, you can perform your own, obtaining results useful for sunspace design. All that you need are all energy bills (electric, gas, propane, oil, wood, etc.) for a typical year. After you calculate the total energy consumption for the heating season from these bills, you can estimate the amount of sun-collecting area that will provide 80 percent of the equivalent heat. To arrive at an appropriate size for the sunspace, consider latitude, variations in sunspace orientation, an allowance for inefficiencies, and the methods of heat storage and transport to the house. The sunspace should not be so large as to overheat the house on most winter days, nor so small as to cover less than one-tenth of your heating needs. If you are planning to grow plants using the sunspace as a greenhouse, it can still be a heat source in the daytime, but provisions must be made not to overheat the plants in day nor to permit freezing at night.

The specific climate and location have much to do with the performance of a sunspace for heating. The outside temperature in winter is not nearly so important as whether the sky is clear on most winter days. If the sun does shine throughout most days, it must not be obstructed by trees or buildings in midwinter. In northern latitudes, the sun stays rather near the horizon and a large glazing area must directly face it to collect much heat. On cloudy but cold days, a good sunspace can collect enough heat for the sunspace to be comfortable, but not enough heat to help heat the house. Further discussion and information on climate is given in Chapter 2 and the Appendix, including maps and data telling how much sun and cloudiness there is anywhere in the United States.

BASIC PRINCIPLES

THIS CHAPTER DESCRIBES, in a nontechnical manner, the basic principles involved in designing sunspaces so that the buyer or builder can choose the best form for projected needs. There is no one ideal sunspace to suit all needs and climates. Designing a sunspace from principles also cannot be done in one straight path. Some careful thought about the many factors will be needed. Studying all of the major considerations together will help to integrate the design. Once the principles are adequately understood, the designer's creativity can take over.

THE GREENHOUSE EFFECT

One of the most important principles underlying sunspace design is utilization of the *greenhouse effect*. Originally named for the concentrated heat that seems to be produced in a glass-roofed building, this term generally refers to the capture of sunlight to produce heat. Glass or other transparent glazing will let light through but keep the resulting heat in (FIG. 2-1).

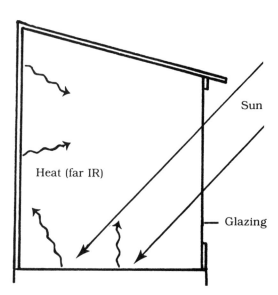

Fig. 2-1. *Capturing solar radiation in a glazed sunspace changes it to heat which cannot escape easily.*

Sun

Heat (far IR)

Glazing

The term *greenhouse effect* has been applied to the atmospheres of Earth and other planets to describe how constituents in the air prevent trapped heat from leaving, especially at night. The 800° F conditions on Venus seem to be due to its thick heat-trapping atmosphere. Scientists are concerned over Earth's average temperature rising about 5° F over the next century as carbon dioxide, methane, flourocarbons, and other natural and manmade gases accumulate in the upper atmosphere and trap heat. The evidence may show that nearly 1° of increase has occurred already. In order to understand the greenhouse effect better and make best use of it, the types of solar radiation must be described further.

The Nature of Solar Radiation

About 50 percent of the energy provided to us by the sun arrives at the ground as light rather than heat. The sun feels warm because sunlight is converted to heat as it falls on our skin and on the surfaces of most objects. The other 50 percent of the solar energy does reach us directly as heat radiation. It is called *infrared radiation*, *near IR*, or *long-wave radiation*. It is similar to the radiation from heat lamps and other hot, glowing objects. We cannot see infrared radiation with our eyes, although our sensitive retinas can feel it and can be injured by it. The hot coals in a fireplace can radiate near IR so intensely that there is discomfort first from looking at it, then from overheated skin. The "color" of infrared radiation is, as the term implies, literally "beyond red." An object need not be glowing so brightly as to have a red or orange color in order to emit infrared radiation. Everything—even objects colder than ice—emits infrared radiation, although the colder the object, the less the radiation. These are weaker forms of infrared radiation called *far IR*.

About 45 percent of solar radiation is visible light. This light is more energetic than infrared radiation, as can be seen by the fading of colored dyes in sunlight. In a greenhouse, the red and blue parts of white solar radiation are needed by plants. Otherwise, for heating a sunspace, the light should be converted to infrared radiation. The conversion readily happens wherever sunlight strikes a nonreflecting surface and is absorbed.

About 5 percent of the sun's energy reaches the ground as still more energetic radiation called *ultraviolet*, literally "beyond violet." It is abbreviated UV or called *short-wave radiation*. Ultraviolet radiation cannot be seen, but looking at a source of it could destroy the sensitive retina in a few seconds or less. A small amount of ultraviolet radiation from the sun reaches the ground after most is absorbed by the atmosphere. This amount does not represent enough energy to be considered when designing ways to capture solar energy. Glazings also absorb much of it, so ultraviolet radiation is not available for tanning in sunspaces. Ultraviolet radiation cannot be ignored in design, though, because it helps destroy most materials, including the glazing itself. A long-lasting structure must have its exterior materials selected for resistance to ultraviolet radiation.

When there is no glazing, a room still can be warmed by the sun because all illuminated surfaces in it convert sunlight to heat (FIG. 2-2). The warmed materials radiate low-grade heat (far IR) at each other and in all directions. The air itself radiates infrared radiation in proportion to its warmth. Adding the glazing (FIG. 2-1) not only traps the warmed air, but also hinders far IR from passing out the roof and wall. In most climates, a sunspace this simple has a net gain: it is warmer at night than the outdoors, provided sun shone that day and warmed its materials.

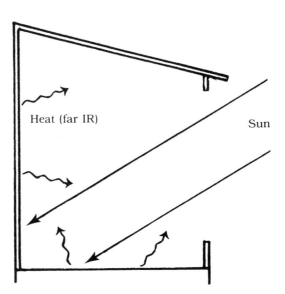

Fig. 2-2. *Without glazing a south-facing shelter captures some radiation, but allows more heat radiation and warm air to escape.*

Heat (far IR)

Sun

Capturing sunlight through clear glazing, trapping it as heat, makes use of the greenhouse effect.

The Direction of Solar Radiation

A sunspace stays in one place with glazing facing south—unless it happens to be a fancy revolving restaurant. The direction from which sunlight enters it varies throughout the year in a complex manner. Substantial solar energy also comes from other directions than where the sun is. On a cloudy day, a sunspace or other solar collector can capture heat from *diffuse* light, that is, the light that is coming from all directions. The overcast must be very thick before no heat is felt behind good glazing. Up to 10 percent of the energy available on a clear day can be captured on a completely cloudy day. On a clear day, the sunlight from the direction of the visible sun is called *direct radiation*. Up to 25 percent of the energy received by a surface is of the diffuse sort and comes from all other directions.

The sun rises and falls in its apparent height above the ground, both during the day and over the year. Its height measured in degrees is its *altitude* (see FIG. 2-3). The altitude starts at zero with sunrise and increases to a maximum at solar noon. (Solar noon is usually not the same time as local clock noon, and might differ by more than an hour, depending on location.) The highest altitude of the sun will be of interest particularly on the shortest and longest days of the year. On the day of winter solstice, about December 21, the sun is low at noon. At summer solstice, about June 21, the sun is nearly overhead at noon. The annual variation in altitude is due to the 23.5-degree tilt of the earth's rotation axis with respect to its motion around the sun.

You can determine the exact height of the sun at noon at summer or winter solstice if you know your latitude. This is an important design value. Any atlas or road map should show your latitude to the nearest degree, which is more than sufficient accuracy. Suppose that you live along the 40°N line of latitude, which passes through the center of the United States (see FIG. 2-4).

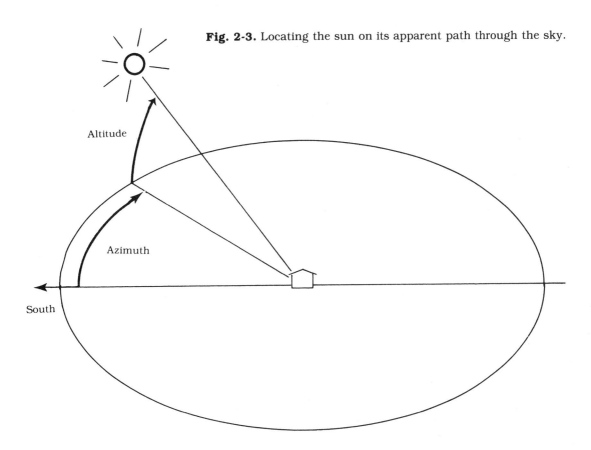

Fig. 2-3. Locating the sun on its apparent path through the sky.

In winter the sun will be overhead (altitude 90°) for people at the Sao Paulo beaches at 23.5°S. The sun is then 40 + 23.5 = 63.5° away from being overhead at your location, making it 90 – 63.5 = 26.5° above the horizon. Similarly, at noon at summer solstice the sun is overhead in southern Mexico, 40 – 23.5 = 16.5° away from your position. At your location it is 90 – 16.5 = 73.5° high. You will see the sun to be 16.5° from your *zenith*, the straight overhead location. These methods of calculation will be useful for designing overhangs for shading. There should always be twice 23.5°, or 47°, between the altitudes at summer and winter solstice. or 47°, between the altitudes at summer and winter solstice.

The location of the sun in compass direction also varies each day and throughout the year in a complex manner. Knowing about this variation can be important in designing a sunspace. At midsummer at middle latitudes (like 40°N) the sun rises well north of east and sets well north of west. North walls receive light in summer. At midwinter when we most need it, the sun rises about 60° from due south on the eastern side and sets at about 60° from due south on the western side. In between, the compass direction of the sun during its path through the sky is called *azimuth*.

The sun's apparent path in the sky is about twice longer in summer than winter, since daytime is twice longer in summer. This seasonal variation is more exaggerated in the Northern United States than in the south. Several aspects of

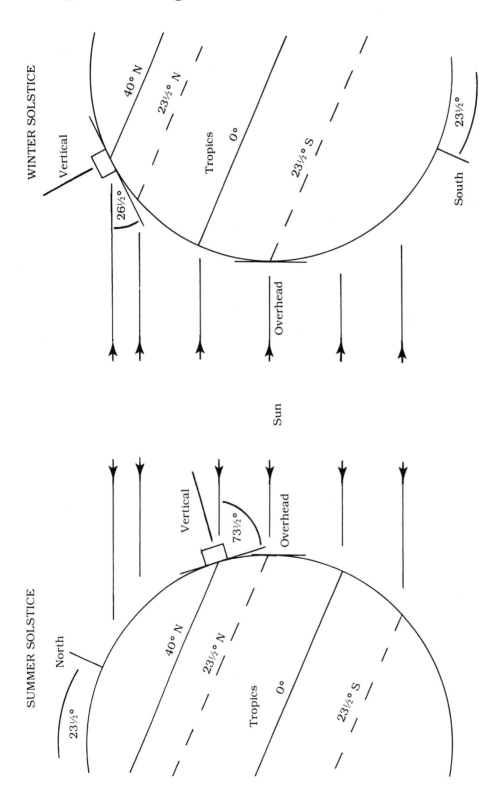

Fig. 2-4. *The direction of incidence of solar radiation varies by 47° between summer and winter, shown for latitude 40°N. Rays from the sun are essentially parallel over the earth and are shown at solar noon. The scale is exaggerated.*

the sun's rays are at their worst in the winter. Then the sun is at low altitudes, it stays near south, it is up for less time, and its rays must go through more atmosphere before reaching us. All these factors result in less total solar energy for the day, and less intense sunlight at any hour.

Solar Intensity

The intensity of solar radiation is sometimes technically called *insolation*, from *sol*, a name for the sun. This term is not to be confused with *insulation*. The strength of sunlight is described in energy terms. In common units, intensity is described in Btus per square foot. A Btu is an energy unit that is rather small: the amount of heat needed to increase the temperature of 1 pound (one pint) of water 1° F. As the sun shines on a surface, the energy the surface receives accumulates over time. Therefore, tables and maps must give values for the insolation over some standard unit of time. This book refers to Btus per hour, per day, and per year. The total insolation accumulated over some period of time must be distinguished from the insolation received in a unit of time, such as an hour.

The amount of solar energy absorbed by a surface depends on several factors, including the angle at which the rays strike, and the absorbing versus reflecting properties of the surface. Light striking a surface head-on (perpendicular or "normal" to the surface) is more intense than light striking at an angle (FIG. 2-5). Oblique rays are spread over more area, depositing less energy per unit area.

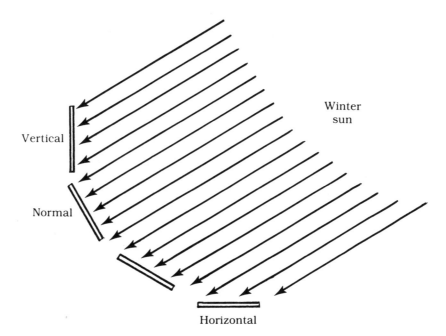

Fig. 2-5. The intensity of solar radiation landing on a surface depends on the angle between solar rays and the surface. The intensity can be judged by the approximate number of rays falling on each surface of identical size in this representation.

Insolation maps and tables will give the intensity for several useful orientations of surface: vertical, normal, horizontal, and selected tilts. For sunspaces, the designer will be interested in vertical surfaces (south walls) and in south-facing surfaces tilted to be nearly perpendicular or normal to the sun at certain times. The normal surface always intercepts the most sun, but it would need to be reoriented continuously as the sun's position changes. Fixed surfaces are usually given a compromise orientation, chosen to aim best at the sun when the sun is weakest and lowest.

As an example, at 40°N latitude at sea level, about 263 Btus strike one square foot of vertical surface at solar noon in one hour on December 21. This should be compared with 208 Btus per square foot per hour at the spring equinox, March 21, and with 98 Btus per square foot per hour on the sunniest day, June 21. Clearly, a vertical surface favors the winter for solar collection. There seems to be a bonus of energy in the winter although the sun shines about half as long. When a total day's accumulation of energy is considered, 1646 Btus are obtained on December 21 and 610 Btus on June 21. You might wonder, then, why a room with plenty of south windows does not get hotter in winter than summer. It could, but usually the heat losses to the cold outdoors and the cold temperatures of the materials on winter mornings prevent full warm-up.

Tables and maps of insolation are available for all regions of the country. Tables, such as TABLE 1 in the Appendix, provide the amount of energy available for a specific latitude at various times of day, month by month all year. It shows how many hours the sun is up and what altitude angle it reaches. Also given is the azimuth direction of the sun at each hour. Insolation tables typically provide the solar energy striking a variety of surfaces. Included in TABLE 1 are horizontal, vertical and tilted south-facing, and normal surfaces. A horizontal surface would approximate a roof of low slope. A vertical surface would approximate a south wall or a slightly tilted south wall. The tilted south-facing surface is provided for designs that use the rule of thumb that the glazed wall should be tilted at an angle equal to the latitude plus 20° for maximum winter sun. The normal surface is of theoretical interest only, for comparing the maximum possible insolation at different times.

Because the insolation varies during the day, the Btus received in a given hour cannot be simply multiplied by the number of hours per day to obtain a daily total. Instead, the measured Btus for each hour are added together to obtain the totals given in the tables. Over a month, the total daily insolation also varies. In order to avoid the need to provide a table for every day of the year, however, the tables list the average insolation, which can be applied to any day of the month. Therefore, you can find a monthly total simply by multiplying the daily average by the number of days in the month.

Insolation tables are for sea level, clear air, and no cloudiness. About 10 percent should be added for each mile increase in local altitude of the land, and about 10 percent subtracted if the air is somewhat dusty or pollutant-laden. If your sky is usually blue, you are getting most of the sunlight. If it is usually white, there is dust and pollution blocking some sunlight. A bonus of energy—as much as 20 percent more—is available from ground and building reflection. Rocky surfaces, masonry and painted buildings, and especially snow can reflect sunlight from other collection areas into the sunspace. Before the clear-day insolation data can be used, they must be discounted according to the amount of cloudiness during the months of interest. MAP 1 in the Appendix shows the average fraction of the sky covered or opaque with clouds each month anywhere in the United States. The fraction of sky cover can be interpreted on the average as what fraction of the time clouds cover the sun. The fraction ranges from 0.2 in the Southwest to 0.8 or more in the Northeast and Northwest. The corresponding amount of time the sun is shining ranges from 80 percent in the Southwest to 20 percent in the Northeast and Northwest. Correcting for cloudiness is discussed in Chapter 3.

An alternative to tables of insolation is a series of maps of the United States, which show the insolation month by month at many locations by means of contour lines. On such maps the average cloudiness and the effects of altitude have been taken into account, and the accuracy is generally expected to be greater than what can be achieved with insolation tables. MAP 2 and 3 in the Appendix give the values for total or global insolation, including the diffuse radiation from all parts of the sky. Ground effects are not included. MAP 2 is for south-facing vertical surfaces. A small tilt from the vertical has little effect on the insolation. MAP 3 gives the insolation landing on a horizontal surface and could be applied to roofs with low slope. You can consult the sources of the maps and tables for data for surfaces with other tilts and with other compass directions.

The contours on the solar radiation maps are marked in units of megajoules per square meter. These metric or International System of Units (SI) units are now the working language for scientific and engineering work, and the latest maps are available only in these units. Therefore to use the maps in familiar Btu units, you will need a conversion. Megajoules per square meter are energy-intensity units, and 1 megajoule per square meter is equivalent to 88.11 Btus per square foot. The time element for insolation enters through the fact that the map gives the insolation for a day. For your location, you can obtain the equivalent of table values by reading the insolation per day and multiplying by the number of days to get accumulated solar energy within each month. If you live between two contours, it is sufficient to estimate whether you are one-fourth, one-half, or three-quarters of the way between two lines and use the appropriate intermediate value. This estimating method is called *interpolation*. Simple applications of this information on insolation will be shown in Chapter 3.

To summarize, the ingredients that would go into determining how much energy a sunspace could capture would include the area of the glazings, the latitude of the location, the angle of tilt of the glazings, the orientation of the glazing with respect to south, the season(s) during which collection is wanted, the altitude, the clarity of the atmosphere, the fraction of cloudiness, and the presence of nearby reflecting surfaces. Examples in Chapter 3 will show how to carry out simple estimates of the energy collected.

Capturing Sunlight

To summarize the principles of capturing sunlight and to give further details of what happens to sunlight as it enters a sunspace, the paths taken by radiation are shown in FIG. 2-6. Here the model of the sunspace has two glazings, a common method of increasing heat retention. The path of a solar ray is traced through several reflections, absorptions, and conversions. Glass and most other glazings reflect about 4 percent of the light at each surface through which it passes. One sheet of

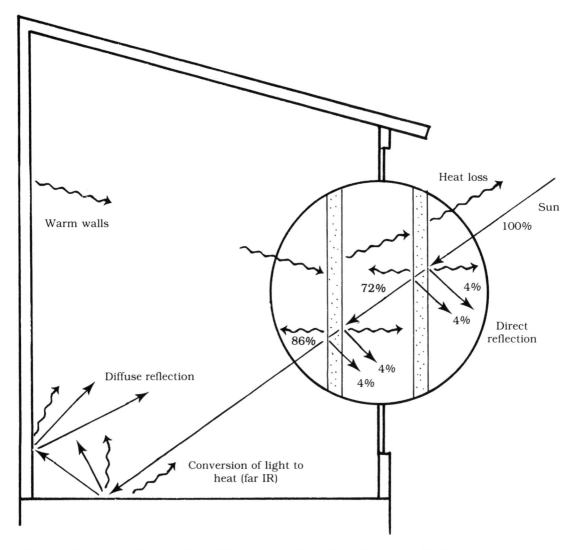

Fig. 2-6. *Trapping solar radiation with double glazing. About 6 percent of radiation is absorbed in each layer of glass and heats the glass directly.*

glass has two reflections, one from the front and one from the back surface, so only about 86 percent of the light would pass through the whole sheet. Another 6 percent or so is absorbed in the glazing and converted to heat, which then radiates away as infrared radiation. After passing through two glazings, only about 70 percent to 72 percent of the light energy remains. (There is more detail to calculating light flow through materials than need be of concern here.) No single sheet of glazing can transmit better than about 90 percent.

Once inside the sunspace, direct rays strike walls and floors and reflect. The amount of reflection depends on the color and other surface properties of each surface. At each bounce some light is absorbed and converted to heat, which then radiates. The radiation striking the glazing is partly reflected back into the sunspace. The air in the sunspace is warmed partly by direct contact with walls and partly by absorbing light and infrared radiation.

The overall performance of south-facing glazing in windows or a sunspace is best illustrated by considering net heat gain of windows facing different directions, comparing daytime insolation that comes through a glazing with nighttime heat loss during the year. Only south-facing glazing provides net gain all year. This holds true all over the United States for double glazing, but not for single glazing during winter in Northern states. Note that, in the North, east, west, and north windows considered by themselves have net heat loss in winter even if they are insulated at night.

HEAT GAIN AND LOSS

Once heat energy has been captured by a sunspace, its loss must be prevented, retarded, or controlled. If the walls and floor had no insulating value and no heat storage ability, warmth could not be maintained in the sunspace. There are four common ways that heat travels from one place to another: conduction, convection, radiation, and infiltration. Materials and methods are needed to control heat loss through each of these independent routes. In Chapter 3, the methods of finding heat loss will be discussed with examples.

Conduction

Conduction is the name for the way heat travels through materials from the warm side to the cooler side (FIG. 2-7). The greater the temperature difference, the larger the amount of heat that travels through. This and other forms of heat flow will continue until there is no longer a temperature difference. The amount of heat flow depends also on the thickness, area, and type of the material. Thick materials provide more resistance to heat flow. Larger surface areas provide more material through which conduction can occur, so more heat flows out. Plastics conduct heat less readily than concrete, and much poorer than aluminum and other metals. Conduction of heat has little to do with how well materials can store heat.

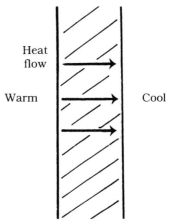

Fig. 2-7. *Heat conduction through a material is caused by a temperature difference between the two sides.*

Heat flow

Warm   Cool

The resistance of a material to heat flow is commonly and somewhat loosely called its *R-value*. Wood is a good insulator and so has a high R-value compared to concrete, but, inch for inch, glass conducts heat about the same as concrete. R-values are needed to find out how much heat flow occurs through walls or other structures composed of layers of one or more different materials. The R-values of the layers are simply added together. For example, an insulated wall of stucco, fiberglass, and gypsum board would have the R-value for each layer added. (What to do about the framework of wood or steel in the wall is a more complex matter.)

The opposite of the impedance of heat flow is the conductivity of heat. The heat conductivity of a building component made of various materials, such as window assembly, is popularly called its *U-value*. Although U-value is not as widely used yet, it is essential for finding out the heat flow out of a room made of different materials for the walls, floor, and roof. The total heat flow for an enclosed volume such as a sunspace can be determined by considering the R-value and U-value of every wall, floor, and ceiling. The enclosed space must be visualized as surrounded by an "envelope" and every part accounted for. The U-value of each part is simply added up to get the total U-value. The equivalent R-value of the room describes its effective performance and can be found by dividing the U-value into one: $R = 1/U$. Conversely, the U-value for any material can be found from its R-value thus: $U = 1/R$.

Heat flow through a material in Btus per hour is found by multiplying the area in square feet by the temperature difference (in degrees F) and dividing the result by the R-value for the given thickness. An example will be given in Chapter 3. TABLE 2 in the Appendix gives the R-values of many common building materials.

Heat loss by conduction is hindered by the use of thick materials and materials that inherently resist heat flow. If a building component is a rather good conductor, its ability to lose heat by conduction can be reduced by incorporating a thermal interruption, or *break*, in it. For example, aluminum window units are durable and inexpensive, but the heavy metal frame is a direct thermal connection between cold outdoors and warm indoors. The inside of the aluminum frame will collect condensation even if the double glazing remains dry. A thin plastic gasket between two halves of the frame will provide an R-value similar to the glass, or about 1, which is much better than the aluminum's R-value of about 0.001.

Convection

Heat flow by *convection* occurs wherever heated air (or water or other fluid) is allowed to flow. If the sun through a window (FIG. 2-8) warms the air and floor in a room, the warmer and therefore less dense air rises, drawing cooler air to a position in the sunlight where it is warmed. A circulating flow is set up so that warm air reaches most parts of the room and the total volume of air (along with the walls) gradually warms up. Convection can occur in very small, closed regions such as between two panes of glass or within a hollow sealed wall. The net result is that the warm side cools down and the cool side warms up. Convection ceases when there is no longer a temperature difference. This is undesirable when the double glazing or the hollow wall is supposed to keep the inside warm when the outside is cold. If it were not for convection, air would be almost as good an insulator as a vacuum. The best way to stop convection where it is not wanted is to fill spaces with substances that block air flow. The substance must also be a poor heat conductor. Hence, the best insulators are made of light and fluffy glass fibers or with a plastic foam of small closed cells. Removing the air completely makes a perfect insulator, but vacuums are impractical in ordinary construction.

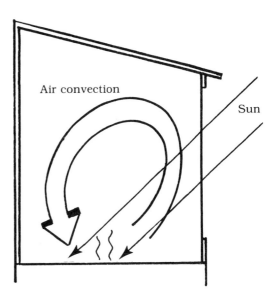

Fig. 2-8. *Heat travels by convection currents in the air, which carry heat upward.*

Air convection

Sun

Radiation

Insulators, except for glazings, appear opaque to us in visible light, but most allow some amount of infrared radiation to shine through. Every material radiates heat energy from its surface (FIG. 2-6), and the *radiation* passes through air about as readily as through a vacuum. At ordinary temperatures, the radiation is the rather unenergetic far IR, rather than the near IR that comes directly from the sun. Cool materials radiate waves so long and weak that they are like weak radar waves. If air could be kept from convecting and conducting, heat would still pass through it by radiation. Heat loss by radiation is best stopped by using special surfaces that either radiate poorly or reflect infrared radiation back toward the warm region (for example, shiny metal).

Radiation is very strongly dependent on the temperature difference between the warm surface and other cooler surfaces. If all surfaces are at the same temperature, they still radiate at each other but there is no net flow of heat. A hot object cools very rapidly at first because of its relatively high temperature. Later other heat-loss modes become more important than radiation. At night the surfaces of buildings "see" (in the infrared) the night sky as very cold and radiate heat away strongly, especially at higher altitudes. Loss by radiation is readily felt by people under clear night skies, as well as in a room with cold walls. It is said that people would be warmed more efficiently by radiation than by heating the air first. This statement has some truth, but the air warms up anyway and it takes (as will be seen) very little heat to warm air as compared to solid objects and people.

Infiltration

Heat loss by *infiltration* (FIG. 2-9) occurs when cold air finds gaps through which to enter a warm room. The cold wind pressure must push warm air out through holes somewhere else, because pressure will not build up appreciably in a room.

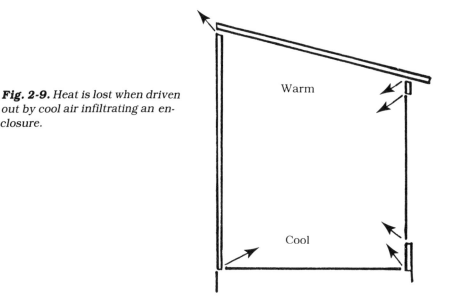

Fig. 2-9. *Heat is lost when driven out by cool air infiltrating an enclosure.*

If there is no wind pressure, warm air inside will still find holes through which to leak out, and the resulting lower pressure in the room will draw cold air in elsewhere. The loss of warm air could be called *exfiltration*. Infiltration has belatedly been recognized as a major route of heat loss and has inspired the use of the *blower door* test to pressurize (or depressurize) a house to find its leaks.

Infiltration is stopped by caulks, tapes, weather-stripping, sealants, paints, house wraps, plastic film, and other means of closing holes. To avoid cold air flow into insulation, the sealing would best occur as near the outside of the structure as possible. To avoid warm, moist inside air flowing into the structure and insulation, another barrier is needed at the inside.

THERMAL EXPANSION

Heat has several effects on materials, creating problems for the sunspace designer and builder. Not only is heat easily lost through materials, but it also changes the material size and might cause deterioration, too. The most common heat-caused damage is from *thermal expansion*. Nearly all building materials increase in length as heat causes their temperatures to rise. This situation would not be so bad if all materials changed length the same amount. Few materials, however, have exactly the same response to temperature. The change in length is proportional to the change in temperature. The amount of the change is expressed with a *coefficient of thermal expansion*.

The values of coefficients for some common important sunspace materials are given in TABLE 3 in the Appendix. Glass, for example, has the coefficient 0.000005 per degree Fahrenheit. This might seem a very small value and nothing to worry about in ordinary sunspace construction, but an example in Chapter 3 will show that major problems are possible because of the larger expansions of some glazings. Thermal expansion can lead to huge forces. Often a material will destroy itself or the framework holding it if it is constrained during expansion or contraction.

The change in length of a material is found by multiplying the length of the given material by the change in temperature (in degrees Fahrenheit) and by the coefficient. Practical problems occur because some materials change much more than others. Commonly, a glazing will expand more than its frame when it heats up. When the temperature swings the other way, the glazing will shrink more than its frame shrinks. The temperature changes involved in sunspaces can be quite large: a −40° F winter to a +140° F overheated sunspace is a change of 180° F.

Materials expand in all directions when heated. Thus, a sheet of glass will increase in length and width. The width increase is handled exactly like the length increase. The overall result is an increase in the area of the sheet. The increase in thickness of the glass is usually negligible. Liquids and solids increase in volume when they are heated. Aside from important changes in air volume (discussed in the next section), volume expansion is rarely of importance in sunspace design. The expansion of heated water can be dangerous in any closed water system or tank, however.

HOT AIR AND HEAT CONTROL

In order for you to control the heat in a sunspace, you need to know some introductory considerations about where the heat goes in a sunspace and the behavior of hot air. The pressure or volume of a given mass of air is proportional to its temperature, other factors being equal. Thus warmed air, when unconfined, occupies more volume and becomes less dense. The air seems lighter and wants to rise above cooler air. If confined, warm air will increase in pressure. Pressure is rarely a problem in sunspace applications since a sunspace cannot be sealed so tight as to prevent all leaks. (If liquids like water are considered, the same principles apply, but with much smaller changes. Warm water will rise to the top of a tank.)

Solar heating of a sunspace does not ensure uniform temperatures from floor to ceiling, despite internal convection. The air motion is too gentle in a closed space. There is a zone of cool air near the floor, warm in the middle, and hot at top, when the sun shines. These zones can remain at night, although each has a proportionately lower temperature. This *stratification* can be especially good for growing plants, since the plants are on the ground in the cool zone. There will also be heat zoning from front to back, with the region in front of the glazing being warmest because it receives direct sun. The presence of the hottest air at top makes it imperative that there be no uncontrolled air leaks at the ceiling. Insulation overhead is needed for nighttime heat retention.

Sunspaces will tend to be too hot at times. You can use the heat zones to promote natural venting of excess heat. When the ceiling is much warmer than the floor, there is sufficient air density and pressure differences that the hot air will rise out of any open vents while cool air is pulled into vents near the floor (FIG. 2-10). Because the hot air wants to occupy more volume, the vents at the top need more area than those at the bottom—typically 30 percent more.

Wind pressure can aid or hinder natural venting. The upwind side, usually the west and south in the warm season, subjects openings to high wind pressure inward. Sometimes the flow is much more than is needed for ventilation. On the downwind side and the roof, wind causes suction, which can help draw air out of vents placed high for heat exhaust.

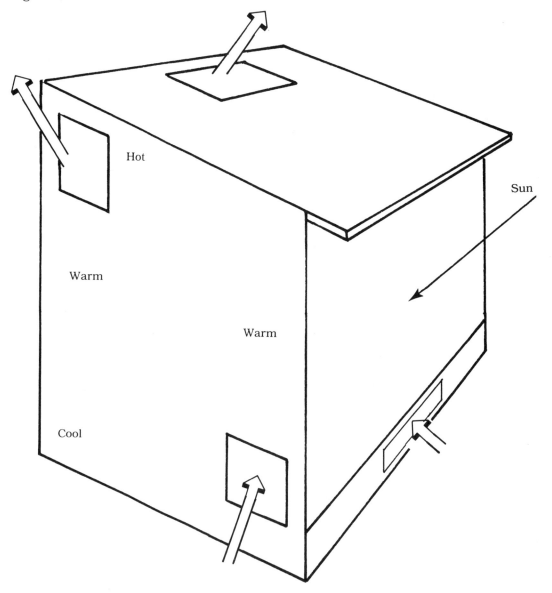

Fig. 2-10. *The natural heat zones in a sunspace can aid in venting out the heat.*

Often it is necessary to take more active steps to control overheating, either by forcing hot air outdoors with a fan or by opening automatic, motor-controlled vents. Possibly, summer venting can be done with the same fan that transfers hot air into the house in winter. The control of venting should be "positive"—that is, there should be tight covers for vents and some hardware should ensure that the vent is held open, shut, or partway regardless of the forces from air flow or wind. Vents are bad places for loss of heat and entry of rain. Insulation and louvers are means of controlling both.

REFLECTION AND SUNLIGHT CONTROL

Sometimes you will want more sun inside, sometimes less. You can use reflection to bring more sun in, and shading to reject excess sun. There are two kinds of reflection: *specular* and *diffuse*. Specular reflection is what mirrors do. If the sun arrives at a certain angle on the shiny surface, it departs at an equal angle. Light-painted walls, sandy or rocky ground, rough wood, and so forth reflect light diffusely. It is scattered in all directions upon reflection, with a mild preference for the direction that specular reflection would produce. Diffuse reflection provides an approximately uniform illumination that is useful for good seeing in rooms and outdoor spaces. Specular reflection is highly directional and provides bright spots of light in a few places and much less light over most of the area. It is rarely useful because people cannot see well in the dazzling changes of contrast, and plants do not receive uniform light for growing.

Not widely appreciated is the specular reflection that occurs at steep angles. Almost any material is a good and directional reflector if light strikes the surface at a grazing angle. The amount of reflection increases as the angle becomes steeper. This fact is especially useful in regard to glazings. A vertical glazing that captures much winter sun when the sun is low will strongly reflect it when the summer sun is high (FIG. 2-11).

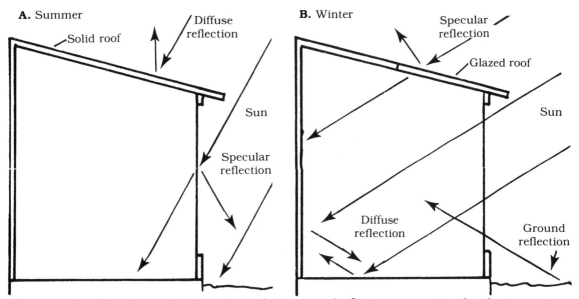

Fig. 2-11. *The effect of ray reflection varies with season, and reflection can assist with radiation capture.*

The tendency of any surface to reflect increases rapidly after the angle between lightrays and surface diminishes below 30 degrees. While about 8 percent of the sun is reflected when the sun shines straight into glass, about 70 percent is reflected from the outside surface when the sun is 70 degrees high in the sky, nearly overhead. Glazed roofs at moderate to low pitches, although popular, make the worst use of this effect. When the sun is low in winter, they reflect most of it away. When the sun is high, they let most in for summer overheating.

In winter, a greenhouse must have more light than its glazing area can put directly on the plant beds. The natural light intensity should be at least doubled. Additional light is obtained if there is snow or light sand on the ground in front. White-painted surfaces outside can be positioned to bounce light around inside and to concentrate it on the region where the plants are. A good greenhouse design, especially if it is free-standing, has the solid north wall properly sloped for reflection of winter sun onto the floor (FIG. 2-12). The inside of the north wall is painted a light color. Glazed roofs that are not pitched steeply on greenhouses are beneficial for collecting diffuse winter light, but otherwise have the disadvantages already mentioned for any sunspaces.

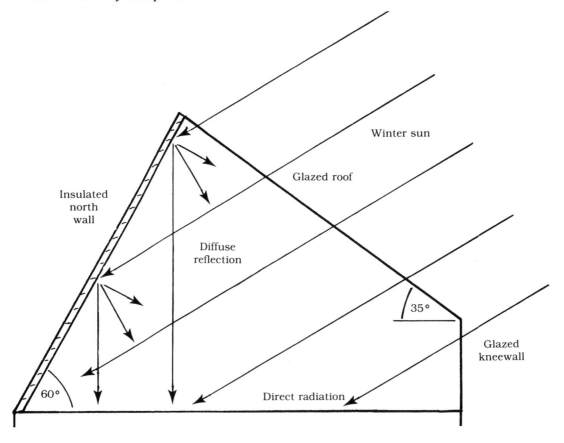

Fig. 2-12. *Reflection used in a freestanding greenhouse or sunspace. (A good design is not limited to the angles shown.)*

The sunspace designer who wants to use reflection can easily check the reflective behavior of sunlight in a particular design by drawing typical light rays coming in and using a protractor or other device to draw the rays after reflection from various surfaces. The angle at which the ray strikes the surface is duplicated as it leaves the surface, as shown in several figures. This method will help find the best arrangement for diffusely reflecting surfaces, too. Often, light rays undergo two or three reflections before reaching the region of interest and before diffusing so much as to be untraceable in their effect. Useful results are obtained quickly by using low winter rays and high summer rays. They should not be the lowest and highest, conditions which apply only a few hours of the year, but rays about 5 degrees above the lowest in winter and about 5 degrees below the highest in summer.

HEAT STORAGE

To be of value at night, excess heat must not only be collected in the sunspace, but also stored. The sunspace, being a newly added space, is also a good candidate for locating the heat storage. Heat storage can be as simple as having a thick brick or concrete floor on which the sun shines all day (FIG. 2-13). The floor should be a medium dark color to absorb heat, but possibly not so dark and dull that it does not reflect some sunlight to strike the back wall. The hot air in the sunspace helps heat all parts of the floor.

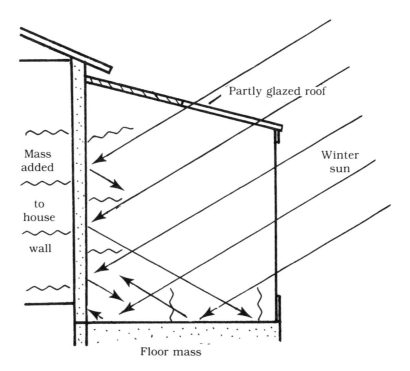

Fig. 2-13. Winter sun can heat floor and wall mass directly as well as indirectly.

If the adjoining house wall is made of brick or other masonry, it can be used for heat storage. Winter sun should be striking the wall directly most of the day. If the wall is dark, it absorbs more heat. If the insulation is removed from the inside of the wall, the heat will reradiate at night into the house, and back into the sunspace. Late at night the wall will be cold and cause heat loss from the house unless insulation is returned to its interior surface. A heat storage wall also radiates heat in the daytime, but it should be so massive as to require all day to warm up enough for noticeable radiation. The heat storage wall would be good for greenhouses, but making it dark might be at odds with plans to use it for light reflection. This is one of many places the designer must make a choice.

A masonry wall with sun striking it is a rudimentary form of a solar collection method known as the *Trombe wall,* which was named for a French solar engineer (see FIG. 2-14). Refinements include making the wall dull black, adding glass in front of it, making it the proper thickness for overnight storage (about 1.5 to 2 feet thick), constructing it for good heat conduction (no gaps, holes, wood, or other thermal breaks), and perhaps insulating the outer surface at night. Vents also can be added.

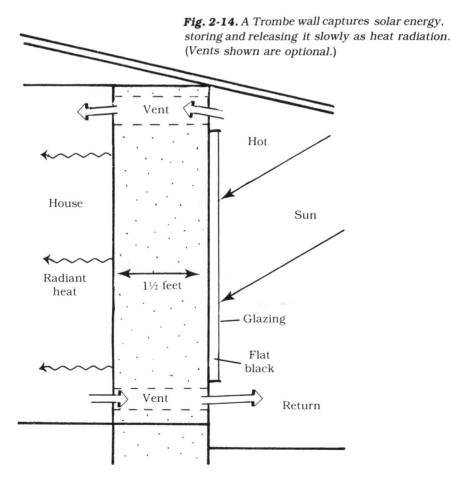

Fig. 2-14. *A Trombe wall captures solar energy, storing and releasing it slowly as heat radiation. (Vents shown are optional.)*

A proper Trombe wall will be a massive structure and will need its own foundation to support it. If you are considering a Trombe wall for a sunspace, you must begin planning for it as early as you do any other part of the project.

Good heat storage is possible because some materials have a high *heat capacity* or a low cost, or both. The principle of heat storage states that the amount of heat energy stored (in Btus) is equal to the weight of the storage material (in pounds) times the amount of heat a pound of material can store (its heat capacity) times the temperature difference between the outside of the storage and its inside. TABLE 4 in the Appendix gives the heat capacities of rock, concrete, water, and other likely materials. For example, concrete, sand, rock, and similar materials based on rock can store about 0.2 Btu per pound for each degree Fahrenheit that the material rises above its surroundings. The table also provides the densities of the materials so you can convert pounds to cubic feet and vice-versa before finding heat capacity. How much storage a sunspace might need is shown with examples in Chapter 3.

Most of the area under the sunspace floor can be used for heat storage. A simple storage will be at least one foot deep and can be filled with rocks or made of hollow concrete blocks. It might be covered with a concrete slab for more storage and should be insulated on all sides and perhaps underneath. Hot air collected at the ceiling of the sunspace would need to be blown down a duct and into the storage during winter days (FIG. 2-15A). The practical arrangement of ducts, rocks, and blocks to promote uniform circulation from one side to the other is shown in Chapters 3 and 4. Cool return air should be forced up near the glazing.

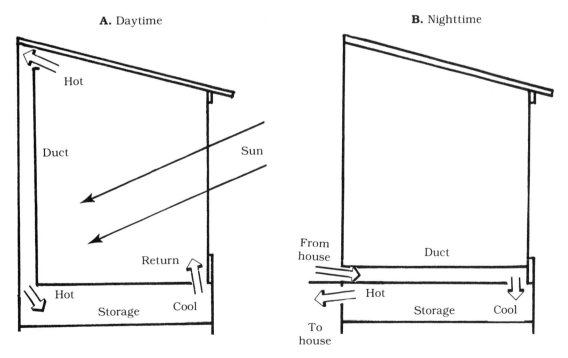

Fig. 2-15. *Heat storage under a sunspace in winter and its transfer to the house. (Two duct systems are shown separately for clarity.)*

At night not much heat will come back from storage unless air flow is reversed and cool air sucked in, forcing warm air out (FIG. 2-15B). The warm air should not be blown at the sunspace ceiling but be sent to where it is needed, either into the house near the floor or back into the sunspace. If the sunspace is used as a greenhouse, this nighttime heating is especially needed, although radiation through the floor from a passive storage area might be sufficient. If circulation of air is not controlled, the natural tendency of the warm air in the underground storage area to rise will cause it to move up any duct, cool off at the cold glazing, and drop into the storage area. This unwanted convection, also called *thermosyphoning*, serves only to lose stored heat back to the outdoors. Methods of control will be discussed in Chapter 3.

A simpler storage material, but with disadvantages, is the earth itself. Unless passages are formed in it, not much earth is exposed for heat storage in a sunspace floor. An earth floor is a part of the outdoors and not to be considered living space. It is appropriate for a greenhouse, but otherwise is a source of dirt to be tracked in and will harbor unwanted creatures.

A more difficult storage material is water. Water does provide cheap storage and holds the most heat of any common substance: five times more than rock. The substantial plumbing and containing problems of using water for heat storage are left to you to research in other sources or experiment yourself.

A simpler form of water storage has been to place steel drums—painted black and filled with water—in sunlight. Control of rust has been a problem, and some steel containers deteriorate rapidly. Plastic bottles, while cheap, do not last one season in sunlight. Glass bottles are long-lived but must be protected from freezing and breakage. They also can focus sunlight and start fires on nearby flammable materials. For safety and best storage, the water should be dyed black, but black water in bottles might seem less attractive than clear water.

When water is put in large, transparent plastic containers stacked against or incorporated in a glazed wall or a house wall, the result is called a *water wall*. It lets light through while moderating the heat flow.

HEAT-TRANSFER SYSTEMS

Moving heat into storage and then back for use is an example of *heat transfer* or transport. Generally an active mechanical means is needed for efficient heat transfer and makes the sunspace system into an active solar system. Letting it run on its own is a passive method. When the passive method involves ducts, vents, and other passages, the heat will move the wrong way part of the time. Active intervention could be as simple as closing vents at night.

A good passive system that needs no attention would use the direct heating of a storage material by sunlight, followed by its reradiation of heat back in all directions at night, for example, a Trombe wall. Some heat is lost to the outside, but there is a net gain. Since hot air rises, storages located underground are not naturally accessible to it. Putting the storage above the ceiling, however, is definitely not the answer. In addition to being very heavy and bulky and needing insulation, the storage cannot be relieved of its heat without artificial means to bring it down.

The value of comparing passive and active heat transport is apparent when you are considering a sunspace-type solar collector that must be "fail-safe." Active systems usually require electric power and complex devices, which can fail in various ways, sometimes at the worst time. Thus, any system, including a sunspace, should be designed to work moderately well in a passive mode.

Passive operation is a good backup for an active system. For example, during a high wind or a snowstorm, the power might go off. During the wind, however, might be precisely the time when an automatic external vent should be closed. During the snowstorm might be just when the air blower should switch to heating the house. Equipment tends to fail when it is too hot or too cold—just the extremes found in a sunspace where the equipment is needed to prevent overheating or freezing. You cannot assume that the human residents will always be on hand to adjust a vent or to serve as backup to power failure. You must ensure there is a reliable backup system.

One such control is a backdraft damper. Whether the damper is called active or passive is irrelevant. What is important is that it automatically does its job in a reliable manner—in this case falling shut under gravity to prevent air from flowing back (backdrafting).

BUFFERING AND HUMIDITY

An advantage of a sunspace is that it provides free heat while not overheating the house. Thus, it serves as an isolation zone, or buffer, between the outside and the living space. Although it is usable part or most of the time, the temperature extremes occur in the sunspace rather than the house. If highly humid activities such as using a hot tub or growing plants occur in it, then the sunspace/greenhouse isolates this humidity from the house. The buffering effect of the sunspace also reduces heat loss from the house by serving as a large extra insulator on the house exterior.

The sunspace will not function as buffer unless it is somewhat isolated from the house. If there is good isolation, however, there will not be passive transfer of heat from the sunspace to the house, especially at night. Sunspace design should include consideration of how the sunspace is connected by means of doors, windows, vents, walls, and insulation. Unless the sunspace is well built and airtight, the house wall, windows, and door are needed to keep insects, rain, and wind out. A door, windows, and vents should be provided as needed to bring warm air in during the day.

In conditions of high humidity, special care is needed to be sure the sunspace or greenhouse is isolated from the house in regard to moisture flow. Water takes up much heat (970 Btus per pound) when changed to water vapor, its gaseous form. The vapor tends to diffuse through the air, whether or not there is convection, to regions where the water vapor is less concentrated. Cold places such as the glazing are places where water-vapor pressure is low. When the vapor condenses back to liquid droplets, all that heat is given off. Thus humid air exacerbates heat loss.

Places such as glazing and frames where the temperature is below freezing act as if they attract moisture strongly and might even freeze it (releasing another 144 Btus per pound to the outside). They also help cause convection of air to move the vapor more quickly. Insulating the glazing makes the problem worse unless the insulation is very vapor tight, because the insulation lets the glazing reach still lower temperatures so that it can attract more condensation. Water vapor will pass through very small openings to reach the cold glazing.

The condensation that runs all over the inside structure, penetrates it, and runs onto the floor can be a nuisance and cause damage. A sunspace with humidity must be made of moisture-resistant materials throughout. Transferring heat to the house with moist air would cause many problems in the house and in every component that contacts the air.

For humidity buffering, vapor-barrier material should be placed on or in the back wall of the sunspace/greenhouse and perhaps in all walls. Plants prefer, even require, 40 to 60 percent humidity, but this level will begin to promote mold and perhaps damage the house. Plants will emit much moisture, and die when their roots run out of water, so water must be returned to the plants. A hot tub will raise the humidity to 90 percent or higher except when it is tightly covered. Wood doors and windows to the house will swell and stick, as well as permit moisture to pass through. Gaskets or special doors and windows might be needed to stop the passage of water vapor.

CLIMATE FACTORS

A set of factors that the sunspace designer must allow for concerns the climate. Cloudiness, rain, fog, hail, snow, cold, wind speeds, wind directions—all with annual cycles that vary from year to year—affect sunspace design, use, and durability. A brief description of how these factors affect design and construction will be given here. Chapters 3 and 4 show construction methods that have been proven to be weather proof.

Areas with cold, sunny winters, generally in the West, have the advantage, but sunspaces have proven useful and energy-gaining in all parts of the country. Maps showing average cloudiness for every month of the year are provided in the Appendix. For any region of the country these maps will give a general idea whether sun is in short supply in fall, winter, spring, or summer.

Most important for sunspaces is whether much of the cloudiness occurs in midwinter or not. It is best to consult local weather services and observant residents, since no map is available with such detailed information.

Another way to assess the amount of sun available in your area is to examine MAP 4 in the Appendix, which shows the total number of hours the sun shines in a year after cloudiness is allowed for. The total ranges from 2000 hours in the Northeast to 4000 in the Southwest, not as large a difference as you might think between Maine and Arizona. Dividing the total by 365 gives the average hours of sun per day. When you compare the average hours of sun per day in your area with the average day length of 12 hours, you can obtain an estimate of cloudiness. Do not expect data from all maps and charts to agree closely with each other or with what you observe where you live, however. Climate and weather data fluctuate unpredictably, and accurate measurement has always been difficult.

The precipitation level and type affect sunspace design. Even if you have low humidity inside your house, if there is a high amount of rainfall in your area, you might need to build the sunspace for high humidity. Some very localized valleys are plagued with low-lying fog in winter. The solar records might state that your area has high insolation, but you might miss half of it because of morning fog. In some areas hail is frequent or severe, and the roof glazing, if any, should withstand the damage.

About half of the United States is liable to heavy snowfalls, so you must build the roof to withstand the maximum expected load. Snow might constitute the most severe loading the structure will get, so you should allow for it (as described in Chapters 3 and 4) whether or not local building codes are enforced. Generally, if the structure can hold a substantial snow load, such as 30 pounds per square foot, it can withstand the worst winds. Another consideration in regard to snow is that extra snow might land on the sunspace roof, having fallen from the main roof. If the house is two or more stories high, the impact can be large. After the snow is pulled from, or falls from, the sunspace roof, where does it go? How high will it pile up in front of the crucial south glazing? Before the snow slides off, it blocks any roof glazing from receiving heat, so you might need to pull it off.

Snow also can be beneficial. It insulates the roof, walls, and ground. In front, it provides vital reflection of low sun into the glazing, increasing the energy collection area substantially.

Since snow usually accompanies very cold weather and clouds, the rapidity with which the sun returns after a deep winter snowstorm strongly affects whether the sunspace is truly usable in the winter. In the northern half of the United States, and in the mountains, a week of below-zero weather with clouds comes at least once a year and is difficult to anticipate. This is very bad news for greenhouses. Do you want to allow for this extreme? On the average, if you expect the sunspace to be comfortable all winter, you can determine its energy needs by the same heating degree day criterion applied to houses as follows.

The severity of climate is commonly measured in its *degree days* for a given location. Degree days are the number of days times the number of degrees the outside temperature is below 65° F and heat is supposedly needed. The count of degree days is taken over the year, although most of them occur in the cold season. Under 4,000 degree days signifies a mild or warm climate. Over 6,000 degree days is a cold climate. This information is available from your local newspaper or weather service. MAP 5 in the Appendix shows by means of contours the heating degree days per year over the United States, so you can obtain a general idea of the severity of your climate. Tables and maps in the references give heating degree days per month if you wish to study a particular month. Heating degree days vary widely from year to year, but maps and tables give a long-term average suitable for insulation and solar design.

If the average inside temperature requirement were relaxed to say 60° F for a sunspace, about 500 heating degree days could be removed from the heating load in the central United States. If you know the level of insulation of the sunspace as represented by its net effective R-value, you can determine the amount of heat input needed to maintain an average temperature of, say, 60° F. If the glazing does not provide for this temperature, the sunspace will not stay warm on the average. Examples will be given in Chapter 3. You also can make the estimate day by day, week by week, or month by month. It might be particularly useful to compare solar input and heating requirements for the month of January, usually the coldest month of the year.

Where the climate is windy, the sunspace structure must be strong. Almost all parts of the United States are subject to high winds of at least 70 miles per hour, if only once a year. Building codes specify the wind load that must be allowed for in each locality. High winds from all directions must be considered when designing the strength of the foundation, framework, walls, glazing, its fastening, doors, and vents. Although this might sound like a major engineering feat beyond the capacity of the most versatile homeowner, using a combination of standardized building practices, simple requirements in building codes, and standardized available materials will nearly ensure success. Design pressures are in the range of 20 to 30 pounds per square foot, so clearly a sunspace made of cheap polyethylene plastic wrapped around a 2-x-2 wood frame is likely to last only until the next big wind.

The worst winds are usually from the west, indicating an east placement of an outside door if at all possible. Lap roof and wall materials so that a west wind cannot catch under them. Give consideration to whether the rest of the glazing and structure will survive if one glazing panel or section is popped or broken out by wind (or by vandals). In such a case the large wind pressure is suddenly transferred from outside to inside the sunspace. The change in stress could overload the structure, where gusty winds alone did not.

Not all the wind pressure is on the outside of the west or south wall. The roof has pressure upward from below during wind, whether doors and windows are open or not. The mere passage of high-speed air over a surface cause a low pressure on that side of the surface. The leeward wall, probably on the east where the wind causes suction, has outward pressure on it. The roof and leeward wall pressures are typically about half the main windward pressure.

Windbreaks are an important supplement to a well-designed sunspace, not only to protect it from damage but also to reduce heat loss at certain times. The house itself is an excellent north windbreak for the sunspace. Coniferous trees, a fence, or other buildings are helpful on the west, as long as they do not block southwest sun in winter. The west windbreak should attach to the southwest corner of the house so that cold wind swirling around the house from the north does not immediately encounter the sunspace.

You should not block all wind, however. Breezes and mild wind pressure are needed to have good natural venting of heat from the sunspace. The cool air intake should face the direction from which most summer breezes come, to aid venting. Of course, if your yard site does not allow for an ideal sunspace location, you should modify these and preceding considerations to obtain the best protection in the circumstances.

PRACTICAL DESIGN

THE BASIC PRINCIPLES OF using solar heat with a sunspace have been presented. This chapter will show how the principles are used to design a practical sunspace. Many examples will be used. The principles determine both the options that are possible and those that are unrealistic. Some mistakes to avoid are given from the experience of builders and owners. It is not possible to anticipate every sort of problem, although the better you understand the principles, the less you are likely to make a serious mistake. Details of construction follow in Chapter 4; however, design and construction details cannot always be separated.

This discussion should be useful whether you are making decisions on a packaged sunspace or planning to build a sunspace. You will not regret having some basic knowledge about materials, structure, operation, and options before you purchase components or a complete unit. As before, the discussion will feature a simple, almost generic sunspace, leaving elaboration to the designer and to the photographs of various sunspaces. No single correct shape or size will suit every owner's needs. Knowledge of how to apply the design principles should leave you free to create a sunspace that functions well and has beauty.

REVIEW OF BASIC CONSIDERATIONS

You should make some basic decisions about the sunspace as to type, purpose, shape, size, capability, location, and structure after you have studied this book. At this point, it would help if you had a general idea what you want to do. If that is not the case, then perhaps by the end of this chapter you will have more ideas about what you want.

The general choice is among greenhouses, hot-tub spaces, and other sunspace uses. The first two uses involve high humidity, with the greenhouse requiring reliable temperature control and much winter light. The other uses could be for energy collection and the wide range of uses of an additional room on the house. A sunspace that is not permitted to become hot in winter might not be a good source of free home heat. The sunspace intended to be hot in fall, winter, and spring for home heating might often be too hot for occupation.

The size of the sunspace will be determined by the size you want and can afford, and also by the size needed to provide a significant amount of energy. The minimum suggested size is 8 feet wide and 12 feet long, giving about 100 square feet of floor area and a similar area of glazing. The better the energy production, the more you will save on utility bills, releasing more cash to spend on the sunspace. The limit of cost-effectiveness generally occurs when about 80 percent of home heating needs are covered. This assumes an ideal south-facing site, which might not be available.

The shape and structure of a sunspace are determined partly by the desired appearance and guided by the existing house, by the site, and by examples. The structural form is also determined partly by the purpose. You should give special consideration to the use of glazing on the roof. Although glazed roofs are popular, you should consider carefully whether a glazed roof is compatible with the expected uses and the local climate.

THE SITE

You can begin the design by determining which of the available locations will best fit the desired uses. If there is only one possible site, then it will dictate much about the sunspace. Walk around the south side of the house and take a careful look at the possibilities. Consider the following questions and others that might arise during site examination. Attaching the sunspace to the house is an ideal arrangement, since it saves building a wall, protects the sunspace, and makes it convenient to the house. If none of the following seems to work out, consider a free-standing sunspace in a better location away from the house. It might be known as a "summer house," or be a greenhouse.

Does your house have sufficient south wall? Does it face nearly south (FIG. 3-1A) or must you work with a house corner that points south while the walls face southeast and southwest? Should the floor plan be L-shaped, wrapped around the house corner (FIG. 3-1B) or tucked into a corner (FIG. 3-1C)? Would you like to include 45-degree angles in the shape so as to obtain a south-facing portion in a wrap-around sunspace (FIG. 3-1D) or in a corner (FIG. 3-1E)? Is there a back porch which could be converted to a sunspace? Is the back porch partly and fortuitously enclosed by sidewalls (FIG. 3-1F)? Unless the south wall is facing more than 30 degrees from south, as will be determined shortly, there is little problem using that wall. Can the back door be covered by the sunspace, making an airlock as well as providing a handy entrance? Which house doors and windows will fit into the sunspace and which might interfere? If the back door is in the wrong place, is there a place or room where you could make a new exit into the sunspace? Converting a window to a door will be easier than making a door in a blank wall.

Does your back door open to the north, forcing you to consider a sunspace on the front of the house? Although privacy might become a problem, sunspaces have been built on the fronts of all sorts of homes in all sorts of neighborhoods, and many look as if they belong that way. Perhaps you have a front porch that just needs glazing. If the front yard is on the south but completely out of the question as a site, do not give up yet. Some unusual solutions have been found that work, such as putting the sunspace on the roof or building up from the back of the house high enough for the sunspace to "look" over the roof.

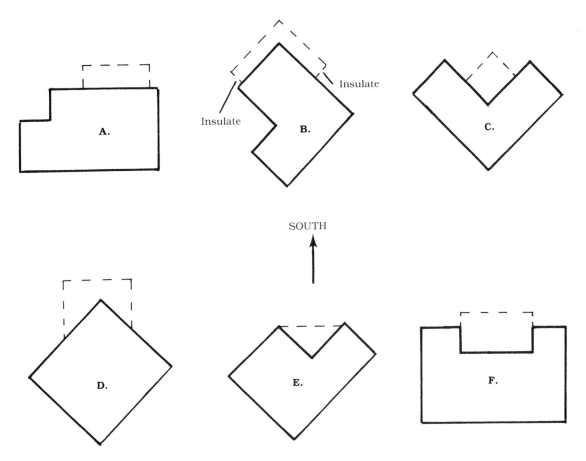

Fig. 3-1. Siting a sunspace with various house orientations and shapes.

Are there obstructions—coniferous trees that block the most wanted winter sun, a tall fence, a two-story house, a one-story house very close, a garage, or a dense tangle of trees that provide shade even with their leaves gone? Can you sacrifice the tree(s)? Would your neighbor remove one or more trees, giving you your right to the sun? Can you build the sunspace far enough above the ground so that it can receive sun hidden by a nearby shed or garage? Is there a place for a two-story sunspace, or could it be put on the garage? Can an outbuilding be moved aside? Does a wing of your house block the morning winter sun? Are some of the obstructions also blessings: will they reflect extra sun to the site in winter?

Look to the west and east a moment. Are there trees, a fence, or something else that will interfere with the setting or rising sun? Little heat is gained in the first hour of sunrise, but the second hour is important in winter. Would the obstacles make good windbreaks? And are your neighbors already watching your actions and likely to find some problem with your plans?

Here are some other aspects to consider about the site. Will your house or some other structure funnel much of the snowfall directly onto your sunspace site? Can you prevent that occurrence? Is the soil good for a stable foundation? Do you know what had to be done to ensure that your house foundation was stable? You might need to repeat that method for the sunspace. Is the soil easy to dig, so that your sunspace can be completely hand-built? Is the soil too poor for growing plants in a greenhouse?

Which way does the ground slope? Could a slope upward toward south be altered favorably by excavation? If your backyard faces south and a tall hill, your winter sun is very limited. Can you use a site that slopes to the east or west, perhaps digging in on one side and having a tall foundation wall on the other side? Will a sunspace lowered below grade level fit your backyard better and give you more room overhead to put a steeper roof? "Pit" greenhouses are better protected from the cold.

After looking over your sites, it is not too soon to discuss your project with your neighbors and local officials, to find out what legal, zoning, and covenant restrictions might pertain. Zoning or building requirements might prohibit use of your site or your intended design, but you might be able to obtain a variance. If you are surrounded by vacant land, consider what might be built later to block your sun. Find out how much sun you have a right to. In addition to privacy, a backyard site might remove your project from the scrutiny a front-yard site would get. It also will remove the glazing from the attention of vandals. Careful attention to the appearance of your sunspace and its fit with the house will make a difference in how well it blends in, making it relatively unnoticeable.

FINDING SOLAR TIME AND TRUE SOUTH

If you are not certain where south is during your site examination, you can use the information in this section to determine true solar south. As soon as you know where south is, sketch a site plan showing possible places for the sunspace. Include as many answers to the preceding questions as possible. A careful diagram of the site should help identify potential problems.

Great accuracy is not needed in finding south for a sunspace. The following methods will help you find south as accurately as you might wish. Simplest and usually most reliable is to examine the survey map of your lot, which will show true north and south. It will be at the county courthouse if you do not have a copy. It might not show how your house is oriented on the lot, but if you can match your property lines on the map with the real ones on the ground, you might be able to draw your house on the map and so find the orientation of its south wall.

If you use a compass, be aware that you must apply a correction of as much as 23° to its north or south indication to obtain true solar south. Compass and true directions agree only on a line through Michigan and Florida. The correction map, sometimes called a *gonometric map*, is available in references (e.g., Alward/NCAT or in *Solar Age*).

You also can determine true south from the sun if you know the time of solar noon. You can find solar time from clock time first by subtracting the hour for daylight savings, if any. Then make a correction for the number of degrees west that your town is from an hourly longitude that is a multiple of 15° (also called a *standard time meridian*). If you live close to such a longitude (e.g., 105°W), your regular clock time is approximately solar time. Each 15° is equivalent to 1 hour of the solar day. Therefore, 1° is equivalent to 4 minutes of time. Subtract 4 minutes from the clock time for each degree that you are located west of the nearest hourly longitude. If you live at 111°W, for example, then subtract 6 × 4 = 24 minutes from your clock to get solar time. When the sun is directly overhead at 105°W, it is not yet overhead (by 6°) at 111°W, although the clocks in your time zone might already show noon.

The calculation of solar time might also be useful if you want to use the detailed insolation tables, although they should not be necessary for sunspace design. For further accuracy, there is a correction for the location of the earth in its orbit. This correction can be as much as 15 minutes, and you could obtain it from a graph in references such as Anderson. Sunspace design should not require this accuracy. Once you know solar noon from clock time, you can use the shadow of a vertical stick at solar noon to point out north and south. There are other procedures using vertical sticks that are not necessary for the amount of accuracy needed with a sunspace.

Once you have found the direction of south, you can determine the region that should be free of obstructions. Use the compass or a protractor to locate 60° east and 60° west of true south, as seen from your intended site (FIG. 3-2). These points are approximately where the sun rises and sets in midwinter in most of the United States. Imagine an arc from the rise to the set points that goes no higher in the sky than the altitude of the sun at noon on December 21. (The method of finding the maximum altitude at winter solstice was to add 23.5° to the latitude, then subtract the result from 90°.) It is difficult to judge angles in the sky, so if you need accuracy, a protractor or other sighting device will help.

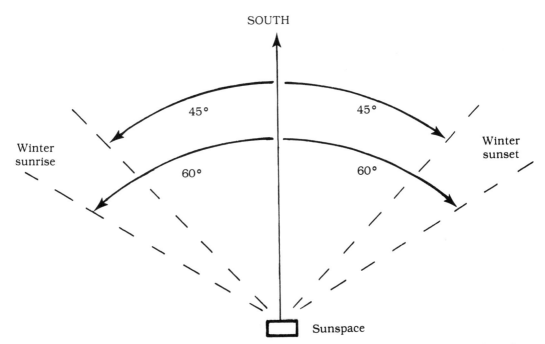

Fig. 3-2. *The south view of the sun as seen on a ground plan in winter. The 45-degree lines from south mark the minimum unobstructed view that should be available for adequate solar heating.*

This arc or sun path shows how high obstacles to the south can be at the time of lowest sun without blocking it. Some of the references (e.g., Alward/NCAT) provide charts that show the altitude, azimuth, and general path of the sun in the sky for every month of the year at various latitudes. Three of these charts are reproduced in the Appendix. If your state has public energy conservation offices, experts might visit your site free or at low cost and provide information about south, sun path, sunspaces, and perhaps much else. Sun path charts are also sold by various companies.

The altitudes and azimuths for each hour of the day and each month of the year, given in TABLE 1 in the Appendix, provide the same information. You can make your own sun-path chart by plotting altitude versus azimuth on graph paper for a latitude near yours. You might just need the path for December.

Watch for trees, windbreaks, buildings, fences, hills, houses, and so forth which encroach on the sun's lowest path. In midwinter most solar heat is provided between the time the sun is at about 45° east of south (about 9 A.M. solar time) and when it is at about 45° west of south (about 3 P.M.). Therefore, if the only obstructions are outside this zone (see FIG. 3-2), there is little need to worry.

SUNSPACE SIZE AND SHAPE

The minimum suggested sunspace size was 8 feet wide and 12 feet long on the side facing south. This size provides room to walk in while leaving room for plant beds, a hot tub, or furniture. It also is a minimum size that collects and stores enough heat to counteract the losses through its walls, with plenty left over. Widths larger than 12 feet are constrained by the rapidly increasing sizes needed for roof rafters. There is no real limit to sunspace length, except possibly the length of the house. You can choose the size of the south wall to provide a desired level of energy collection. The next section will help analyze the size you chose or help tell what size you should build for energy purposes.

Choosing the height will require some thought. House walls are usually 8 feet high, with an overhanging roof eave (FIG. 3-3). The house sits on a foundation about 1 foot above grade. The house sits higher if there is a basement partly underground. The sunspace roof must slope down enough to shed rain—a 2-inch drop for every 1 foot of width, for most kinds of shingles. In 8 feet the roof should fall 1.3 feet. Then the south wall of the sunspace will be less than 7 feet high, unless you take further steps to gain more height. Glazing at the ground is nearly useless, so 1 foot of wall might be unglazed at the base and called a *knee wall*. The remaining area for south glazing is as little as 6 feet high.

FIGURE 3-3 shows that the floor of the sunspace would need to be set 2 feet below the house floor to obtain adequate roof slope and glazing height. Typically, the south glazing area will be less than the floor area. If you want a steeper roof or taller glazing, you must build the sunspace lower into the ground or tilt the south wall. If the house wall is two stories high or is the gable end, then obtaining sufficient height is much easier.

Many building materials, including glazing, come in sizes that are multiples of 2 or 4 feet. The route to the most efficient use of materials at lowest cost is to design the structure to have a length and width that are multiples of 4 feet. Unfortunately, doors and windows are almost never multiples of 2 feet in width, so there are structural complications around them. Before you assume, however, that your sunspace is, for example, exactly 12 feet long, consider the later discussion of how the corner posts are located around the chosen glazing.

Fig. 3-3. *A profile view of a simple sunspace with optional roof and 65-degree tilted glazing (8 feet wide and 8 feet high on the south; some framing not shown).*

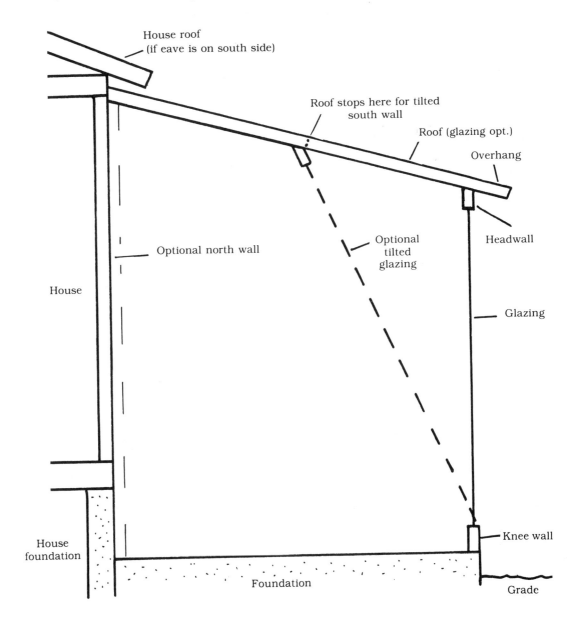

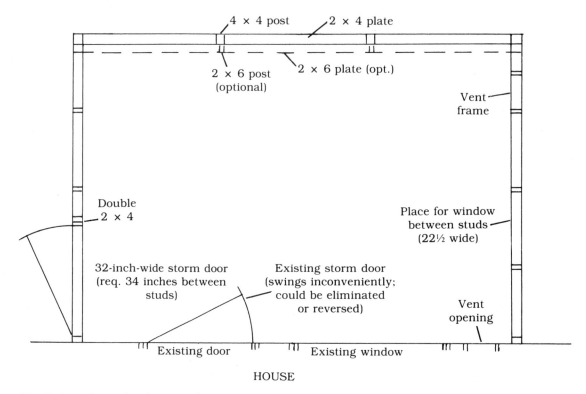

Fig. 3-4. *A floor plan for a simple sunspace 8 feet wide and 12 feet long showing the features that must be located accurately.*

You should start your layout of the sunspace with a floor plan. This plan can be as simple as a rectangle showing locations of doors and windows, to scale (FIG. 3-4). Be sure to include existing doors and windows in the house. A more elaborate plan would show the locations of permanent furniture, the hot tub, equipment, or plant beds. Particularly in the case of a greenhouse for growing food, space is at a premium and the location of every species of plant might be preplanned (see the references for details). A greenhouse could have a subgrade walkway for easier access to plants. Other details needed on the plan are the location of vents and any east or west glazing, as well as the locations of any large posts. You should draw the floor plan large. It would be wise to lay out the preliminary plan on the actual site with stakes to be certain everything fits.

Next you should determine the profile of the south-facing part. Draw the edge view of the house wall and its roof line (recall FIG. 3-3). You might need to climb and measure what you have. It can be important to measure accurately, to the nearest ¼ inch. Be sure to include whatever foundation is exposed. If the ground slopes east or west, it is easiest to assume you will build a level sunspace and choose the lowest ground level for planning. Removing high ground is easier than filling in low areas unless you will have drainage problems. With the ground line for the sunspace established, draw how high you want its foundation. It should be several inches above the ground. A building code might require 6 or 8 inches. Unless you have a reason for a higher foundation, every extra inch of sunspace foundation reduces the height available for roof slope and south glazing. Be sure that sizes agree on the plan and profile drawings.

Now is the time to decide if you want tilted south glazing. Vertical glazing provides the best heat control, but tilted sunspace walls have become popular nevertheless. Tilting the glazing also provides another foot or so in the height available for glazing (recall FIG. 3-3). The angle of tilt is measured from the ground. The rule of thumb has been to tilt glazing at an angle equal to your latitude plus 20 degrees for maximum heat gain, and insolation tables provide data for this tilt. This is an extreme tilt, however, and a value more like 70 to 75 degrees is recommended for appearance if not gain. With any tilt the heat gain might be excessive in midfall and midspring, especially below 40°N latitude. In northern areas, the heat gain will be somewhat reduced in midwinter for tilted glazing.

You must balance appearance against heat control in this choice, keeping in mind that what looks good perhaps also should work best. Tilted glazing has proven difficult to seal tightly against rain leaks. Structurally, a vertical wall is easier to build and will be stronger. (Chapter 4 will show you how to design a tilted wall.) In cold northern climates with a long, cold spring, a good compromise is to use vertical wall glazing and steeply sloped roof glazing so that the sun penetrates more directly through some part of the glazing in fall, winter, and spring. During part of the year, shading will be necessary on the roof glazing.

Draw the thickness of the walls on your plan and profile. This thickness will depend on your structural plans. It is conventional to use nominal 2-x-4 framing, so that structural members are 3½ inches wide and 1½ inches thick. The extra insulation provided by 2-x-6 framing would be wasted because of the large glazing area. You might, however, find 2-x-6 framing necessary in the south wall. The spacing of framing members will be covered in Chapter 4, but in general it is 2 or 4 feet. If you plan to join some walls at angles other than 90 degrees, there is little complication in design but more in actual construction. Decide if you want a kneewall. It looks nice, saves on glazing, provides a place for vents, and generally keeps things away from the bottom of the glazing. If the lower part of the glazing would be in shade in winter because of obstructions, the kneewall can replace that part with insulation.

With the south wall set, you can draw the roof profile. You may assume 2-x-4 rafters for it, but if the sunspace is wide or the snow load heavy, you must leave space for thicker rafters, as discussed in the section on roof framing later in this chapter. You might be permitted to fasten these rafters to the house wall under the overhang, or even to the house rafters themselves if they are exposed. You might prefer, or be required, to build a new wall along the house on which the rafters sit. Be sure the roof pitch will provide the minimum necessary slope for the shingles, glazing, or other covering you plan to use. Most shingles require a slope of 1:6 (a 2-inch rise over 12 inches). Thus, an 8-foot-wide sunspace roof should rise about 1⅓ feet.

Tentatively determine the amount of roof that will be glazed, if any. A fully glazed roof is an extreme heat burden in summer. In the most northern climate, 4 feet of glazing would be as much as you might want. If the sunspace is mainly for heat collection, glaze most or all of the roof and plan for it to get hot in winter and hotter in summer! Also plan on much storage mass. A partially glazed roof provides shade in the rear part of the sunspace in summer. A fully opaque roof can shade the whole sunspace in summer. The joint between normal, solid roofing and roof glazing is a bit tricky and liable to leak—another consideration.

The overhang of the sunspace roof over its south wall is a good way to control summer sun. As shown in the section on using shade later in this chapter, you can design an overhang that shades the glazing completely in June without losing any winter sun. If this is to be a greenhouse, however, there will be too little light for most plants.

The practice in the construction industry is to look at the floor plan and estimate construction costs on a per-square-foot basis. Because of its different construction, sunspace costs cannot be estimated in the same way house costs are. A disproportionate amount of value is incorporated in the glazing, which might or might not have an area similar to the floor area. In addition, sunspace costs might be much lower or higher than typical residential construction costs. Here costs will continue to be indicated on the basis of floor area, using values appropriate to sunspaces. Later, costs of glazing and other major materials will be discussed so that you can make more direct estimates.

The owner/builder can reduce the cost to as low as $10 per square foot. (Lower costs are possible but appearance might suffer.) Fancier structures could be $20 to $30 per square foot. Contractors would start at about $30 and go up. Manufacturers of kits start at about $30 or more per square foot, not including a foundation and some other necessities. (See the references for the latest listings of manufactured sunspaces.) The bronzed aluminum-framed units are $60 or more per square foot without the extras. The example with 100 square feet of sunspace would cost a minimum of $1,000. If that sounds like an underestimate, consider the costs of roofing and glazing for that area. All the materials in a typical shingled roof cost about $1 per square foot. Some of the better glazings cost $3 per square foot. Adequate money remains to do the framing, walls (any sort of exterior finish is about $1 per square foot), and other necessities, such as foundation, insulation, a simple door, and simple vents.

ENERGY GAIN AND ENERGY NEED

Suppose you have chosen a certain size of sunspace and you want an estimate of the solar energy it will collect. If the result is not enough for your needs, then enlarge the design and try again. Let the example sunspace be 12 feet long with glazing about 7 feet high, positioned vertically. This area of 84 square feet will gather $84 \times 0.33 = 28$ million Btus during the seven cold months October through April at 40°N latitude.

The 0.33 million Btus collected per square foot was found by adding the monthly totals of insolation in TABLE 1 of the Appendix for the seven months. The result of 331,000 Btus is divided by 1 million to convert it to 0.33 million Btus. This keeps the figures small and simple when dealing with months' worth of energy. No more than two-digit accuracy is needed or justified. You will only need to do this chore once for your latitude for the months you need heat.

To be more realistic, you should correct the result for the cloudiness in your area, as well as the altitude and clarity of sky. If clouds cover the sun about 40 percent of the time (0.4 opaqueness for the months of interest from MAP 1 in the

Appendix), then the insolation per square foot would reduce to 60 percent of 0.33 million Btus, or about 0.2 million Btus. Polluted air might reduce it 10 percent; high altitude would increase it about 10 percent per mile; and ground reflections might raise it 10 to 20 percent. Chances are, in your area, the available insolation is nearly the table value, unless all the factors are against you.

Another approach is to use the maps for insolation on south-facing vertical surfaces—MAP 2 in the Appendix. These maps also provide both direct and diffuse (global) insolation, but this time the effect of local altitude and clouds is also included. Suppose you live in western Nebraska near 40°N. The insolation per day for the months of October through April has the values in megajoules per square meter of 15, 13, 13, 13, 14, 13, and 13, respectively. When those figures are multiplied by the number of days in their months and summed, the result is 2,846 megajoules collected per square meter over seven months. This energy intensity is converted to Btus per square foot by multiplying by 88.11 to obtain 250,000 or 0.25 million Btus per square foot. This more realistic amount includes the effects of cloudiness, altitude, and other regional factors.

The 28 million Btus collected in the example sunspace might seem large, but compare it with home heating needs. First consider that at least half of the energy will be lost before it ever enters the house. An efficiency of 50 percent is typical and difficult to improve upon. So about 14 million Btus are usable. You should not view the quantities obtained in these examples as highly accurate. Because of variabilities in weather and efficiency, high accuracy in solar matters is nearly impossible and rarely needed or meaningful.

A typical medium-sized moderately insulated and weathertight house (very early 1970s practice, before the first big energy panic) might have gas heating bills of about $550 for the season in a climate of 5,000 heating degree days. If you happen to know the net effective R-value of the house to be $R = 7$ (much less than the rated insulation put in the walls and ceiling), and if you have found its total envelope area (walls plus floor plus ceiling) to be a typical 3,000 square feet, then you can find its total heat throughput during the heating season by multiplying envelope area times degree days times 24 hours and dividing by net R-value. The result in this case is 51 million Btus. (You multiply by 24 hours to convert degree days to degree hours, to be compatible with the hours used with R-value.) You can determine the heating degree days in your area from local information or from MAP 4 in the Appendix.

Thus, the 14 million Btus net gain from the small sunspace would make a 28 percent contribution to the total need of 51 million Btus for this example house. That amount burned as gas in the typical furnace for this house would cost about $130 per year, using the national average gas cost of $9 per million Btus (TABLE 3-1). The rule of thumb given earlier that solar heat is good up to about the 80 percent level indicates that this sunspace could be scaled up. Tripling its size of glazing would bring you near the 80 percent level and save about $400 per year.

You also can estimate the *payback time*, the time to recover the cost of the sunspace from the energy savings. If the 100 square feet sunspace costs $1,000 without frills, then it will pay for itself in about 7 years, ignoring details of interest, taxes, etc. As the sunspace is scaled up, the payback remains the same in this example. Since electric heat costs two to three times more than gas, this sunspace would be a blessing for those burdened with electric heating bills.

————————Table 3-1. Costs of Useful Energy at Typical Efficiency.————————

energy source	efficiency	cost per M/Btu	conversion of common units to Btus	
Natural Gas	60%	$ 9	1 ccf (hundred cuft) =	83,000 Btus
Propane	60%	$15	1 gal =	90,000 Btus
Heating Oil	50%	$15	1 gal =	140,000 Btus
Kerosene	90%+	$12	1 gal =	135,000 Btus
Coal	20%	$20	1 ton =	24 MBtus
Wood (soft)	20%	$20*	1 cord =	20 MBtus
Wood (hard)	20%	$30*	1 cord =	30 MBtus
Electricity	100%	$22*	1 kwh =	3,413 Btus

Notes:

Useful or usable energy is defined as that delivered within the heated space, after chimney and duct losses are discounted. The typical efficiency is shown for the average heating appliance in use. Fuels have less recoverable heat content when used at higher altitudes.

The conversion factors are for total heat content of the fuel, regardless of losses. 1 MBtu = one million Btus. Pricing is mid-1980s level for residential use. * denotes pricing varies widely over the US and an average is used. Values are rounded.

Kerosene is assumed used in a portable heater without vent. However, window ventilation must be provided.

20% efficiency for wood and coal burning applies to a moderately low efficiency woodstove but would be high for a fireplace.

Electricity is generated from one of the other listed fuels, from nuclear energy (similar cost), from hydroenergy (low cost), or (rarely) from solar energy (high cost).

———

If all you know is your gas and other energy bills for the season, you can convert that information to your total heat use. Prices will vary, so check locally. Many areas have public agencies with information on energy pricing. TABLE 3-1 gives the cost ranges for various energy sources per million Btus actually used (not sent up the chimney) for costs that prevailed in the mid 1980s. This table assumes that the energy is used in appliances of typical efficiency. Some areas will have higher energy costs, especially large eastern cities. Others, perhaps with hydroelectric power, will have lower. The table also gives the conversion from fuel units purchased to energy units consumed. For example, if you use 1-kilowatt-hour, that is equivalent to 3,413 Btus. This is the way to obtain your energy usage from the consumption readings on the bills. Be sure to use a set of bills covering all the months you want heat. If one year was unusual, average bills for several years.

Nearly all the electric and fuel energy that you buy ends up as heat in the house, but for accurate comparison you will need to estimate what proportion went directly for space heating, if any. If you use a gas-fired water heater, perhaps 10 to 30 percent of your gas energy went to it, depending on usage. At a smaller scale of energy usage, a gas furnace blower uses substantial electric energy, which would be saved if the furnace were rarely used. A sunspace heating system also will need blowers, although smaller ones.

To finish the example, at the rate of $9 per million Btus actually used, a gas bill of $550 represents 61 million Btus. If a modest 10 million Btus went to the water heater in this case, with most of that energy leaving through the drains or as steam, then 51 million Btus remain as provided by the furnace. The energy analysis balances out neatly, as you might expect in a textbook example.

If you prefer to determine the size of sunspace you need from your energy needs, then you can calculate the area of the glazing by dividing the amount of energy wanted per year by the solar gain per square foot on vertical glazing (or glazing at the tilt in the insolation tables). Then multiply the resulting area by two to cover the estimated 50 percent efficiency of the process. Note that these analyses work best over long time periods. The weather is likely to permit the calculated amount of solar energy to be gained over the seven months. However, there will be fluctuations month by month, and especially day by day. Seasonally, the sunspace is likely to gain a bit too much energy in fall and spring and run short of your goal in midwinter. To go further and allow for, say, four days of clouds following just one day of sun, you would need a sunspace and storage system four times bigger than the one designed for overnight heating. The payback time lengthens by the same factor.

If you can find the solar gain per square foot, you can estimate the sunspace payback time directly per square foot built. Suppose each square foot collects 0.3 million Btus at 50 percent efficiency during the seven-month cold season. The resulting 0.15 million Btus is worth about $1.50. If it costs $30 to build that square foot—remember, floor area is at least similar to glazing area—the simple payback time is 20 years.

In summer, zero solar heating is preferred. The same vertical glazing in the example produces 0.13 million Btus per square foot in the warm five months. This heat might result in overheating simply because the losses are much less and the weather is hot. If you are planning tilted or roof glazing, you might want to work out the heat gain through those surfaces. Use the horizontal insolation data from the table or maps for a roof with low slope. The likely conclusion is that vertical glazing controls solar gain best over the year.

GLAZINGS

Probably the most important component to select is the glazing—both the material and the method of mounting it. Cost, clarity, transmittance, lifetime, strength, resistance to ultraviolet radiation, and appearance are the main factors to consider. *Clarity* refers to how well you can see clear images through the glazing (aside from reflections from its surfaces). Some glazings are *transparent*, passing most light and providing clear images. Others are *translucent*, passing most light but diffusing it so that it seems to come from all directions and blurring any images. *Transmittance* refers to how much light comes through, including far IR, near IR, visible, and ultraviolet. Ideally transmittance would be poor only for far IR and ultraviolet light.

The *lifetime* of a glazing refers to how long it lasts when exposed to the weather and sun. Conditions are more severe in some areas than others, so lifetime can vary by many years in different parts of the United States. Lifetime should be longer than a few years, since reglazing can be a challenging and expensive project. The strength of a glazing is pertinent to how it responds when struck by rocks, hail, gusts of wind, and the like, as well as how it holds up with a snow load on it. Strength is related to what a fracture does when started in the glazing—whether a crack grows until the whole sheet fragments or whether cracks stop by themselves.

TABLE 5 in the Appendix lists most of the commonly available glazings and their special features. That information is expanded upon here. FIGURES 3-5 through 3-9 give a first look at glazing cross sections and some rudiments of their mountings. There is no perfect glazing that suits all requirements. You must decide, from the advantages and disadvantages given, which features are most important for your application, and then select the glazing that has most of them. For example, if growing plants is the main purpose, then clarity is not needed but good insulating properties are. If the sunspace is for a hot tub in the front yard, you might not want clear glass. If cost is the major factor, the first glazing could be polyethylene, to be replaced in a year by a better material (or more of the same).

For glazing intended to last many years, you need to consider the method of fastening it. Each glazing has its own unique mounting requirements, and these are described briefly to help you make choices on materials and framing. Unless a material is specifically suggested, it makes no difference whether the underlying frame is wood, aluminum, steel, or something else suitable. Details of mounting for actual construction are given in Chapter 4. You must plan the mounting before you either choose or build the frame. Water and air leaks and thermal expansion are principal problems you must consider. See the references by Alward, McCullagh, Yanda, and many others for additional glazing details for special situations.

Glass Glazings

In most climates where sunspaces are needed, *double glazing* is justified. Double glazing consists of mounting two layers of glazing close together. They need not be the same material. The separation can be narrow, ¼ to 1 inch, so that the air between the two layers serves more as an insulating blanket rather than as a convector of heat from the inner glazing to the outer. The air blanket has been the most cost-effective way to reduce heat loss through a clear material, since pumping out the air layer is rarely feasible. The inner glazing can be inexpensive polyethylene sheet, at some loss of clarity. The outer glazing would protect the polyethylene from some ultraviolet degradation and from wind and damage. If the inner glazing is added separately, then it is likely to be easy to remove, repair, and replace from the inside without disturbing the outer glazing. On the other hand, moisture between the two layers is likely to be a problem, and the framework should resist deterioration by water. Some manufacturers sell assembled double glazing of glass or plastics, sealed with dry air.

Insulating glass does not refer to the insulating properties of glass itself. That is worse than you might think, since glass itself conducts heat as well as a similar thickness of concrete (and concrete is a pretty good heat conductor). Instead, insulating glass is simply double glazing: two sheets of glass permanently sealed together to prevent water from entering between them. The trapped dry air serves as an insulator with an R-value of about 1. Excluding condensation is nearly impossible between other glazing materials.

In addition to obscuring the view and looking as if something is wrong with the glazing, water vapor within double glazing contributes to heat loss because water transports heat as it evaporates from the warm side and condenses on the cold side. The trapped water also can damage the structure.

Window units for well-insulated houses have been increased to three or four layers of glass, with modest increases in R-values and large increases in price. This upgrading would not be justified on a sunspace. Radiation is the dominant heat-loss mechanism through some double glazings, so a radiation barrier or low-e (low emissivity) coating has been developed for placement between the two layers of glass (e.g., Heat Mirror). It reflects the far IR back toward the warm side. Again, the cost is high (an additional $7 per square foot) for a modest improvement in efficiency. Heat-barrier glass would not be cost-effective for a sunspace until the material is much cheaper and can be applied to the inside by anyone. Further improvements are expected in special "selective" coatings for glass and perhaps plastics, and the cost is likely to fall.

Since a heat barrier affects radiation loss and not heat conduction, it is not strictly accurate to refer to it as gaining one unit of R-value. In terms of overall heat loss in typical installations, however, this is its approximate contribution.

Heat-barrier film presently is factory-applied in a delicate process and should not be confused with the common sun-control films widely available. The latter are broad-spectrum mirrors that reflect some percentage, usually 50 percent, of all types of solar radiation. Although it will prevent some heat loss from the inside, reflective film also prevents a comparable amount of solar gain from the outside and is not selective or one-way.

Overglazed sunspaces that are overheating might benefit from reflective film applied on the inside south glazing and any roof glazing. Glass is available with the reflective element (a metal powder) embedded in it. It has various colors, depending on the metal used. "Smokey" glass that appears dark without reflecting would not be as good to control overheating since it gets very hot itself. It works more by absorption of sunlight than by reflection, and the heat could damage seals and mounts.

If you select glass, the "best buys" in glass are the standard sizes of tempered double-glass units costing $3 to $4 per square foot. These units are available 76 inches high and 34 or 46 inches wide, and were originally intended for regular and large patio doors. These patio units are manufactured in large quantities, are well made, widely available, low in cost, of convenient size, and expected to be available for the foreseeable future. The standard height might seem short, but it leaves room for a vent above or below the fixed glazing. Tempered double-glass units in custom sizes are very expensive, if available at all. Single sheets 8 feet high are available, and were made originally for solar collectors.

Tempered glass cannot be cut after it is manufactured, a disadvantage you must accept in order to gain its superior strength, impact resistance (to soft objects), and flexibility. Tempered glass is nearly immune to hail in vertical mountings, but is easily broken by sharp, hard objects and will transform with a "bang" into a pile of safe glass gravel. You must design the sunspace to accommodate the special sizes and mounting requirements of these units, but they are worth it. The tempered units can endure the widest range of temperatures of any glazing and last the longest (indefinitely except for the seal).

Some sunspace makers have used patio doors themselves for glazing. These units come 6 or 8 feet wide and 80 inches high, like any door. Older or used ones might have leaky frames or worn tracks. You could caulk the leaks shut, and the sliding part would rarely be moved in a fixed installation. Using a series of patio doors as glazing might not have the appearance you want, but the cost, ease of installation, and ease of replacement are advantages. The framing and sealing of the glass has already been done for hardly more cost than the glass itself. For good summer ventilation, each unit can be half opened and most are provided with screens (although the screens are usually not very durable).

If you can find single sheets of tempered glass at a bargain price, you might be able to assemble your own double units. You can space them by caulking strips of cedar or redwood (cross section about ½ × ½ inch) between clean sheets. Moisture cannot be excluded in this simple process, however. It would be better to find old patio doors with double tempered glass and remove the glass unit (carefully) from the frame. Another bargain to look for is large salvaged windows from commercial or institutional buildings. You might find tall single- or double-glazed window units about 3 feet wide with an operable vent window (sometimes called *Anderson-style*, after one maker).

Tempered double units are very heavy (over 100 lbs. for 46 × 76 inches) and are mounted resting on two hard synthetic rubber blocks in a frame. Various thicknesses of the sealed unit are available. The minimum recommended is ⅝ inch, giving about ⅜ inch of air space. The unit is held in place with wood or other soft battens (FIG. 3-5).

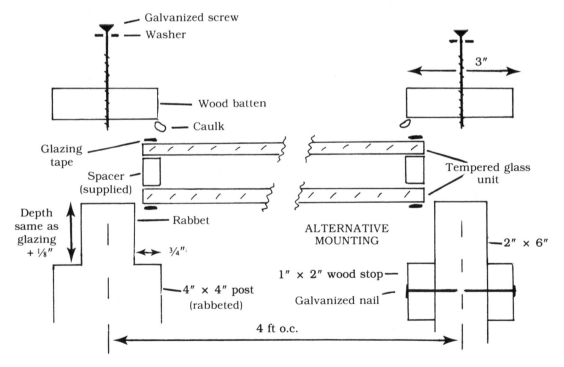

Fig. 3-5. *Mounting double-tempered glass between 4-x-4 wood posts and on 2-x-6 posts (cross-section view).*

You can frame and batten it from the inside or the outside. Apply *glazing tape*, long-lived sticky black strips ⅛ inch thick, to both sides so that the battens can squeeze it into the frame and form a seal. Be sure to maintain a ¼-inch clearance all around the glass in the frame so that if the frame distorts slightly, it cannot apply stress or bring a nail into contact with the glass. You need to take great care to keep screws and nails from accidentally deflecting into the glass during mounting.

Wood frames are difficult to build to high precision and squareness—another reason for the clearance around glass. Also, wood frames are difficult to form flat, that is, in one plane. Fortunately tempered glass will bend slightly to allow a fit anyway. You can place the glass against a smooth aluminum frame with care, since aluminum is softer than glass. The frame joints must be very secure so that there is no perceptible step in the surface of the frame. You should consider carefully how the glass is mounted, what problems could develop, and even how the glass is to be maneuvered into place for mounting. You should not put 46-inch-wide double units on a roof, just those 34 inches wide. Double units that are 46 inches wide flex alarmingly under their own weight, and the seal will creep and fail.

You should use tempered or other strong and safe glass for overhead applications. Building codes are likely to require protection from broken glass overhead. Glass also comes "wired" or laminated with plastic film to prevent broken pieces from falling. These forms might be difficult to find for individual use, although some sunspace manufacturers are supplying them.

The more expensive sunspace systems with aluminum frames now feature curved glass at the eaves. Instead of the glass roof having a small overhang, the last roof piece curves gently downward to form the top wall piece. Although plastics have been used in curves, only tempered glass has the low thermal expansion to maintain a seal around a curve. Use of a curved glazed eave is mainly an aesthetic choice, although it provides less place for leakage.

You can obtain untempered, or *annealed*, glass cut to any size and made into double-glazed units at about $4 per square foot. Glass thicknesses are 3⁄16 inch for large sheets and ⅛ inch for small. The sealed unit should have at least ⅜ inch of air space, although ¼ inch is used in many of the lower cost window units. Single sheets of glass are only about $1 per square foot. Annealed glass would be suitable only for vertical glazing, and even there would endure only the smallest hail. Caulking into wood frames, or using glazing tape, is the best way to mount annealed units. Again, there should be clearance all around, with the glass resting on rubber blocks. Old window units with single annealed glass do not work well in tilted walls, and especially not on roofs, because water collects in them and rots the frames.

Reasons for selecting glass are clarity, ease of getting a good watertight seal (except on roofs), appearance, and low thermal expansion. Reasons for not selecting glass are its liability to catastrophic breakage (damage usually is not limited to a crack or hole) and its clarity (when privacy or diffuse light is wanted).

Plastic Glazings

Plastic glazings cannot match the performance of glass in trapping far IR or in long life. Some plastics are cheaper, and some are more expensive. You might choose plastic because some types are not clear, or because it is resistant to breakage. Even a large rock will leave a limited hole in most plastics. Heavy hail on plastic roofs is bad news, however, because the roof becomes all holes.

The naming of plastics is complex (see TABLE 5 in the Appendix). Each material has a chemical name, a more common or generic name, and several brand names. Although development continues, no substantially new and better glazing plastics at a reasonable cost have entered the market in many years. The ones described have been available a long time and seem destined to remain available for the foreseeable future. You can choose any of them with confidence in the availability of replacements.

In thin, flexible sheets there are translucent polyethylene (about $.02 per square foot) and clear polyvinyl chloride ("vinyl," about $.10 per square foot). Both are recommended in the 6 mil (thousandths of an inch) thickness. Ultraviolet-protected polyethylene is made, but more difficult to find (e.g., Monsanto 602 and 603). Vinyl lasts longer and is sold in small widths for temporary storm windows. Polyethylene is available in very large rolls. Other thin plastics are polyesters (e.g., Mylar) polyvinyl fluoride (e.g., Tedlar), and fluorocarbons (e.g., Teflon). These are expensive and of no greater advantage in sunspace applications. As outer glazings, their thinness and large thermal expansion would show up as ripples and sags, and any impact with a sharp object would leave a tear that could grow.

To mount thin plastic sheeting, fasten every 2 feet with wood battens (FIG. 3-6).

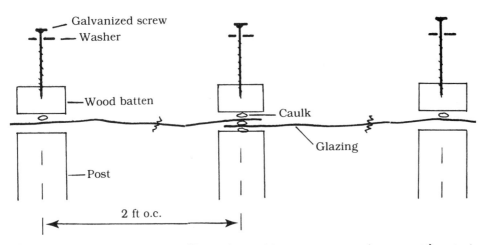

Fig. 3-6. *Mounting thin plastic film with wood battens on posts (cross-section view).*

Tight mounting will not work because when in use they become hotter and will sag, and when cold they will permanently stretch or tear. Heat loss is much reduced in an inexpensive sunspace using plastic film if it is doubled. You can separate the layers with wood or metal spacers. Unusual designs use air pressure.

Sheet acrylic (methyl methacrylate, about $2 per square foot) is ⅛ inch thick, flexible, and difficult to break. It is sometimes used for storm doors and windows and widely available. It is clear with an initial transmittance better than glass. Double-walled acrylic is ⅝ inch thick, with the two sides joined by ribs at ⅝-inch or 1¼-inch intervals (e.g., Exolite, $3 to $4 per square foot). The latter form is relatively clear and provides a semidistorted view. Double-walled acrylic is 47¼ inches wide and comes in lengths of any multiple of 2 feet from 8 to 22 feet. It has proven adequately strong for impacts and high winds. It is especially suitable for long roof runs since there do not need to be joints. Roof rafters need not be spaced closer than 4 feet for this material, but they must be extra thick to hold the required roof load. The lifetime is 10 years or more. The temperature should not be permitted to exceed 160° F, which is unlikely in a sunspace.

Stronger than acrylic, with slightly less transmittance and higher temperature tolerance (240° F), is polycarbonate. It is available as sheets or double-walled with ribs. Polycarbonate is slightly yellowish, degrades in appearance faster, and costs more than acrylic (about $6 per square foot).

You need to mount the double-walled plastics in special aluminum T-channels with either a vinyl cap strip pressed onto the molding and glazing (FIG. 3-7) or an aluminum batten containing a gasket bolted on. The sheet width of 47¼ inches is intended to fit the T-channel 48 inches from the center of one channel to the center of the next (termed *on center* and abbreviated o.c.) without touching the narrow center rib. A total sideways expansion of ¼ inch is permitted. The mounting is more expensive than the glazing itself and is designed to provide a rain seal while allowing thermal expansion. The seal has not proven perfect in practice, but the channels are also designed to drain small amounts of moisture. The cap strip deteriorates in a few years, depending on how hot it gets. The tightness of the mounting is critical; it cannot be too tight or too loose. No simpler and cheaper method has been found to satisfy these conditions. You cannot screw battens down against this glazing. No caulk will remain sealed against it. As the material heats and cools, thus changing its length in the mounting, you hear it pop and snap.

Double-walled acrylic provides an important case for examining the thermal expansion of glazings. The expansion is substantial, up to ½ inch per 8 feet of length for an extreme change from −20° F in winter to +120° F in summer.

The glazing is likely to be somewhat warm during installation, so the mounting must provide room for a little more expansion. Suppose that the acrylic is at 80° F during mounting on a roof and that it might get as hot as 140° F (only 20° less than its rated limit of 160° F). The coefficient for thermal expansion is 0.0004 inch per degree per foot of length (from the glazing table). A temperature change of 60° would lead to a length increase of 0.19 inch (less than ¼ inch) over 8 feet.

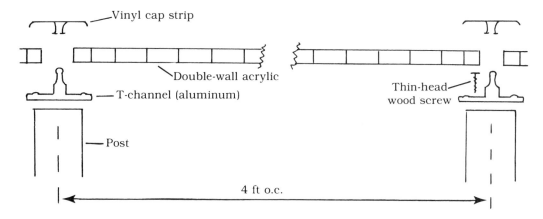

Fig. 3-7. *Mounting double-walled acrylic glazing on posts (cross-section view).*

The mounting system can accommodate that change.

Also consider the winter extreme. Then this glazing shrinks $0.0004 \times 100 \times 8 = 0.32$ inch over 8 feet. The mounting system can accommodate just about this much shrinkage before the glazing pulls out. Clearly you must measure the installed length carefully to avoid problems at either extreme of temperature. The frame also expands when hot, but not nearly enough to keep up with the glazing.

Fiber-Reinforced Glazings

Combining some of the features of glass and plastic is fiber-reinforced polyester (FRP). The fibers are glass, and enough is used to make it somewhat opaque to far IR. Despite its cloudy appearance, FRP transmits sun almost as well as glass. Several grades are available, from $.20 to over $1 per square foot. The best grade is the only one that lasts 10 years or more during exposure to the sun. It usually has, and should have, a coating that helps protect it from ultraviolet light. FRP comes in flat sheets 0.04 inch thick, which might sound thin but is sufficient for a very durable material. Thicknesses of 0.025 and 0.06 inch are also available but of little advantage. The corrugated roof style is thinner but rigid by virtue of its shape. The flat sheets are available up to 49½ inches wide in 50-foot rolls, so large areas can be glazed without joints. With age and exposure, FRP weathers so that fibers are exposed, leading to a worn-out appearance that has little to do with its transmittance or strength. It should remain hail-resistant at least 10 years, and it can be recoated for better appearance and lifetime.

You should support sheet-form FRP every 2 feet, but still it will sag or bow because of substantial thermal expansivity. You can overlap, caulk, and batten adjoining sheets (FIG. 3-8) or assemble them in an interleaving synthetic rubber gasket held by metal battens.

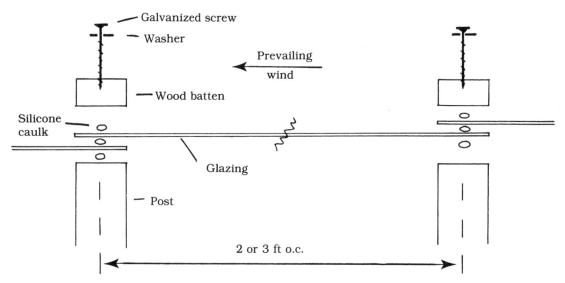

Fig. 3-8. *Mounting thick plastic sheets (e.g., fiberglass-reinforced polyester or FRP) on posts (cross-section view).*

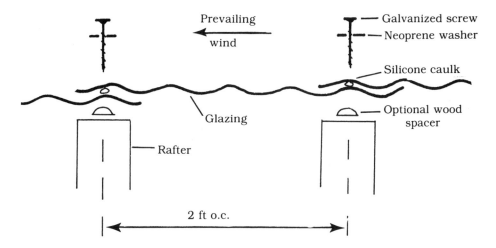

Fig. 3-9. *Mounting corrugated FRP on roof rafters. Put screws in the valleys when mounting on wall posts (cross-section view).*

Mount corrugated sheets with screws or nails that have neoprene washers. (Screws are much easier to remove for reglazing.) Put the fasteners through the peaks of the corrugation on roofs and in the valleys on walls. The corrugations are no simple fraction of a foot apart, but the sheets are 26 inches wide and designed for 2 feet o.c. spacing. You will need to use wavy trim boards to form a good seal between the corrugations and the frame (FIG. 3-9).

Precautions for Glazings

You should add glazing in large units, since small window frames or recycled windows might introduce excessive shading because of the frames. Glazing cannot, however, span such a large distance as to be unable to withstand wind or snow loads. Support single-walled plastics every 2 feet (in one direction is sufficient). Double-walled plastics are designed for 4-foot spacing. Some manufacturers make double-glazed units using FRP, which require a minimum of construction to assemble as a sunspace. These units are 4 feet wide and can be almost any length.

Teflon film does not seem to have a place in sunspace glazing. Although it is very strong, very clear, and very resistant to ultraviolet light, it is also very expensive, about $1 per square foot in 1-mil thickness. Very thin Teflon film succumbs to tears started by some sharp edge or minor accident. The inner glazing of a sunspace would be bumped with objects, so a weak plastic film is not recommended there. Polyvinyl fluoride film is translucent but otherwise a good inner glazing. It costs about $1 per square foot for a 4-mil thickness. Another good inner glazing, too stiff to wrinkle but still translucent, would be the thinner 0.025-mil FRP.

Some additional comments are needed on the thermal expansion of glazings and their frames. As TABLE 3 in the Appendix shows, glass and wood have the lowest (and similar) coefficients of expansion. A change in temperature from −20° F to +120° F would expand an 8-foot sheet of glass only about ¹⁄₁₆ inch. The similarity of expansion for glazing and frame material is more important than the lowness of the coefficients. Loss of seal is less likely when the frame and glazing expand about the same. Wood and steel frames are compatible with glass, but an aluminum frame expands twice as much. The plastics have expansions hopelessly larger than frame materials (except other plastics, which are not usually available for this use). Note that the expansion of the underlying structure is what matters, not the expansion of channels or battens attached to the frame. An aluminum channel screwed to a steel frame will bow slightly when hot if it was originally fastened during cold weather.

GLAZING ROOFS AND OTHER WALLS

A glazed roof is an extreme heat-collecting measure that is more effective in seasons other than winter. It is best used in cold, cloudy northern climates. It is also a major source of heat loss at night, since warm air collects under the roof. Therefore, you should have some means of moving insulation over the glazed ceiling at night. A partially glazed roof (FIG. 3-10) might be helpful for obtaining enough diffuse skylight for plants in winter, but it will provide no heat. You must make a careful seal from the shingled roof to the glazing to avoid penetration of rain or melting snow. You should never glaze a northward-sloping roof, and in fact you should avoid designing a sunspace with a northward roof.

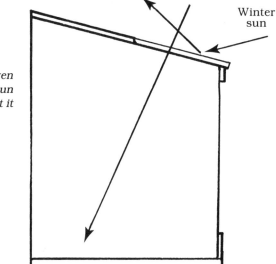

Fig. 3-10. Roof glazing, even partial, accepts most summer sun and rejects most winter sun (but it provides more winter light).

Glazing part of the east or west walls will require some thought. Studies have shown that, on the average, more heat is lost through such glazing than is gained (if no insulation is used). If you plan to use the sunspace in early morning or late afternoon, however—perhaps for work, rest, or meetings—then you could glaze the side the sun is on during this use. It is better to glaze just part of the wall—that part nearest south. If you plan to have a glazed storm door on the east, that might let in sufficient early sun to warm the sunspace before the sun swings to the south. If large, glazed storm doors are too expensive or do not have enough glazed area, then you can make your own oversized door frame and attach one of the glazings to it. Adding glazing by means of ordinary operable window units rather than by total wall glazing would be a good way to gain some sun on the east or west and also would make night insulation easier.

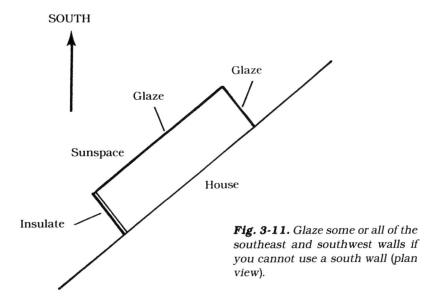

Fig. 3-11. *Glaze some or all of the southeast and southwest walls if you cannot use a south wall (plan view).*

If your site has no place for a south-facing sunspace, then you should add glazing on the walls favored by the sun. For example, a sunspace on a wall facing southeast should have glazing on what is now the southeast wall of the sunspace, and on the southwest sidewall (FIG. 3-11).

PROTECTION OF THE SUNSPACE

The sunspace as a whole and its glazing in particular need protection. The protection should be against cold weather and damage. Placement of the sunspace on the south side of the house and provision of windbreaks will help. The glazing, being the most expensive and visible component, should have additional protection. Sometimes you might need to provide wire screening, although screening usually detracts from the appearance and reduces the amount of sunlight by up to 10 percent. You should not place the sunspace so that trees which lose limbs are located above or upwind from the glazing. Summer shade by deciduous trees is desirable, but you should choose the type and location of the trees carefully (if possible). A glazed sunspace cannot readily share a yard with a baseball game. Car tires on the street can send small rocks at high speed toward the glazing. The builder might note other unusual dangers to the glazing.

USING SHADE

Not only is quality glazing the most costly material per square foot, but it also permits much more heat loss at night than will an insulated wall. Also, it is liable to damage and breakage. Therefore, the glazing area should be kept to the minimum that admits all wanted sunlight. Careful use of overhang and other shading in the summer can keep much sunlight out, while admitting all available sun in the winter.

FIGURE 3-12 shows how summer sun can be prevented from striking even the bottom of the glazing because it first strikes the substantial roof overhang. The summer solar rays are drawn at the angle for the highest altitude the sun reaches in the sky. In winter the rays are no higher in altitude than some low maximum angle, as shown. The overhang prevents these rays from striking any higher than a certain position. Therefore you can make the wall above that point solid, rather than glazed, creating a "headwall." If you want some sun through the glazing in summer, then you can shorten the overhang. Remember, however, that at other times of the day than noon, the sun is lower and will enter more glazing. You can eliminate sun most of the day through shading design, but you will need extreme overhangs.

The designer can make two triangles, one with an angle matching the highest summer sun altitude and one with the highest winter sun altitude. Then he can retest and redraw a profile drawing of the sunspace until the desired shading behavior occurs, as shown in FIG. 3-12. Using the scale of the profile drawing, he can measure the height of the headwall and the length of the overhang.

Fig. 3-12. *Size the overhang to control the summer sun, then size the headwall to admit winter sun past the overhang without wasting glazing. Use the sun altitude at summer and winter solstice for your latitude.*

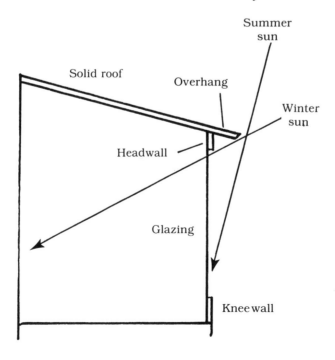

There are many other ways to control summer sun by means of shading. You should plant deciduous trees, which gain and lose their leaves at convenient times of the year, if they are not already present. The solar landscape designer should learn how far the limbs of selected mature trees will reach in the locality, then place the trees so that the limbs just intercept summer sun without overhanging the sunspace (FIG. 3-13). Also important is the expected height of the tree.

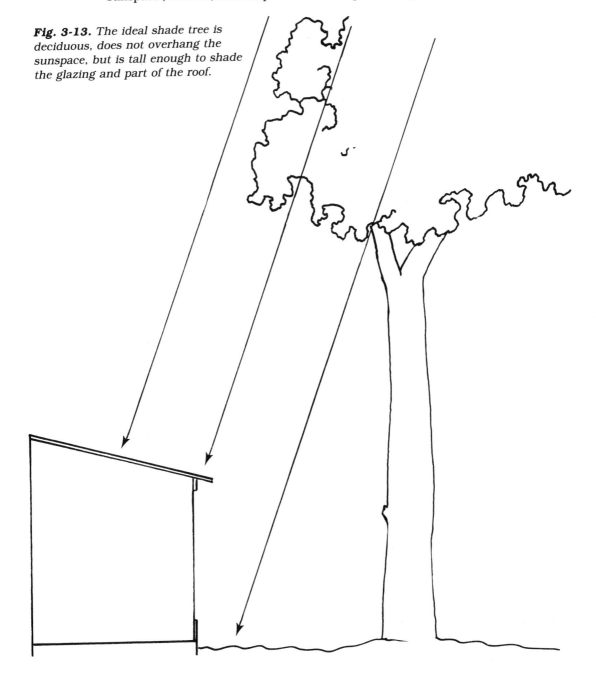

Fig. 3-13. *The ideal shade tree is deciduous, does not overhang the sunspace, but is tall enough to shade the glazing and part of the roof.*

Unfortunately, unless your backyard already has the right trees in the best places, it will be a long wait for deciduous shade. If possible, position the sunspace site to take best advantage of existing long-lived trees. Also plant replacement trees to be ready for the time when the mature ones die or fall down.

Shade is best produced outside first. Overhangs are outside, and that is where you can build wood lattices. Annual vines grow much faster than trees and will climb and cover a lattice before summer. Perennial deciduous vines will need a few years to provide shade. Some plants, such as sunflowers and corn, grow tall rapidly each year. (Weeds do, too.) You can attach roll-down bamboo or metal-slat shades (FIG. 3-14) outside the glazing, although it is a nuisance to roll them up and down as often as you might need in fall and spring. They also manage to loosen and to flap wildly in the wind. Special shade paint, akin to whitewash, will stay on glazing a few months in summer and wash off by fall. You can mount wood or metal louvers, preferably adjustable, over the glazing. You can set louvers to pass winter sun and block the sun when it is higher in the sky in other seasons. Aluminum "screen," which consists of many small fixed louvers stamped in aluminum sheet, is available in some areas.

Fig. 3-14. *Metal, slatted blinds can be rolled down to provide summer shade outside the glazing.*

If you do not have outside shade, then you can attach inside shade inside the glazing in the form of sunproof shades, blinds (FIG. 3-15), or curtains (FIG. 3-16) of light color. Roll-up shades made of reflective film are available. Manufacturers of glazed-roof sunspaces often provide a means of shading the ceiling to reduce overheating. You can pull covering along tracks in the aluminum frames. Some indoor shade designs prevent heat loss in winter as well as excessive insolation in summer (e.g., Window Quilt, Insulider); however, they must shut tightly in winter but permit ventilation in summer. Avoid tightly covering the south wall or glazed roof to form a solar collector, because heat could build up to a dangerous level. You must permit some air passage to the sunward side of sun-blocking material.

Fig. 3-15. *Rolled blinds can control summer sun from the inside. A ceiling fan helps bring winter heat down. (Notice the intensity of the sun, as seen in the bottom lefthand corner.)*

Fig. 3-16. *White curtains reject summer (and winter) sun.*

Reflective curtains, film, or panels will reject more sun to the outside than ordinary fabrics and slatted blinds. Fabric shades and plastic blinds vary widely in the degree to which they withstand color fading in the sun and actual deterioration. Reports (see *"Fabrics and the Sun,"* in the Articles section of the References) on which materials perform better are available. Some shading systems can be made to close and open automatically, at substantial cost.

FOUNDATIONS AND FLOORS

These sections on the structure are intended to provide an introduction to what is involved in installing a sunspace, so that you can choose whether to buy or build and to understand some of the choices. The information provided will enable you to determine cost estimates. Chapter 4 will include details of construction. Enough of the construction is discussed here so that the designer will know how to choose the sizes of various parts of the structure.

The foundation you choose depends in part on the framing method you choose (discussed in the following section). The foundation, however, is what holds up the sunspace and helps keep it together, hence its introduction here. Building officials in some areas will require that the sunspace be built to the same specifications as any room added to a house. Others will classify it as an auxiliary, or even a temporary, structure. Thus, the permanence and durability of the foundation depend on how stable you want the structure to be and on what is required. For the most part, exact sizes are not given here because local codes might vary on sizing.

The most common foundation is the poured concrete wall, possibly with footing and reinforcing (FIG. 3-17). In most areas with cold winters, officials will require that the foundation extend below the *frost line*—the depth at which the ground freezes in the worst winters. In the United States, the frost line can vary from a few inches to 5 feet. Generally no compensation is granted for the fact that a sunspace that truly stores heat in an insulated foundation will prevent freezing of the enclosed ground. The problem with freezing of the ground is that, especially for wet soils, the soil expands upward and applies pressure sideways. A structure resting on this part of the ground will move upward in winter and will likely not settle back in summer.

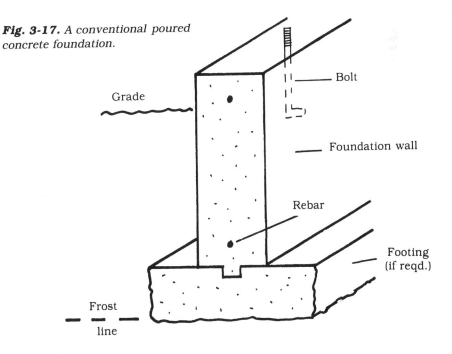

Fig. 3-17. A conventional poured concrete foundation.

Grade

Bolt

Foundation wall

Rebar

Footing (if reqd.)

Frost line

The sunspace would need to be structurally isolated from the house if the sunspace foundation permits it to move as a result of frost. It might touch the house and be sealed to it, but there should be no permanent connections and no rigid alignments. Its foundation also might need to resist breaking under sideways soil-ice pressure. To prevent such breakage, use the standard 6- or 8-inch-wide concrete foundation. Footings might not be required for a sunspace because the weight to be supported is minimal and nearly all soils can hold it. The concrete foundation wall itself usually will be much heavier than the rest of the sunspace that sits on it. Footings matching those under the house might be needed, however, to ensure that the sunspace is affected by ground changes and motions the same as the house.

Although a slab or deck already present might be a tempting no-cost foundation on which to put a sunspace, it is recommended that you use a proper frostproof foundation to avoid problems. A low-cost foundation, such as railroad ties, would also create problems due as a result of the motion of frozen ground. If you are using an expedient foundation, be certain nothing can be torn loose on the house if the sunspace moves. Also consider what would happen to glass glazing if an insecure foundation would move or heave.

Excavation to the frost line for building even a small foundation could be an arduous job by hand and would take many weekends. If you can hire an excavating machine and operator by the hour, the whole job will take only about two hours with careful planning. If the dirt is placed where it will not prevent concrete pouring but is near the foundation, then you can fill around the foundation by hand in a few hours. Excavation should be just to the bottom of the foundation or footing and no farther. The foundation should rest on undisturbed soil, which supposedly is firmly packed and fairly dry. If you must build on fill, compacting is necessary first, and is best done without much water. Add sand and gravel and avoid loose, wet clay soils.

Much of the work on a concrete foundation is in constructing wood forms in the excavated trenches. If these forms are not strong and straight, the concrete foundation will be irregular and difficult to adapt to. You can simply pour the footing, if any, on the dirt first, adding the means to connect it to the foundation wall. Once the forms are built, you can closely estimate the amount of concrete needed for the poured foundation by calculating the cubic feet of concrete for the form, converting to cubic yards, and using the price per yard or reasonable fraction of it. Usually the quantity needed is far too large for home mixing, and delivered ready-mix concrete is worth the extra cost.

You should have several helpers, wheelbarrows, finishing tools, and some experience with concrete projects before you attempt to pour a foundation. Also be certain that a concrete truck can reach most of the foundation. Usually the trucks carry chutes that can reach about 16 feet maximum from the rear of the truck. Check whether the truck can pass over fragile sidewalks, travel along narrow side yards, and aim the chute at the work. Soft ground and lawns will be permanently packed and show the tracks. For extreme cases, you can hire a concrete pumping service that will move the concrete through a large hose a long distance to your pour site. Another alternative is to have several people with wheelbarrows wheel it around the house—on firm ground and over smooth, strong planks—to the site.

The foundation requires a second look if you want to put a floor in the sunspace and heavy loads—plant beds, a large hot tub—on the floor, which then rests on the foundation. Generally it is assumed that a sunspace does not have a floor separate from the ground. This choice keeps the cost low, preserves the idea that the sunspace is partly outdoors, and helps couple the solar energy input to ground storage.

Another type of foundation is one made of concrete blocks on a footing and used much as a concrete foundation wall would be (FIG. 3-18). It must have a cap of concrete or a treated wood sill to hold it together, and probably also reinforcing steel bars (*rebar*) through some of the empty cores of the blocks. You might need to fill the cores with concrete. The cost to do all this work might be similar to that for a poured concrete wall. Only the work to install forms is eliminated. If you own a small concrete mixer, you can spread out the pouring work for a concrete block foundation over time and between two people. Before you replace dirt fill on the outside of a concrete or block foundation, you should insulate the foundation, as described later.

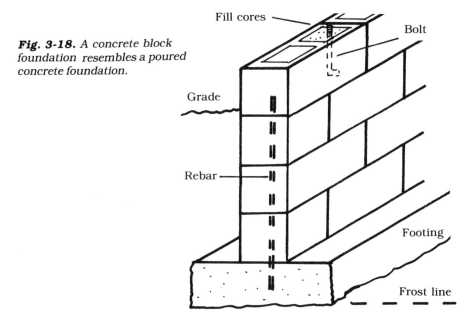

Fig. 3-18. *A concrete block foundation resembles a poured concrete foundation.*

The preceding foundations provide a continuous wall in the ground, which could also serve as a kneewall and is a continuous resting place for wall frames. The continuous foundation also can hold heat storage material. If you build the sunspace by the post method, with the main structure supported by posts 4 or 8 feet apart, then you do not need a continuous foundation wall. You can set in the posts or fasten them to concrete piers about 1 to 1½ feet square or round (FIG. 3-19).

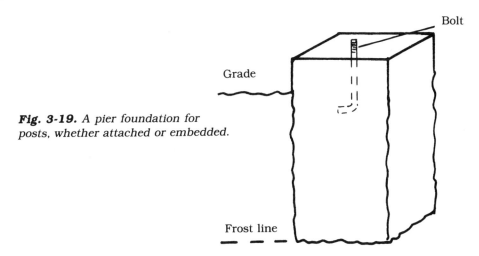

Fig. 3-19. *A pier foundation for posts, whether attached or embedded.*

You can pour piers in place or purchase and drop them in holes. Positioning must be accurate. Regardless of the frost line, posts 4 feet o.c. should be anchored at least 2 feet deep; those 8 feet o.c., 3 feet deep, to prevent tipping. In more casual construction, just put the posts a couple of feet in the ground with concrete tamped around each post in its hole.

To make the structure frostproof, the piers should go to the frost line. Otherwise, they will "float" on the soil, and the sunspace might move relative to the house. There is no foundation to insulate, but you should excavate a deep trench between and around piers or posts for the insertion of insulation. Putting wood posts into concrete can cause trouble, even if the posts are treated. The wood will swell when wet and break the concrete, either during setting or later. It is better to insert steel bolts or hardware designed to attach posts to concrete, or to use nonrusting steel pipes. Do not plan to rest the structure on a foundation without connecting it, since wind loads can tip or raise the sunspace when a heavy foundation is not holding it down. Posts in soil are just as inadequate.

Placing the sunspace as a unit on the ground also makes it liable to overturning or lifting by wind. Some sunspaces are manufactured and advertised as being ready to place on the ground. If this procedure is permitted in your area, you need some means to tie it down with heavy weight. Stakes would have to be very heavy, thoroughly protected from rusting, and driven deep. Sunspaces have been built with railroad ties or treated wood beams as the only foundation. This should be considered a temporary approach at best. If you layer, pin together, and bury railroad ties, the foundation can be frostproof and you can treat it as a continuous one. The effort and expense involved, however, might better go into the more permanent concrete foundation.

A wood foundation requires quite a different method (FIG. 3-20). The wood must be pressure treated for underground installation with chemicals that do not harm plants or emit toxic fumes. Use only wood treated with copper arsenate, which

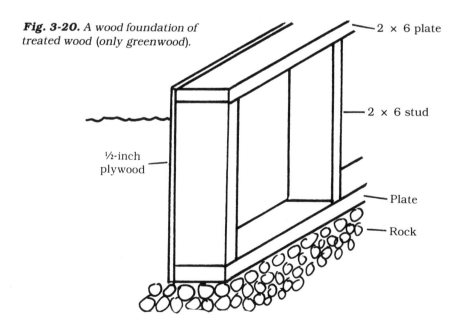

Fig. 3-20. *A wood foundation of treated wood (only greenwood).*

2 × 6 plate

2 × 6 stud

½-inch plywood

Plate

Rock

acquires a green color, hence the term *greenwood.* An arsenic-based treatment sounds dangerous, but studies have shown that very little leaches out of the wood. Be sure you understand the ratings on the wood you get. It must have been treated for underground use. When the wood is cut, the chemical should be seen to have penetrated the wood fully. Greenwood costs typically about three times more than conventional lumber of the same dimensions.

A greenwood foundation wall of 2 × 6s and plywood is built to do the function of a concrete wall. It must be strong and straight, and extend to the frost line. It should rest on about 6 inches of tamped crushed rock. Since the weight of a house is not on this foundation, just a sunspace, you might best place rock over its bottom wood plate to help weigh it down against uplifting. Wood foundations cost somewhat less than the equivalent in concrete and have been found to be adequate for houses and similar structures in all parts of the United States. You must consider, however, that with wood the heat storage of concrete is gone. On the other hand, the wood wall conducts heat to the outside poorly compared to concrete.

If the floor is not earth, then you can set some other durable waterproof floor on the ground. The floor might be a concrete slab (about $1 per square foot). It can be 3 inches thick to handle most loads and should have sand and a plastic vapor barrier under it. Another type of floor is made of paving brick set on sand and a vapor barrier. You can use the bricks ($1 or more per square foot, depending on style) loose or mortared. You can cement clay tile ($1 to $2 per square foot) to a concrete floor. You can color and finish concrete floors to look like tile. (See *"Sizzling Slabs,"* in the Articles section of References.) Masonry floors are excellent heat storage elements. More heat storage can be under the floor, as described in the section *Heat Storages* later in this chapter. You can build a sunspace with steel frames, including steel floor beams, or *joists.* You then can make the actual floor wood or wood underlaying floor tile or outdoor carpet. You can lay wood joists across the foundation and use them for a floor. You can fasten wood 2 × 4s to any flat concrete slab, nail a wood subfloor on top, then lay carpet or tile.

Almost any floor will cost $1 to $2 per square foot. Only outdoor carpet will withstand the rigors of a sunspace. Chapter 5 gives more details on special floors.

FRAMING METHODS

Several possible types of framing are suitable for sunspaces. In addition to the conventional wood stud wall, with wood roof rafters, there is the post-and-beam method and masonry structures. Posts and beams can be of wood, steel, aluminum, plastic pipe, or combinations of these materials. The steel or aluminum can be in the form of rectangular or round tubes (pipes), angles, channels, or I-beams. Plastic PVC pipe should have 2-inch or larger diameters; there is no well-established construction method for PVC pipe.

Masonry includes concrete block, brick, and adobe (unfired clay). If you build masonry walls, you need to use framing, as covered here, to hold the glazing and the roof. You are invited to invent a new framing method, but be forewarned that code enforcers are very conservative about new methods. You should carefully study the established methods, and the reasons for their components, before you try any variation.

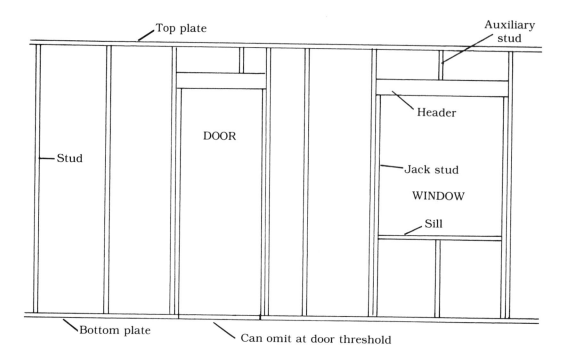

Fig. 3-21. *Conventional wood framing in face view.*

Conventional framing uses wood 2 × 4s, plywood, and other lumber. A bottom plate, which will be bolted to a continuous foundation, has 2-x-4 vertical pieces, or *studs*, fastened between it and a top plate (FIG. 3-21). For a sunspace, you can space the studs 2 feet o.c. Fasten with nails whose length is at least twice the thickness of one board. Nail a covering, or *sheathing*, to one face of the framework to bind all the parts together and make it rigid. This structure resists collapsing or distortion (called, loosely, *shear*) as in FIG. 3-22, although it can be twisted somewhat. A wood foundation wall is built to perform similarly.

If the planned length of this wall structure exceeds available lumber (usually 20 feet), then you can build it in separate sections and nail end studs together. Bolt the bottom plate to the foundation. You must study foundation bolt placement carefully to avoid having a bolt interfere with a stud or post location. Codes usually require bolts to be about 1 foot from each end of each separate bottom plate and not more than 6 feet apart in between.

This framing method is good for the east and west walls of the sunspace, but the sheathing interferes with glazing on the south. If you will mount the glazing 2 feet o.c., then the vertical 2-x-4 studs will serve as the framing posts (also called *mullions*) for the glazing. If you will mount the glazing 4 feet o.c. or use other spacing, then you need a thicker beam along the top to support the roof. The beam can be two 2 × 6s on edge, as would be used for the header in FIG. 3-21. Also, the studs or posts must be stronger to make up for the wide spacing. Here 2-x-6 framing is recommended, or you could use 4 × 4s. (Chapter 4 will provide more details on how the overhead beams are mounted on the posts.)

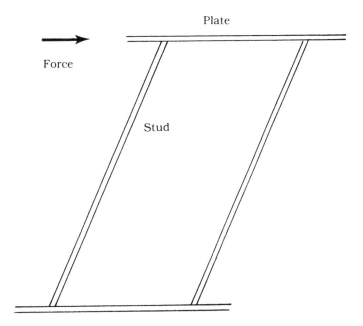

Fig. 3-22. *Distortion (exaggerated) of a frame by forces when not braced.*

The south wall framing carries much of the load of the roof and must be strong. Sometimes a second top plate is required, not so much to add more strength but to hold together the first top plate, which might be in two pieces. Joints must be staggered. The glazing does not brace the south wall and you should not expect it to do so. Something should brace the wall to keep wind load from distorting the frame and harming the glazing. A solid roof is rigid and can provide some bracing. In extreme cases, you might need to add a rigid steel rod or angle piece diagonally near each end of the south wall frame to prevent distortion. These pieces might appear unsightly, but when you see that a few manufacturers have provided such corner bracing, you should wonder why others have not.

The total length of a wall will not work out to be an exact multiple of 2 or 4 feet, although you will install glazings in such a width. The reason is that the spacing of studs or posts 2 feet o.c. causes the outer edges of the end ones to be located beyond that distance. For example, 2- x -4 studs would add an extra ¾ inch to each end of the wall.

Another consideration in wall length is whether the south wall matches the stud pattern on the house so that the east and west walls can be attached to house studs. Sometimes this condition is simply impossible to meet. (Chapter 4 will discuss options.)

Further study of the glazing method shows the need for refinements in wall length. For example, 46-inch-wide tempered glass would have just the right clearance between 2- x -6 studs 48 inches o.c., since there would be 46½ inches between the studs. (Backup trim will be provided to actually hold the glass.) The end studs would provide an additional ¾ inch at each end, as discussed (FIG. 3-23).

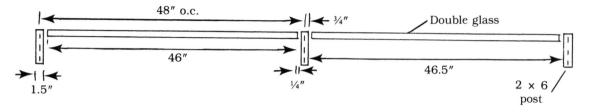

Fig. 3-23. *Planning post spacing for tempered glazing that cannot be cut, in this case, 46-inch-wide units.*

If the south wall had been designed with a different way of interpreting 4 feet o.c. so that its total length was a multiple of 4 feet and no more, then the space between an end post and the next post would not be 46½ but 45¾ inches—too small for the glass.

Using 4-x-4 posts (actual size 3½ inches square) would require cutting *rabbets*, rectangular grooves along the edges of the posts in the front faces to provide clearance for the glass in the preceding example. With this method, 1½ inches of wood, the thickness of a 2 x 4, would remain uncut in the posts. The rabbet should have a width of 1 inch and a depth the same as the thickness of the glass plus ⅛ inch. The designer should verify by drawing that each end post would add 1¾ inches to the total length of the wall unless the rabbet is cut deeper on them. You could mount the glass outside on the face of the posts. If you are using 47¼-inch-wide double-walled acrylic sheets, then face mounting is possible on 2 x 6s, and you need to use a mounting channel, as discussed earlier.

When you take into account the corners formed by connecting a south glazing wall to a sidewall, more length might be added to the south wall, depending on the type of corner you want. FIGURE 3-24 shows three possibilities. In FIG. 3-24A, there is a "blind" region at the end of the sidewall. You can add an additional stud as shown to close it or provide an inside nailing surface. In FIG 3-24B, the blind region is in the glazed wall and allows glazing as close to the end of the wall as possible.

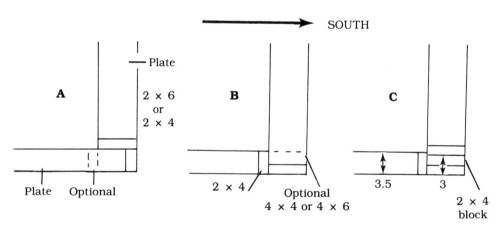

Fig. 3-24. *Three different ways to construct a corner in framing. A 4 x 4 or 4 x 6 also can be put in the corner (plan view).*

In FIG 3-24C, the blind region is filled in by a spacing block and another stud. Now there are 3¾ inches from the center of the last glazing stud to the end of the wall, which adds 7½ inches to the total length of the south wall. Another option for corners is to use 4-x-4 or 4-x-6 posts, although you must still deal with the sidewall end stud. If you are mounting the glazing on an unusual spacing, for example 3 feet o.c., these same considerations apply to the overall design of the wall.

If you want doors and windows on east and west walls (FIG. 3-21), then you need an additional feature, the *header*, which carries the roof load over the door and windows. There is not much load on the sidewalls of a sunspace, but you still need headers as if a full snow load were bearing on these walls. The header rests on two auxiliary, or *jack*, studs. The basic 2 feet o.c. is kept, and other vertical members are put in where required regardless of the odd door and window sizes. Rear exterior doors are fairly standard at 32 inches wide, plus 2 inches for jambs around them. Windows can be any size within reason. Note that this discussion in terms of east, west, and south walls is to be modified for other orientations of the sunspace. For example, if the corner of the sunspace points south, then two adjacent walls might be fully or partly glazed.

Wood post-and-beam framing (on a larger scale sometimes called *timber framing*) uses larger posts and beams to hold up a longer span of wall. As shown in FIG. 3-25, heavy top and bottom beams (names will vary) span the 4 or 8 feet between posts. Use two 2 × 6s or 2 × 8s fastened together, or whatever the code requires.

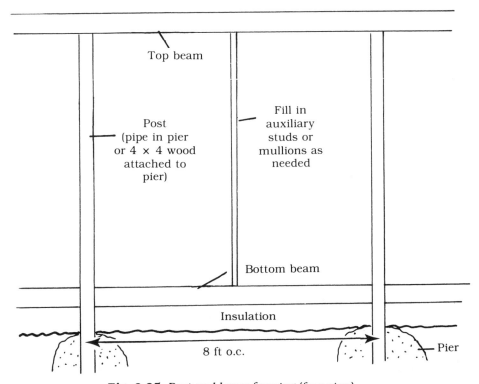

Fig. 3-25. Post-and-beam framing (face view).

You can use wood studs or auxiliary posts to fill in between bottom and top beams to support either a solid wall or glazing, as needed. Some building codes do not specifically describe the post-and-beam method yet, but the information is implicitly given in the code if conventional lumber is used. Wood 4 × 4s and 2 × 6s or 2 × 8s are the largest lumber likely to be needed for a sunspace.

Solid walls between posts have also been made as a "foam-core" panel or sandwich. This element consists of thick foam insulation, perhaps 3½ inches in this case, to which is glued ½-inch exterior plywood or waferwood on both sides. (See References for details.) Solid walls are difficult for the homeowner to construct, although home-constructed versions would be sufficient for sunspace structure. Building codes are just now adjusting to these ways of building.

If the south glazed wall is steeply tilted, rather than vertical, then you must reexamine its connection with the roof, if any, and with the knee wall and foundation. In FIG. 3-26, substantial forces are trying to tip over the knee wall.

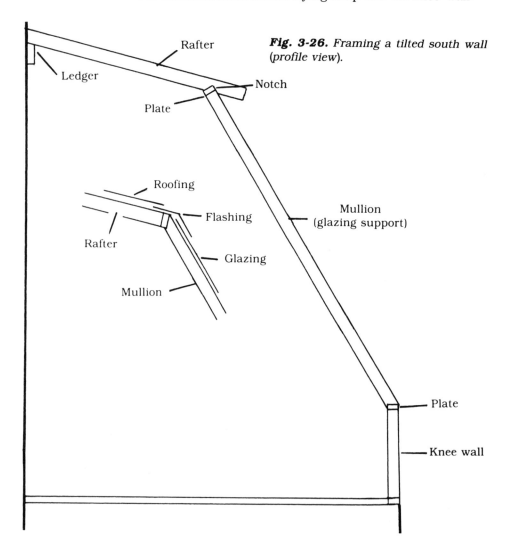

Fig. 3-26. *Framing a tilted south wall (profile view).*

You cannot string bracing through the sunspace to tie the knee wall to the backwall. The solution is to keep the kneewall very low, perhaps 1 foot tall, tie it very securely together with plywood, and fasten it securely to the foundation with metal plates and bolts. A better method might be to plan a taller concrete foundation on which to fasten the sill and tilted studs directly. At the upper end, at least two connection methods are possible. You can put a plate on the tilted wall studs, on which notched rafters rest (as shown), or a plate can connect the ends of the rafters, against which the studs abut (see inset). In the latter case, there will be no roof overhang, and only metal flashing hangs over the wall or glazing to control rain.

This information about wood framing should give you an idea of what sort of work and tools might be involved and should enable you to estimate the lumber and materials needed and, therefore, the cost. Standard lumber has been stable around $1.50 for an 8-foot 2 × 4, with all other sizes in proportion. Standard lumber has been examined and graded to meet minimum building requirements, but avoid using the tempting "economy" studs. They will probably bend and crack before you can even use them. Information about putting weatherproof exterior siding on the outside and finishing the interior walls is covered in Chapter 4 and the References.

If any framing is to be exposed to weather or if you are planning a humid sunspace or greenhouse, then you should make framing from cedar, redwood, or "green" treated wood (underground grade is not necessary). These woods cost two to three times standard lumber made from pine, spruce, fir, and many other species. Sometimes cedar and redwood are available in rough form, not sawn smooth, and having true-size dimensions. The extra strength of the larger dimensions is needed, as these woods are water and weatherproof, but weak in strength. Check the lumber available in your area before finalizing your plans. If the redwood or cedar is of poor quality, you will need to select carefully or use larger sizes.

You can replace the wood posts in post-and-beam construction with galvanized steel pipes 2 or 3 inches in diameter. Except for different attachment methods, you can then build the walls with wood as before. You also can bolt or weld the entire sunspace framing together from steel pipes, channels, rectangular or square tubing, angles, I-beams, or a combination of these materials. You should carefully clean and well-prime the steel before assembly, then fully prime it again.

You can obtain the equivalent members in aluminum with more difficulty and at higher cost. High-grade aluminum is weaker than steel, so members must be thicker for roof loads. Commercial manufacturers have developed many sunspace designs using systems of aluminum or steel framing. The use of aluminum eliminates any rust problems, but aluminum also corrodes unless it is protected by baked enamel or anodizing, resulting in a colored finish rather than the mill finish, the usual silver-grey color. The costs will be high, but the results are beyond the reach of all but the most resourceful of individual builders.

You can build the sidewalls and kneewall of concrete block, brick, adobe, or other masonry. You can include windows and glazing in this construction, and fasten the framing into, or around, the adobe or other block material (FIG. 3-27). The roof will be held up by beams or headers resting on masonry. With masonry, the resulting wall has a low R-value and needs insulation, preferably on the outside, and an additional exterior finish. You also can put the insulation between courses of blocks, bricks, or adobes. Double adobe walls would be about 2 feet thick and have R-10 by themselves. Concrete blocks with new shapes that allow cheaper and more efficient insulation within the blocks are becoming available. If you want to pursue a masonry sunspace, check the References for further information and construction methods.

Fig. 3-27. Solar windows framed into an adobe wall. The adobe is wired for stucco.

It is possible to imitate the concrete-block foundation method in building more of the sunspace. Build it higher and attach durable wood sills and plates securely. Avoid placing ordinary lumber against any masonry that could become damp.

The principal reason to consider interior and exterior finishes at this time is to allow for their thicknesses and identify any need for moistureproof ones. Interior finish of gypsum board is typically ½ inch thick; paneling without backup, ¼ inch; boards, ¾ inch; exterior siding, ½ inch, exterior plywood siding, up to ¾ inch; and exterior plaster (stucco), up to ¾ inch. Use exterior materials inside if the humidity is high. If you will apply brick to the walls, then additional foundation is needed. Consult the References and your local building code.

ROOF FRAMING AND ITS LOADING

Roof rafters are needed 2 feet o.c. for solid roofs and for some glazings. In areas with moderate snow, the usual required snow-load capability is 30 pounds per square foot, which amounts to snow several feet deep, depending on the pack. The roof might seem too strong unless you consider what happens when an avalanche drops on the sunspace from the house roof one or more stories above, or if someone walks on the roof. Also, if there is roof glazing, you cannot permit much flexing or bending of the roof or seals will open and worse damage occur. Check local codes, but 2 × 4s usually are permitted for roof spans of 8 feet; 2 × 6s are needed up to 12 feet; and 2 × 8s up to 16 feet. As the length of any beam increases, the thickness needed to withstand bending increases more rapidly. It is beyond the scope of this book to show you how to calculate the correct rafter size for a given span, but most codes include tables giving the results.

If you are putting glazing on the roof on 4-foot centers, then you must double the size of these widely spaced rafters. If you do not want deep rafters, such as 2 × 8s or 2 × 12s—which make shadows—then you can reduce rafter size by putting a roof support beam under the center of the roof. It, too, must be strong, perhaps a 2 × 12 supported every 16 feet or a 2 × 6 supported every 8 feet, or it can be a steel beam or pipe. Attach this intermediate roof support to posts set on piers as deeply as the rest of the foundation. The heaviest glazing, tempered double-glass units at about 4 pounds per square foot, is still a small part of the required design load. Glass in particular, however, needs support every 3 feet or less, requiring unusual rafter spacing.

If you are using steel for rafters, building codes usually do not list explicitly the spans permissible for each size and shape of steel member. An engineered design might be required. As a rule of thumb, a 2- × -2 steel tube (true dimensions of hollow, rolled ⅛-inch steel) will perform better than a wood 2 × 4 (nominal size measures 1½ × 3½ inches), and the steel can be spaced twice as far apart. You might need a steel 2 × 5 or 2 × 6 for 16-foot spans.

The south ends of the sloping roof rafters rest on a top plate or beam (FIG. 3-28). If there is a top plate, then the rafters must be directly above studs; otherwise, a header is used beneath the top plate. The header can be two 2 × 4s or one 2 × 6 on edge resting on jack studs if the main stud or post spacing is 4 feet o.c. If the span is 8 feet, then the minimum required header or roof beam is two 2 × 8s or one 2 × 12 on edge. Local codes might vary on these requirements, especially if the local snowfall is very heavy.

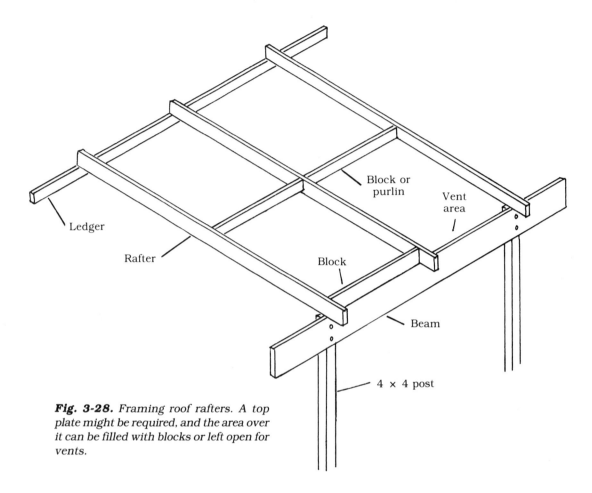

Fig. 3-28. *Framing roof rafters. A top plate might be required, and the area over it can be filled with blocks or left open for vents.*

For wide roofs, roof rafters larger than 2 × 4s set on edge tend to lean over under load. Wood blocks or other means of support must be placed between rafters on long spans (FIG. 3-28). They are also needed to control separation of 2-×-4 rafters carrying glazing. When these blocks support roofing or glazing, they are also called *purlins*. Steel x-braces are one means of holding rafters vertical while not blocking much light. No glazing serves as good roof bracing, whether to keep rafters from leaning over or to prevent distortion.

It is not sufficient to rest the roof on the south wall. It must be connected to the wall in such a way that the roof cannot pull upward from the wall because of wind uplift. By the same token, the wall must not pull upward from the foundation. Simple metal hardware for tying down rafters is now widely available, perhaps even required. It replaces the old-fashioned and insecure methods of nailing at this vital place.

If you are building the sunspace on a frostproof foundation tied to the house foundation, then it can share structure with the house if code permits. The upper ends of the roof rafters can rest on a rafter support, or *ledger*, bolted securely to the house frame. Nailing sunspace rafters to house rafters is not usually permitted.

If the sunspace is permitted to "float" on a rudimentary foundation independently of the house, then it needs its own back wall frame to hold up the roof. You can use a simple stud wall frame and fasten the bottom plate to the rudimentary sunspace foundation. You do not need to cover and finish the wall frame. The house wall can serve as a back wall. You should seal the sunspace roof to the upper house wall, but do not structurally connect them. If there is much movement, the seal of metal flashing and caulk will tear loose without major damage to the house or sunspace.

If you are building the sunspace freestanding with a double-pitched roof sloping both north and south, then you need additional roof structure. The pitch can, and should, be steeper on the north than on the south. You can make or buy roof trusses, or use standard framing methods for double-pitched house roofs. You must use some method of preventing rafters from separating at the peak as a result of wind uplift. Also, the outward forces the rafters put on the walls must be counteracted with horizontal beams, or *ceiling joists*, that hold the walls together.

A solid roof is usually constructed by putting a layer of ½-inch exterior plywood on the rafters, then adding roofing paper and shingles. The plywood serves as lateral bracing, helping the structure resist distortion from wind pressure. Most shingle systems are not recommended for pitches less than 1:6 (2 inches of rise in 12 inches of run) since heavy rain can flow in reverse up through them. The sunspace designer already might be constrained to a low-pitched roof to fit the available space. You can build the roof as if flat in regard to drainage (e.g., with tar and pebbles), or find another compatible roofing method. The usual solution is to lower the sunspace with respect to the house, rather than accept a low ceiling, so that minimum roof slope can be maintained.

HEAT STORAGE

Sufficient mass for heat storage would hold heat for one or two days. You can estimate the amount needed from the heat capacities of water, masonry, and so forth given in TABLE 4 in the Appendix. For example, suppose that 50 percent of the daily insolation reaches the mass in a 100-square-foot sunspace. (Let glazing area equal floor area in this example.) The mass might be the floor, or it might be located underground and warmed by forced air. In January, with insolation at 1,700 Btus per square foot per day, about $1,700 \times 100 \div 2 = 85,000$ Btus are collected in one day through vertical glazing at 40°N. Concrete stores 0.22 Btu per degree rise. To store all possible collected heat by letting the concrete rise from 60° F to 90° F, $85,000 \div (30 \times 0.22) = 12,900$ pounds are needed. It is assumed here that the mass is insulated from the ground.

This mass might seem like an alarming amount, but when you consider the density of concrete, 144 pounds per cubic foot, the volume is $12,900 \div 144 = 89$ cubic feet or 3.3 cubic yards. That is equivalent to 100 square feet of floor 11 inches thick. This is still a lot of concrete, and in slab form it is much too thick for the heat to penetrate fully in a January daytime of about 7 hours. Most of the heat penetrates only about 4 inches into rock or concrete in that time. The usual 3-inch-thick concrete floor, however, will be much less than sufficient storage. The inside surfaces of a concrete foundation 1 foot high and exposed all around the 40-foot perimeter of the sunspace add only about 40 more square feet—hardly an improvement.

If the storage consists of a bed of loose rocks 2 to 3 inches in diameter, the storage is much cheaper and might not seem as large. Typical rock has a density of about 95 pounds per cubic foot. You should purchase rock by the pound or ton so as not to be fooled by the fact that loose rock is about 30 percent empty space. If spread over an insulated subfloor in the sunspace instead of put into a bin, 12,900 pounds, or 135 cubic feet, of rock would be about 1.3 feet deep (FIG. 3-29A). You should cover the rock with a slab that also holds heat; therefore you need proportionately less rock. If there is a blower and ductwork to expose the enormous surface area of this rock bed to the day's heat, much of the heat will be absorbed. A 30° F rise in temperature of a properly built and insulated rock bed or bin is not difficult to achieve. Wash and screen the rock for uniform size. It must have no sand or dust and should be dry. Chapter 4 gives more details of building this and other storage methods.

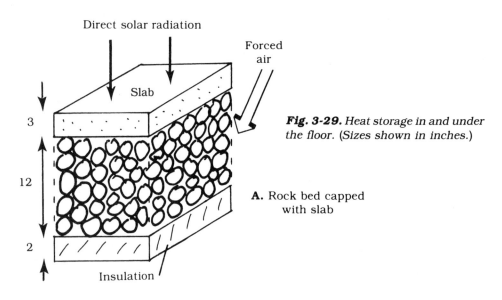

Fig. 3-29. Heat storage in and under the floor. (Sizes shown in inches.)

A. Rock bed capped with slab

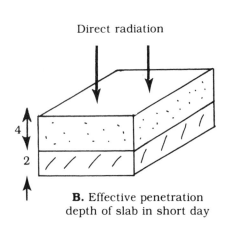

B. Effective penetration depth of slab in short day

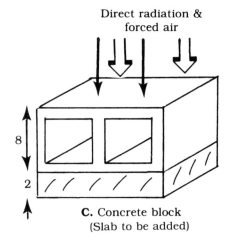

C. Concrete block (Slab to be added)

A slightly different approach will show how insufficient a slab or brick floor would be as storage. Again, 1 square foot of the glazing in the example admits about 900 Btus net per day to the sunspace, after inefficiencies are taken into account. Concrete or brick will take up about 30 Btus per cubic foot of material for each 1° F of rise. As before, only about 4 inches of heat penetration can be obtained in a short day. So only ⅓ cubic foot participates in heat storage under each square foot of floor area (FIG. 3-29B). Therefore, the concrete or brick floor is good for absorbing about 10 Btus per square foot per degree rise. Suppose the floor varies between 60° F at dawn and 90° F in late afternoon. Then the floor can absorb about 30 × 10 = 300 Btus per square foot. This is three times less than the heat available. Clearly the storage must expose about three times more area than the area of the glazing.

A way to put more heat into a concrete slab more quickly is to embed hot air tubes in the slab when you pour the concrete. To triple the exposed area—that is, to gain another 200 square feet in addition to the top surface—you would need 16 tubes 4 inches in diameter in the 8-foot width of the floor. This number of tubes would need to be jumbled into a thick slab, almost piled on top of each other. Although 4-inch plastic drain pipes are inexpensive, the thin plastic is a poor heat conductor and substantially slows down heat transfer from the air to the concrete. Galvanized steel tubing would cost more, but conducts heat much better through its walls.

A different approach might seem more attractive: use concrete blocks set on their sides so that their "cores" form ducts (FIG. 3-29C). Concrete blocks (not to be confused with cinder blocks) have a little less than the optimum thickness to take up and release heat. Each 8-x-8-x-16-inch block occupies about 0.9 square foot and exposes about three times more area in its cores than does a solid block (more if it has three cores). This matches heat storage needs very well. Concrete blocks cost about $1 each, so our sample 100 square feet floor would cost a little over $100 for the storage mass. You should cover the blocks with a finish floor, however, so you need another 33 cubic feet of concrete.

If water is the desired storage medium, then its heat capacity of 1 Btu per pound per degree rise is used. Water is more than four times better than concrete at storage, so the amount can be proportionately smaller. The simple approach with water is to put it in storage containers, preferably containing about 5 gallons each, rather than the popular 55-gallon drums. Large containers require too long to warm up. The heat-transfer methods consist of natural convection of warm air around the containers and solar radiation on them. Few suitable water containers are available. Steel cans rust even if given rust protection inside and out. Plastic containers degrade rapidly, except for expensive ones of fiberglass, polypropylene, or acrylic. Glass breaks if the water freezes. You can darken water in transparent containers (try clothes dye) to absorb sunlight better. If you want to put the water in one big insulated tank, you should consult some of the more technical books on active solar systems. The air-to-water heat transfer plumbing, tank, and freezing problems present a situation beyond the scope of this book.

Still another storage method is to use *phase-change*, or *eutectic*, *salts*. These special salt mixtures (not ordinary table salt, but different chemicals) store latent heat when they change from solid to liquid. The process is comparable to melting ice, but it happens at a higher and more convenient temperature, such as 80° F, and less heat is stored. Later, when the temperature outside the phase-change salt falls below 80° F, the material begins solidifying, giving up the stored heat in the process. Phase-change salts provide heat storage without heavy weight for above ground and second-floor applications.

The salt is usually kept in a plastic tube or box since it will corrode most metals. The container heats the air and its surroundings by radiation. At least one manufacturer has packaged phase-change salts in narrow black plastic boxes that fit between wall studs, enabling a wall to store heat. The storage is many times greater than the equivalent masonry; how much depends on what temperatures you compare. Study manufacturers' specifications carefully since the material is very expensive compared to rock and water storages. Generally dozens of packages at about $30 each are needed for adequate heat storage.

If you want more than one day of storage, then you should increase proportionally both the amount of storage and glazing. If the glazing is unchanged, a larger amount of storage mass is simply heated less. Also, the heat stored will not last longer than one day. With storage, as large a temperature change as possible is wanted to raise the efficiency of putting the heat in and getting it out. The practical limit for air systems is not far over the 30° F design value used in the examples here.

If the ground is to hold the heat, you must consider that soil holds somewhat less heat than rocks, sand, or concrete. Again, the area exposed on the ground or floor is far too small to store the heat introduced by the comparable area of glazing. The problem is always one of accessibility of the storage medium to the heat supply. A floor surface provides too little exposure, hence the emphasis on forcing air into a storage chamber where the mass has a large exposed area. If several sunspace walls are made of masonry, the potential storage area is more suitable, but the sun will shine on only parts of these walls for parts of the day.

UTILITIES

It is likely that you will want electric power in the sunspace for lighting, fans, controls, and recreational equipment. You might want plumbing for cold and possibly hot water if there is a pool or many plants to water. A hot tub would be a particularly heavy user of electric power and occasionally would need water and a water drain. You must plan for these utilities and install them early, at the framing stage if you want to hide the runs. Framing time is also the time to plan and do the wiring for convenient telephone and television cable jacks, and for doorbells, alarms, and the like.

You might be able to obtain permits to do the work, or a licensed electrician and plumber might be required to do it. These services could cost a major part of the otherwise self-built sunspace. Shop around for estimates, since the pricing varies substantially. Some building inspectors are willing to show homeowners exactly how to meet the electrical code. Since electric power is a major source of danger, most inspectors and codes are especially concerned with the way the electrical work is done. If you plan to add electricity and plumbing later on your own, keep in mind that there are safety aspects which should be inspected and that it will be harder to have the runs hidden from view and protected. Exposed wiring is considered more dangerous than wiring in the wall.

Electric wiring should have tight conduit if high humidity or sprayed plant water might get into the connections. The components sold for outdoor electric line protection do not seem sufficiently watertight, and extra caulking in all holes and joints is suggested for humid environments. Any steel conduit and fixtures might rust over time, so you must find nonrusting versions. Ground fault interrupter breakers and outlets (GFIs) are very sensitive to the leakage of current that occurs in shocks and faulty equipment. These are a good idea in wet areas and might be required. The version mounted in an outlet box is much cheaper than the breaker version.

In a greenhouse, a drip irrigation or other individual automatic plant watering system might be convenient. The water used in a greenhouse must ultimately exit. Either it soaks into the ground and evaporates, or it runs out through drains, or the plants emit it as vapor so that it condenses on glazing at night and runs down. There should be control of all runoff so that it does not accumulate in unwanted places or rot the structure. Plan the drains before you plan the foundation. You might need a permit if you will connect a drain to existing drains. The runoff is not large, however, and could be piped outside under the lawn or spilled on the ground away from the house.

DOORS, WINDOWS, AND VENTILATION

You can control the movement of air to and from the sunspace with doors, operable windows, and vents. With careful planning, it is possible to construct sunspaces where most of the glazing is removable in summer and replaced with screens. If you plan to use the sunspace exit much in winter, you might want an *airlock* or vestibule. This is a system of two doors with space in between so that a person can pass through one door while the other is closed. It is particularly helpful in preventing cold winter air from shocking a greenhouse of plants. If security is of concern, you will want to consider whether the sunspace will aid or deter burglars from attempting to enter the back door of the house proper.

A large outside door is necessary if you need to carry wheelbarrows of dirt in and out of a greenhouse, or if you must move large equipment into the sunspace (e.g., a hot tub). It also provides the new rear exit when the sunspace has covered the old one. The door can be a storm door with a screen in the bottom half so that venting can be controlled. As discussed earlier in regard to climate, the outside door is usually best on the east, to avoid problems of using a west door during high west winds.

FIGURE 3-30 shows nine types of vents and locations; you should not use all nine in a given sunspace. Vents near the ground on the south and west take advantage of prevailing summer winds for ventilation. Vents must be able to be tightly closed and insulated in winter and securely fixed or closed in wind. Exit vents should be high on the sidewalls (a *gable vent*), on the roof, or possibly above the south glazing. Some manufacturers incorporate a ridge vent all along the upper end of the roof. Air flow through it follows an S-curve, so that rain cannot enter. Also popular, but more liable to leaks in rain, are pop-up vents on the roof, which open on hinges.

The rule of thumb for natural ventilation in average climates is about one-tenth the floor area devoted to exit vents. A 100-square-foot sunspace should have 10 square feet of exit venting. That sounds like a lot until you want to open window after window on an overheated summer day. The intake vent area should be about 30 percent smaller. To help prevent stagnant regions, use *cross ventilation*, with air entering on the west and exiting on the east. You also need vents to let hot air into the house and return cooler air to the sunspace. The need for positive control and screening also applies to them. The next section discusses details of this venting as it pertains to heat transfer.

Roof vents could be turbine vents, which increase the effective venting area if the slightest breeze is blowing. Simple vents would have hinged covers on the outside. Low intake vents on walls would have the cover hinge downward. High exhaust vents should have the cover hinge upward, but then it is difficult to exclude rain. If you do not want moisture in the sunspace, then the vent design must exclude blown rain and snow automatically. (Vents that close automatically during rain

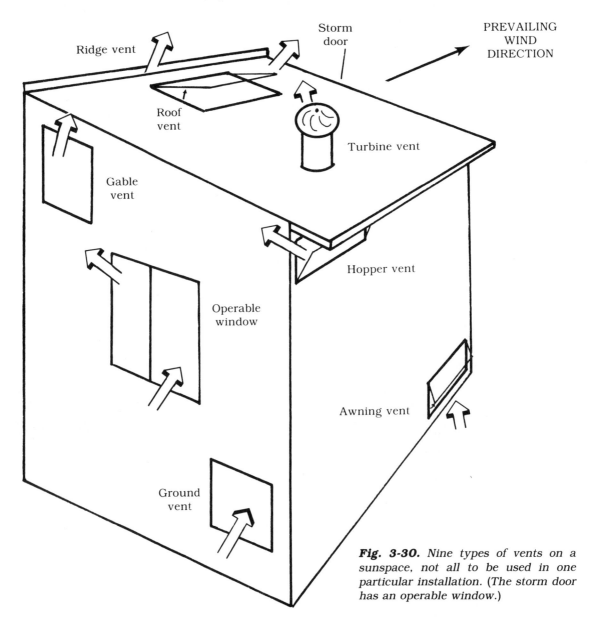

Fig. 3-30. Nine types of vents on a sunspace, not all to be used in one particular installation. (The storm door has an operable window.)

are feasible but expensive.) Louvered vent covers are available (FIG. 3-31) and can be motor-controlled to respond to temperature. All vents should be screened against insects. You can promote stronger natural ventilation with a ventilation chimney, whereby a solar collector is built into a tall tower to heat its air and draw more air up from below. (See *Alward* in the Books section of the References.)

Fig. 3-31. *Exterior louvers on a vent (closed).*

Nonelectric control of vents is possible with the thermal vent opener, often called by a name belonging to one manufacturer, the Heat Motor. It is a mechanical device that moves a lever arm as it warms up (FIG. 3-32). This device can start opening at 80° F and is rated to push about 20 pounds. If it is properly and securely mounted and not overloaded by high wind on large vents, this opener is more reliable and cheaper than electric controls. It will close in winter when a warm period suddenly ends and can help prevent plants from freezing. Large versions have been developed that use cylinders of Freon to control vents and the like.

Fig. 3-32. *A thermal vent opener holding a triangular vent of double-walled acrylic.*

Another method independent of utility power is photovoltaic-operated, motor-driven vent controls. Here sunlight is converted to electricity to operate a small motor to open or close a vent. It might be controlled by a thermostat. Photovoltaic methods are still expensive compared to other methods. Controls that depend on the power line and develop more force are discussed in the next section.

DUCTS, BLOWERS, AND CONTROL OF HEAT TRANSFER

Electric blowers and fans will help control sunspace overheating, regardless of prevailing breezes or lack thereof. One blower might be sufficient in a small sunspace, located either in a cool place near the bottom to suck air in or near the warm ceiling to blow air out. The blower will have a longer life if it is located at the intake where cool air flows, but this is contrary to using the blower to positively exhaust hot air, regardless of leaks elsewhere. Other uses for blowers and fans in sunspaces include forcing warm ceiling air into underground heat storage, pulling it from storage, and directly blowing warm air into the house.

Blowers (see FIG. 3-33) are compact, cost $30 to $60 in modest sizes, and tend to be noisy. They can develop the high pressure needed to force air through ductwork or through rock storage. Fans occupy a large area, move more air at lower speeds, are often quieter, and use less power. A fan would be good for ventilation unless wind pressure overpowers it. Many homeowners have made do with ordinary low-cost window fans to pull warm air from a sunspace through a window into the house.

For serious plant growing in greenhouses, about 5 to 10 air changes per hour (ACH) are needed to control heat and carbon dioxide levels on warm days. Natural ventilation, even boosted by a solar chimney, would not be able to meet this need.

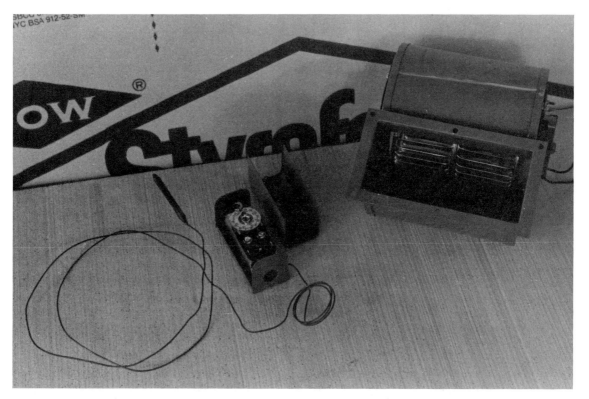

Fig. 3-33. *Remote-bulb 120-volt ac thermostat control and 450-cfm blower against a backdrop of extruded polystyrene foam (for underground use).*

Sunspaces would need less ventilation. Blowers and fans are rated in cubic feet of air per minute (cfm). Once you have estimated the volume of the sunspace, you can calculate the appropriate blower size. If our small 1,000-cubic-foot sunspace is to be moderately ventilated, a very small, 100-cubic-foot-per-minute blower will provide 6 ACH, far more than enough for fresh air.

Possibly the sun is heating the air faster than it can be exhausted. Air typically can carry 0.02 Btu per cubic foot for each degree Fahrenheit it is warmed. Thus, 100 cubic feet of air warmed by 40° F carries 80 Btus. In one hour, exhausting 100 cubic feet per minute will exhaust about 5,000 Btus of this warm air. The sun, however, is putting in about 20,000 Btus per hour through 100 square feet of glazing on a spring day at noon. (Find the hourly rate of 200 Btus per square foot from insolation tables.) Insolation on vertical glass is a little less in summer, but a 100 cfm blower clearly will not be able to keep ahead of solar input. Some of the energy is lost by the other heat-loss routes discussed, but a larger blower is indicated.

A means of cooling and ventilating automatically is provided by the evaporative cooler. This product works well in dry climates (Western United States) and uses little power or water. Large sunspaces might be most effectively cooled in this way. The heat taken up by evaporating water is much greater than that moved out by the air alone. Evaporative coolers are not failproof, however, and you should not rely on one to protect greenhouses without monitoring.

Transferring sunspace warmth to the house involves properly positioning blowers or fans, ducts, and thermostatic controls. It is rarely sufficient to have an open vent at the top of the back wall and another at the bottom (FIG. 3-34A). Flow will be weak, and it reverses at the wrong times. Having a simple fan at the top, pushing hot air from sunspace to house (FIG. 3-34B) is better. The heated air will mix and circulate if the return flow is drawn from the basement or another room. Since it is best to introduce warm air at the floor, a duct in the sunspace with a blower can draw hot air at the ceiling and pull it down (FIG. 3-34C). The return duct or vent should be in another room near the floor. The basement can serve as storage if the warm air is dumped into the basement instead, where it partly will be stored in the massive walls and partly will rise into the rest of the house. Although it is an arduous task, you should insulate the basement walls on the outside if you are using them for storage.

If the sunspace has its own storage, then heat must be put into storage in the day, and brought out and pumped into the house at night (FIG. 2-15). You will need two blowers and motorized dampers or an air handler (see the References, for example, the Department of Energy manuals). Hot air must go into one end of storage, then be brought back from that same end. Parts of ducts can be shared, but then you will need an elaborate switching of blowers and air-flow direction. The less experienced solar designer might best keep the systems separate as shown. Each system would have its own blower and control. Each system must have two dampers, which close ducts when the flow tries to reverse. (Dampers will be discussed shortly.)

Here is another example of how to estimate the size of the fan or blower needed to carry heat. Nothing is gained by being very accurate. You should assume that no more than half of the solar heat gain will be transferred as hot air, the rest being lost. Moving air can carry 0.02 Btu per cubic foot per degree of rise. Suppose 10,000 Btus per hour is available at 100° F, and this air is to be used in a 70° F house.

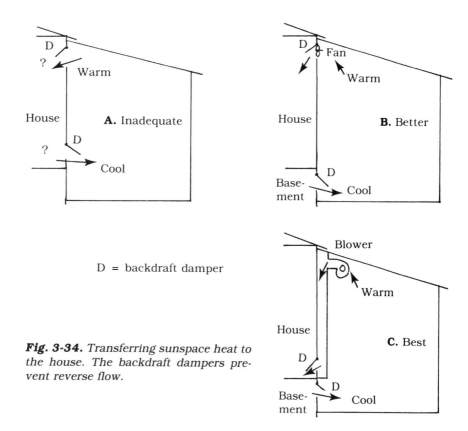

D = backdraft damper

Fig. 3-34. *Transferring sunspace heat to the house. The backdraft dampers prevent reverse flow.*

Then 30° of temperature rise are available. Each cubic foot can carry about 0.6 Btu, so about 10,000 ÷ 0.6 = 16,000 cubic feet must be moved per hour. This amounts to about 260 cubic feet per minute and indicates the needed blower rating. Use the next largest available blower.

Blowers below 500 cfm are of modest size and will not consume much power. Moreover, sunspace blowers and fans are in use less than one-third of the day. The blower should have its own automatic overheating protection, which can prevent damage or a fire. However, you should not rely on electrical equipment to prevent an unusually overheated sunspace, and you should have other more passive means of control. If the blower is used in front of a locking or controlled vent, be certain that the blower cannot be operated if the vent is locked shut for the season or when the control for the vent has shut it.

Manual operation of blowers and vents is a nuisance. Quality thermostats possess the necessary patience for this task and are very reliable as long as electric power is available. Locate thermostats for room comfort about chest high. Locate thermostats to control the circulation or venting of hot air near the ceiling where the warmest air is. If you do not want to get the ladder every time you examine such a thermostat, "remote-bulb" versions are available that allow just the temperature sensor to be put in the desired location (FIG. 3-33).

A greater variety of thermostats is available than this book could cover. If possible, check what other people use in their sunspaces. You should not use the usual furnace thermostat because it is meant to control a low-voltage system, not 120 Vac equipment. Provided you find a thermostat meant for 120 Vac that will handle the blower current, almost any will do. The cost will be in the $20 range (see the References for catalogs). Avoid those that require a temperature swing wider than about 10° F between on and off. If you want to move solar-heated air, you need a thermostat that switches on when the temperature rises. If you want to bring warm air from storage, you need a thermostat that switches on when the temperature falls. If you have a storage system, you might have more than one blower and control. The functions can combine simply, interact complexly, or fight. See the References for more guidance.

The sunspace designer must consider what material to use for ducts. The conventional sheet metal is costly and can appear unsightly. Metal is not needed because no combustible fuels are involved, and metal loses heat everywhere the duct goes. Plywood siding and wood siding are possible duct materials, perhaps with safe insulation inside (to be discussed shortly). Some solar builders have persisted in using ductboard or other fiberglass insulation in air streams, but this makes "itchy" air quality. The shape of the ducts can be anything reasonable, and duct area should be about 1 square foot (more for big installations). Small ducts and high-pressure fans make a noisy system. There should be no need for inspection of ventilation ducts since there is no high temperature or other safety problem. However, wiring thermostats and blowers should be installed carefully and might require an electrician and inspection.

Backward air circulation at night is best counteracted by a gravity-operated backdraft damper. You can make a backdraft damper from light, but durable, plastic film that self-hinges when clamped at the top (FIG. 3-35). You can glue or caulk on

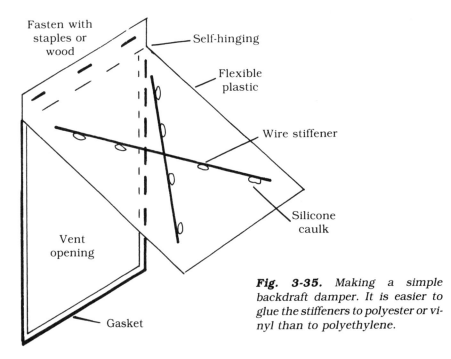

Fasten with staples or wood

Self-hinging

Flexible plastic

Wire stiffener

Silicone caulk

Vent opening

Gasket

Fig. 3-35. *Making a simple backdraft damper. It is easier to glue the stiffeners to polyester or vinyl than to polyethylene.*

wire stiffeners to prevent wild flapping. When no blower is on, its own weight causes the damper to fall shut against a vent opening. The edges of the opening should have a simple gasket for a tight seal. When the blower turns on, the damper is easily sucked open or blown open. You must locate the damper where this action can occur. The designer should draw and redraw duct and blower locations until a place is found where this simple mechanism can work. If the house is warm and the sunspace is cooling down at night, then any open vent or duct is likely to permit a flow of house warmth toward the cold glazing. Suggested locations for dampers are shown in FIG. 3-34.

To estimate the heat loss through a vent accidentally left open on a cold night, you can use previously discussed methods of calculating the heat carried by air flow. Suppose the inside air is 70° F, maintained awhile by floor storage, and the outside has dropped to 20°. Then each cubic foot of air can carry $0.02 \times 50 = 1$ Btu, and will be eager to dump this heat outside. If natural convection builds up to 1 ACH, which is possible where a vent is open at top and bottom, then 1,000 cubic feet will flow out each hour, losing 1,000 Btus per hour. (For comparison, 100 square feet of glazing are losing heat at about twice this rate in the same conditions.) The air speed through a 1-square-foot vent in this example would be about 16 feet per minute, or about ⅕ mile per hour. The air movement can be almost imperceptible and yet carry away substantial heat over long periods of time.

USING REFLECTION

The principle of obtaining more heat and light by means of external reflectors has been discussed. See the References for the variety of unusual ideas and solutions that have been suggested. Some practical advice is that these methods must be durable in the weather and wind. External reflection also has been used when the sunspace location or orientation is unfavorable. A nearby house, garage, or fence painted white could bring in winter sunlight that otherwise would be missed. In a crowded neighborhood, sometimes when one house blocks the sun another is reflecting it toward the sunspace. Light-colored rock might be placed outside on the ground in front of the kneewall to increase ground reflection to the sunspace.

If you need much light in winter for plants, then you can use internal reflection, as well as glazing on part of the roof. You should paint the ceiling and back wall with durable, flat white paint. The designer can check how well the reflection will work in the sunspace by drawing noontime midwinter solar rays at the appropriate low angle (FIG. 2-12). The principle that the angle at which a ray strikes a surface is equal to the angle at which it leaves is useful even if the surface diffuses the light well, because it tells which angles are favored upon reflection. Use a protractor to measure the incoming angle and draw the equal outgoing one. Repeat the procedure for a number of parallel solar rays to see how well or poorly the floor or other desired area will be illuminated by reflection. Repeat again if the first reflected rays strike another white wall, to see where they go. If rays do not land where you want, you might need to redraw your sunspace profile many times, adjusting the walls and ceiling until the rays do approximately what you want.

Reflection, mostly external, also can be quite a nuisance. Glare from sunspace glazing sometimes reaches the eyes of neighbors or motorists. If possible, shading and concealing methods should confine glare to your lot. Nonglare coatings may become available that cause more light to be transmitted through the glazing. Such optical tricks, first developed for camera lenses, are expensive at present. Tempered low-glare glass is available in 4- x -8-foot sheets for solar collectors. It has a rough surface and would collect dust easily. Avoid glass or coatings that absorb light, since such glazing would become very hot.

INSULATING AGAINST HEAT LOSS

You should consider insulating the foundation, walls, back wall, ceiling, glazing, storage, vents, and ducts. TABLE 6 in the Appendix lists general features of some common insulations relevant to sunspace construction. Unfortunately, there is as yet no ideal insulation material for some applications.

If the concrete foundation and concrete, brick, or earth floor are to store heat, you must reduce loss to the cold ground outside. The only suitable insulation at this time is extruded polystyrene foam, which should not be confused with white beadboard. Styrofoam extruded foam (FIG. 3-33) is light blue and was developed by Dow Chemical Company. Foundation insulation should be 2 feet deep and 2 inches thick. The foam comes in 4- x -8-foot and 4- x -9-foot sheets, and is easily cut in half lengthwise with a sharp knife. Beadboard sheds beads of foam with most cutting methods. Extruded foam does not absorb water and lasts at least several decades in the ground. It must be covered to prevent sun exposure and physical damage.

In the sidewalls, ordinary fiberglass insulation gives an adequate R-11 (3½ inches thick) or R-19 (6 inches thick) level of insulation. The sidewalls are relatively small, and more insulation there will not make up for the large losses through the glazing at night. Sheet foam insulation over studs greatly improves the R-value of a wall, too, but is not justified for sunspaces. It does provide a different way to obtain a good vapor barrier on the inside. If you are framing the walls by the post-and-beam method, then thick foam insulation is an established way to fill between posts, although it is more expensive.

The ceiling should be well insulated if the warm air that drifts up there is to be retained at night. R-19 is the minimum level in colder climates. If the sunspace or greenhouse is a separate structure, then you should upgrade its north, east, and west wall insulation. R-19 would be the minimum recommended level. The north sloping roof, if any, should have more.

The back wall is usually the house wall and is already insulated, typically at the R-11 level. If the back wall is wood-framed, then insulation is necessary for the sunspace to serve as a buffer for the house. With insulation, as the sunspace heats up during the day, the adjacent house room is not overheated. As the sunspace cools during the night, the adjacent house will not cool as much. Other possibilities such as using a Trombe wall on the house have been discussed. If the house wall is uninsulated and you allow the sunspace to cool at night, then you should have *movable insulation* on the house wall that is moved away when the sun shines.

Movable insulation can have many forms and uses. It can consist of rigid sheets of foam insulation that are moved aside during the day. You can remove and store the sheets by hand, or fold them back on hinges (FIG. 3-36). Movable insulation can be any sort of curtain designed to retard heat flow. Unfortunately, any practical insulation material with advantages for a particular application also has disadvantages for the same application. A major source of ideas on movable insulation is the book of that title by William K. Langdon in the References. Chapter 4 provides a few details for preparing movable insulation.

Movable rigid insulation can cover walls such as a wall intended to conduct heat to the house, but it is more commonly used on glazing, windows, and vents. Except in extreme cases, it does not need to be moisture resistant and so can be expanded foam or beadboard. Keeping large amounts of foam insulation lying around is a substantial fire hazard. The insulation also degrades in the sun, acquires physical damage, and might look junky. Cover it with foil, cloth, plywood, gypsum board, or some other material. With some difficulty and at considerable cost, you can obtain snap-around plastic or metal frames for rigid foam boards. Sometimes you can glue on wood frames (use glue without solvents). The best coverings make the sheets heavy and, therefore, not so movable. When the panels are for small windows, there is negligible hazard in simply painting them (latex paint) or gluing on decorative cloth or wallpaper. Magnetic and Velcro fastening methods are available for holding and sealing movable insulation panels and quilts.

Another foam to consider is foil-faced polyisocyanurate. Some forms (e.g., Thermax, developed by Celotex Corporation) have thick, shiny foil and fiberglass reinforcing, and pass fire tests as well as thin gypsum board. The foil reflects heat extremely well, making the sheet perform better than just the insulation it contains (already the highest R-value per inch of any common insulator.) Whereas some

Fig. 3-36. *Shutters of foil-faced polyisocyanurate hanging on a tilted south glazing wall.*

amount of infrared radiation will "shine" through white foam, it is blocked by the foil. Foil-faced insulation is useful in summer as well as winter. You will need to have an air space if it is used in walls, or the radiation barrier will not be effective. You also can foil-tape the foil surface to its neighbors and serve as a vapor barrier. When used as loose sheets or pieces, the foil on this foam gets banged up quickly and the exposed edges of the foam disintegrate. They will burn, too. No inexpensive edge protectors seem to be available. You could wrap self-adhesive aluminum tape around the edges, or glue on thin strips of wood. At least one brand of polyisocyanurate, Thermax, comes with a tough aluminum surface embossed and finished with white enamel, ready to serve as wall surfaces or movable panels. This form is about three times more costly, however.

It is desirable to insulate the glazing at night and on cold, very cloudy days. This, however, is the most difficult challenge of all energy control in sunspaces. Some manufacturers have developed quilted material or insulated shades, such as Window Quilt, invented by Appropriate Technology Corporation. This material can move in tracks along the glazing, from floor to ceiling (in the case of glazed roofs, all the way to the highest point). The shade is wound on a roller, and can be rolled by hand or with a motor (FIG. 3-37).

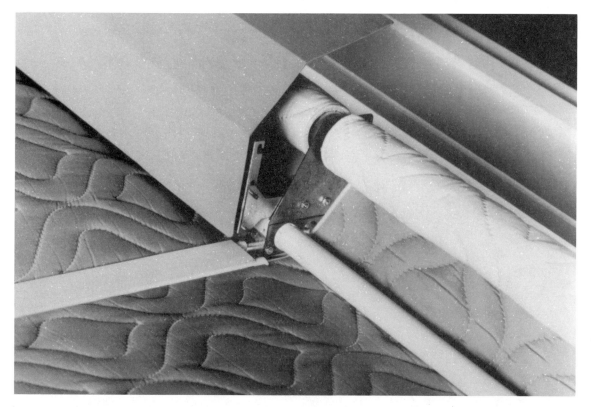

Fig. 3-37. A quilted insulated shade rolling system on the rear ceiling of a sunspace. The edge of shade slides in a track at the bottom of an extruded aluminum rafter (Courtesy of Appropriate Technology Corp.).

As insulation, the quilted shade plus a trapped air layer is only thick enough to function at about R-2, but the material also contains reflective foil, which can control most of the radiation loss. Wherever foil is used, it is bonded to Mylar and can serve as a vapor barrier, or it can come pricked with many tiny holes so it can breathe while still reflecting infrared radiation. The vapor barrier should be on the side of the shade that faces the living space.

Another fabric-based option is an insulated version of the Roman shade, developed by Warm Window. Again, the term *shade* is intended to refer more to the function as an insulated curtain than to summer sun control, but these systems can work in all seasons. Good sunspace shades of any type will have ultraviolet-resistant material on the outside. Insulating Roman shades consist of two fabric layers separated by an air layer of 1 inch or so. Each fabric layer can include thin insulation and foil. When the shade is drawn up and down in tracks, a reasonably good air seal is attained. The trapped air layers plus insulation result in R-3 or better, as well as control of radiation loss. The shade bunches up when raised by a drawstring, and does not use a roller. Some forms might have four or more fabric layers, all of which separate when the shade is down.

Jaksha Energy Systems has found a way to combine the virtues of foil-faced polyisocyanurate with the convenience of a roll-up insulating shade: the Insulider (FIG. 3-38). The foam is cut into long strips and the segments are held together with

Fig. 3-38. Segmented polyisocyanurate foam shades with fabric covering. Motors inside rollers can control any number of shades separately or together (Courtesy of Jaksha Energy Systems, Inc.).

fabric glued on for appearance as well as function. Again, you need side tracks for a seal, and the roller is understandably rather large. This system adds R-6 to the glazing.

Also available is "bubble-pack" polyethylene plastic, sometimes with a foil coating, which performs somewhat better than a quilted shade but might not look as good. Types intended for pool covers or solar use are treated to last more than a year in the sun, and the cost is lower than quilted fabric.

Summary articles listed in the References compare various window insulators. If the sunspace designer does not want fitted insulating quilts or shades, then the choice is between ordinary drafty and poorly insulating heavy drapes or foam panels. A foam panel that fits tightly over each glazed panel will make a large difference in heat loss. At least 1 inch of foam is recommended, resulting in a performance at the R-10 level for foil-faced polyisocyanurate. How to make such panels fit against the glazing is difficult to work out, and you must use ingenuity to design a good system. Even if foam, quilting, or shades are well fitted, moisture will leak behind them to condense on the glazing. Therefore, any use of glazing insulation must be accompanied by ways to control or mop up condensation to avoid interior damage. The problem will be much worse if the sunspace has any source of moisture. The next section gives an example of the large moisture-condensing ability of glazing.

An expensive solution is the Beadwall, invented by Zomeworks Corporation. Foam beads are blown into the space between inner and outer glazing at night and sucked away as the sun arrives. The system can probably be kept dry, but not too dry, but the cost starts at many hundreds of dollars. Research continues on other solutions, such as glass that reflects like a mirror at night (the opposite of solar-sensitive sunglasses) or becomes reflecting by electric control. The moderately expensive solution of using a heat-barrier coating with glass has been discussed.

A different, drastic, and cumbersome approach to insulating glazing has been to put it on the outside. There is room to build large insulated covers—4 × 8 or 8 × 8 feet—consisting of foam sandwiched between exterior siding or other durable material. When open, the covers would best lay on the ground, and can provide reflection too. At night they can be pulled shut with pulleys and ropes.

Whatever method you use, glazing insulation needs much attention. You should close it if dense clouds arrive, reopen it if the sun returns. In winter the sunlight period starts after you might leave for work and ends before you return. For a greenhouse, the insulation must never be left off on a cold night, or you must design the greenhouse to work without it. Sunspaces without plants are simple because you can abandon trying to insulate the glazing and suffer the heat loss.

You should insulate the heat storage system, if you are using one. Use extruded polystyrene underground around the sides of any rock bin and underneath. Two inches, giving R-10, would be sufficient. This foam can hold the weight of a very thick concrete floor or a very large bin without crushing. Aboveground storage can have insulation protected by an attractive wood box or cover. A round water tank would have to be wrapped with fiberglass or many layers of thin foam. Small water containers would be tedious to cover and uncover everyday.

You should tightly cover vents to the outside and to the house with rigid foam insulation at night. You can use a "pop-out" form of insulation or one that is hinged and latched, as will be shown in Chapter 4. Since the ducts are not used at high temperature, any of the foams could line their insides. There is no advantage to the relatively expensive fiberglass ductboard. It must be tightly sealed on the inside or the fiberglass will enter the airstream. Despite its name, duct tape is not a permanent sealing tape. Its adhesive deteriorates and the tape falls apart with time. The foil tapes last the longest, but do not trust that any adhesive will not come loose.

In unusual situations, a door to the sunspace will not be on the south, east, or west, and not be glazed for passing sunlight or seeing through. Then this door can be solid and should be insulated. Well-insulated steel doors are now available at a reasonable cost (about $100) in prehung form. You can construct and insulate a door by assembling a sandwich of foam insulation between two sheets of thin plywood attached to a 2- x -2 frame. It is difficult to make doors at home that are flat. You can glue rigid foam to one side of any door, but in some cases fire safety might require that a layer of gypsum board be put over the foam. Such a door would be thick and heavy. Obviously, you must place these on the side of the door that does not strike the stop molding in the jamb.

VAPOR CONTROL

Particularly if you have plants or a hot tub in the sunspace, you must protect both the insulation from moisture absorption, and the structure from water damage. Any heated space used by people or open to the house will collect moisture. Therefore, a *vapor barrier* is needed all around the inside—that is, facing heated living space. The cheapest form is 4- or 6-mil polyethylene sheet fastened all over the inside of the insulation and covering the frame. You should seal every hole, since even small holes attract moisture that might freeze in the wall. The vapor barrier is also the last barrier to air infiltration. You should caulk and staple joints. Openings for electric outlets have been a special problem, not only for leaking cold air in but also for letting humidity into the walls. The partial solution has been to caulk the sheet to the box, or run it behind the box and caulk around the electric cables. Also see the new types of tight boxes becoming available.

Other ways to form a vapor barrier include taping foil-faced or plastic-filmed insulation together, or using a complete coat of oil-based paint. The tar-filled kraft paper backing on fiberglass insulation is not sufficient and cannot be effectively sealed together. Paper-based barriers on large rolls are available, however.

Only a durable interior finish goes inside the vapor barrier. In high humidity, this should be exterior siding or gypsum board with oil-based primer, or the expensive "marine" gypsum board for showers. You will need good exterior paint, since the compound used to finish gypsum board is also sensitive to moisture. Redwood or cedar siding, tiles, or bricks are also possible.

Give attention to the type of nails to use. Only hot double-dipped galvanized nails or stainless steel nails or screws will withstand continual high humidity. Other nails and screws will rust away. They also will leave stains on the acid redwood and cedar. Note that a shiny finish is not an indication of corrosion resistance in a fastener.

Glazing is a good vapor barrier, but its framing and mounting might not be. You must caulk the plastic vapor barrier with water-resistant caulk, preferably silicone, directly to water-resistant framing next to the glazing or battens. Even if you use cedar or redwood for wood framing and battens, it will pass moisture unless deeply sealed with polyurethane or other sealers. Insufficient care has been given to the integrity of vapor barriers where glazing is involved, and there is room for innovation by the builder. The commercial aluminum-framed sunspaces are a success in this regard in that the all-aluminum frame tightly sealed to the all-glass walls provides a very good vapor barrier. Still, some water passes through, so the frames have internal drains to let condensate flow down and out through "weep" holes. Moreover, water does not easily damage glass and aluminum.

It is difficult to keep moisture from between double glazing. Factory-sealed double-glass units have a good chance of staying sealed for many years, but site-sealed glazings are bound to collect moisture. If you are not able to seal and caulk sufficiently the wood frames holding double glazing, then provide an appropriate weep hole for condensate to run back out. Trapped moisture makes endless problems as the sun changes it to vapor each day. At night when it freezes it pushes components apart. To avoid frame damage, it is better to have both glazings mounted outside the structural frame and let the wood spacers between glazings take the damage.

If the sunspace/greenhouse has high humidity, you should protect the house with a vapor barrier also. The barrier in the house wall is on the wrong side and probably inadequate. Now a barrier is needed outside the house, too, but the wall must be permitted to "breathe." You should attempt to have barrier continuity at doors and windows, although these are difficult areas. Vents are unavoidable penetrations of barriers.

The undesirability of using hot, humid air from a greenhouse to heat the house has been discussed. If the humid air is dumped in the basement, it will leave much moisture on the cold walls. An air-to-air heat exchanger, costing as much as a small sunspace, is one technological solution when you want heat without humidity. The better versions use elaborate methods and materials to separate the water from the air without corroding the exchanger. Water vapor itself should not be dumped outside if possible, since it represents a large loss of heat. When condensed to water, the heat is recovered.

An example is given here of how to estimate the ability of cold glazing to collect water vapor and condense it to water. Suppose that a typical double glazing is used that performs with an R-value of about 2. Suppose that, on a winter night of about 12 hours, a temperature difference averaging 40° F occurs between inside and outside. Then 1 square foot of glazing can remove $1 \times 40 \div 2 = 20$ Btus per hour. Overnight this square foot removes about 240 Btus. Water vapor must give up about 970 Btus per pint or pound to condense to liquid. Therefore, this square foot can condense about ¼ pint of water from the air overnight, and 100 square feet of glazing could potentially remove 3 gallons of water.

That glazings do not wring much water out is because greenhouse atmospheres do not have that much water in them as the air cools. The glazing might remove all available water vapor in the first hour that the glazing is cold. Water vapor that never reaches the region near the cold glazing is not condensed, but ubiquitous convection currents ensure that most air and water vapor does visit that region in a few hours. (Technically, water vapor will condense when the temperature falls below the dew point for the humidity level of a particular atmosphere. The dew point is rarely below 40° F.) Also, the temperature difference across the glazing might not be as large as assumed in this example unless there is much storage mass giving off heat all night.

Paradoxically, insulating the glazing makes the condensation problem worse. Water and ice collect behind the tight insulation because the glazing is much colder than it would be without the insulation. In the morning all this water runs off. You must carefully collect or mop up this water if the sunspace structure is liable to damage. Sunspaces under some conditions might best have a drain installed beneath each glazing panel!

DURABILITY, MAINTENANCE, AND APPEARANCE

Sunspaces are very susceptible to damage and deterioration by sun, water, wind, hail, rocks, tree limbs, air pollution, and other agents. Only glass, masonry, metals, and some unusual synthetic materials can withstand ultraviolet radiation indefinitely. The best gaskets are synthetic rubber. The best caulk is silicone rubber. (These rubbers are not the familiar rubber as used in tires.) Ordinary woods require routine cleaning and repainting. Cedar and redwood will benefit from a preserver or sealer. Considering the durability of materials during design will make for a sunspace that will have low maintenance and will keep its attractiveness.

Make sure glazings and other sunspace components are easy to replace. Always keep this thought in mind as you work out the details of the design. Nails are difficult to remove without damage—although they readily creep out on their own—so you should screw on replaceable parts with noncorroding screws. You cannot count on finding every conceivable fastener—for example, short, strong noncorroding nails in the ½- to 1-inch range for glazing trim—so it is best to purchase likely fasteners before deciding on final plans.

To make a good impression on the neighbors, perhaps the best key to a good appearance is a careful design with quality materials. Materials that last can be made to look good. This means high-quality glazing, careful and tight trim, straight lines, sensible placement of features, and so forth. The exterior finish of the sunspace walls should match or complement the house so that it seems part of it. The roof should be the same color and style. There is a link between performance and appearance. Joints that look leaky probably will be leaky. Glazing, doors, and vents that flap in the wind might come loose in high wind and endanger the neighbors. These simple aspects of design and construction make the sunspace durable, fit the house, and look like a permanent improvement.

CONSTRUCTION

IF YOU PLAN TO build the sunspace or to personally supervise the construction of it, you will need to know many construction details for the practical design approaches given in Chapter 3. This chapter contains these details, as well as giving more information on maintenance and discussing more problems encountered in building sunspaces. Not all possible ways of building a sunspace can be covered in one book, however. Hopefully the designer/builder can extend the basic methods to special projects and circumstances. Many procedures given here might need modification where unusual conditions or building codes apply.

At this point, you should be planning either to prepare or to purchase large detailed drawings of the project. You do not need neat and professionally labeled drawings, but accurate ones are highly recommended. Sketches might not be sufficient either to obtain a building permit or to avoid a major design flaw. For example, suppose you forgot to specify the rabbet grooves to be cut into posts, between which tempered glass must fit. You will be dismayed when the time comes to fit the glass to posts already in place. There should, however, be no need to go to an engineer or architect to prepare the drawings for a project such as a sunspace. The simple floor plan and profile drawings already prepared in the design process, supplemented with a few drawings of special details, should suffice, as long as you are on hand to interpret them.

BUILDING CODES

Nearly all new construction and renovation, including residential additions such as garages and sunspaces, are controlled by sets of regulations known as *building codes*. Several sets have been written by national building and engineering organizations and are intended for adoption in whole or in part by individual cities and counties. They are usually updated at long intervals to try to keep up with evolving building practices. Local governments might choose to create their own codes, select parts of national ones, modify and add to national ones, delete parts of codes, or (rarely) have none at all. Many areas are now known for strict enforcement of code; some areas are overtly or covertly known for laxity, especially in regard to private residential projects.

Ideally, building codes and inspectors have nothing to do with preserving community appearances and property values, but everything to do with safety. The codes are extremely detailed and the safety aspects might easily be lost from view. You, the private builder of a small project, probably will not be expected to master, or even read, the local code. The primary goal of codes is to regulate new construction so as to minimize the possibility of injury from fire, structural failure, earthquakes, wind, and other hazards. A secondary goal, remotely relevant to sunspaces, is to promote healthy and comfortable environments with light, heat, fresh and clean air, clean water, adequate ceiling height and room size, and so forth.

The common and widely adopted codes are the Uniform Building Code (UBC) by the International Conference of Building Officials (ICBO), mostly in the western half of the United States; the Standard Building Code (SBC), by the Southern Building Code Congress International (SBCCI); and the Basic Building Code (BBC), by the Building Officials and Code Administrators (BOCA), mostly in the Northeastern United States. No one book contains "the code." There are a variety of supplements and test reports. Those on new materials such as glazings and insulations, those on solar use, and those on revived methods such as post-and-beam construction could be relevant to sunspaces.

In addition to the codebooks on structural matters, there are voluminous electrical and plumbing codes, which would be almost futile for the novice to examine. You can find simple, generic versions of good electrical and plumbing practices in the library, bookstore, or hardware store. The building inspectors for electrical and plumbing are probably the simplest source of the few bits of vital local information you need. Of course, you should not assume that all materials and components sold in local stores are permitted by the local code. You cannot assume that store clerks know the code requirements, and they usually will not answer questions on requirements.

No book on construction can specify the one correct way for any building procedure, since methods will be correct in some codes and wrong in others, especially when local interpretation is involved. This book can show only some basic practices that have been long established, both in codes and by builders. Some procedures and dimensions used depend on local conditions, and therefore are controlled by local inspectors. The sunspace builder has little choice but to contact the entity enforcing the local code. The "building inspection department" or whatever it is called is likely to be helpful, discuss your project, tell you if code applies, and much more. Officials might have a condensed and simplified version of the residential code which they will sell or give to you. They are unlikely to have a suggested sunspace construction plan, but residential construction methods are almost entirely relevant. They will answer any specific questions you have while you are planning your project. Without them you probably cannot complete your design in an acceptable manner.

Sunspace as an entity is not mentioned in many codes. The nearest term is *greenhouse*, but that can be interpreted as a commercial free-standing structure of traditional design: a frame covered with panes of glass. In areas where little solar energy development has occurred, you might need to explain your project carefully to be certain it is classified properly. If they call it a greenhouse and use existing code statements about greenhouses, that is both good and bad. The structural requirements for traditional greenhouses are lax, but they assume it will not be lived in or regularly occupied. It might need to be detached. To establish communication with building officials, try some other terms than *sunspace*, such as *sunporch, solarium, hothouse,* or just a *room addition.* The old-fashioned term might be *conservatory.*

BUILDING INSPECTORS AND PERMITS

After you have discussed your project with building officials or inspectors and finalized your plans, you are ready to apply for a building permit. The permit will cost a fee, which can vary widely from area to area. Usually, the larger and more stringent the city, the higher the fee. It can approach 10 percent of the project, in the same range as an architect's fee. To apply, you are likely to be asked to provide a sketch or drawing of what you will build. Ask what quality of drawing is expected. Building officials probably do not want to send you to an architect or engineer for precise plans. If they do, discreetly find out whether they are being unreasonable. Ask other solar builders or local engineers and architects what you should do so that you can personally do the work necessary to obtain a simple permit for a sunspace. You also might need to make a sketch of exactly where the structure will sit on your lot—a *plot plan* as in FIG. 4-1.

Issuance of the permit might be contingent upon the approval of a city or county planning or zoning department. This step might be as simple as establishing that what you are building is okay for the zone you live in (see next section), or it might mean having your plans approved by a planning official or committee, this time to satisfy criteria such as drainage, interference with traffic, or perhaps appearance or other characteristics.

If the local building officials allow owner-built residential structures—not always the case in urban areas—then you are thought of as a *self-contractor.* This status will pertain to work on the structure, but not to the electrical and plumbing work. You might be able to obtain owner's permits for electrical and plumbing, too. You need not be the person who does all this work. You can *subcontract* it, as informally as you wish, to friends, relatives, or even professionals. As permit holder, however, you will be held responsible to see that all the work is done properly before inspection. If you do not want to have anything to do with certain aspects, then inform the issuer of permits that, for example, so-and-so, a licensed electrician, will obtain the permit for the electrical work. Then the electrician will be fully responsible for the work and the inspections. Although your neighbor might be in the electrical or plumbing business, he might not be licensed locally and could not obtain permits. You could consult the telephone book or ask to see the current list of licensed subcontractors if you do not know whom to choose. It would be best, though, to ask a friend for a recommendation.

At the mention of ductwork, the building official might assume you will be using sheet-metal work appropriate to a gas furnace and require that work be done by a licensed gas or sheet-metal worker. This opens up a large technical, but unnecessary, area of concern for sunspaces. If possible, do not mention ventilation, blowers, or ductwork. Just be certain they are legally installed in regard to electrical work. When the inspector visits, your use of ductwork for solar-heated air might be obvious and of little concern.

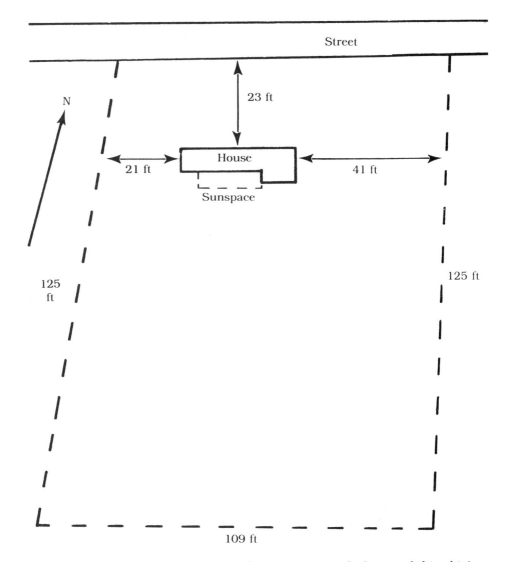

Fig. 4-1. An example of a plot plan of a building site, which is needed to obtain a building permit. (Looking up the lot at the courthouse also provides the direction of true north and south.)

Once the permit is displayed, you can legally begin work at your site. Touchy neighbors can no longer harass by quietly calling the building department and asking whether you have a permit. There follows a series of inspections, which vary from place to place. The first is likely to precede any pouring of concrete in the foundation, to ensure that it will be deep and strong enough. The second—inspection of the "framing"—might not occur until the frame, roof, sidewalls, and perhaps all of the glazing is on, making the sunspace nominally weathertight.

At the same time wiring and plumbing might need inspection at the "rough-in" stage. At this stage, the wiring must be run into boxes, but no fixtures need to be attached yet. A similar rough stage of work applies to plumbing: the pipes are fastened in place but fixtures are not yet in place. If in doubt, ask the relevant inspector what must be seen at what stage. Inside walls and ceiling should not be covered yet, so all work can be seen. Last comes a set of final inspections, first of electrical and plumbing, then of the finished structure. If you stucco walls or lay brick, that procedure might require separate inspections.

Building inspectors are usually looking for problems that affect the safety and security of the structure. They will not care about appearance, nor are they engineering troubleshooters who can help you find and correct unusual mistakes. They might not look at your plans beforehand or at all. What counts is what they see built at certain stages. If the inspectors are rather stringent, then they will not approve any work for which there is not a statement or table in the code. You could indirectly feel out the local building department beforehand as to its strictness. Then you will know whether to ask about something before building it or to risk that what looks right and obviously will perform properly is accepted. The worst situation to fall into is to be asked, several times, to hire a professional engineer to provide approved plans of a particular method after the method is already built. This is expensive, very time-consuming, and embarrassing. With unusual structures where you misjudge both the design and the inspector, a traumatic experience can develop without warning.

Before the framing inspection occurs, it is possible that you have incorporated major problems then installed roof and glazing over them. The burden is on you, for the "privilege" of doing your own work, to anticipate where you might not know what you are doing and to ask ahead of time whether a procedure will be acceptable. To save much time and trouble reinspecting faulty construction after it is corrected, inspectors are usually glad to answer questions in their office or on the telephone. They might even give you one free preliminary site visit.

Building inspectors are expected to have infinite patience with the exasperating construction industry, and budget usually makes them short of staff and time. The less you add to their load, the better. They are usually empowered to charge fees for extra trips. Try not to think of your project as urgent or the most important activity in the county, so that you can always give them a few days to respond after calling for an inspection. Let them know it can be done at their convenience when other calls bring them into your area. As long as the permit card is available to him, no one needs to be at home when an inspector comes. It is better to have someone there to get a first-hand report if there was any adverse reaction to your work or to explain the work if the inspector missed seeing something that you did properly. If you cannot be present at each inspection, call the inspector the next day when follow-up is needed.

If your project is sufficiently large and unorthodox—not likely for a sunspace—it is possible to run into major problems obtaining approval. Perhaps building inspectors in your town are unusually testy, dislike solar energy, or have had too many fights with owners. Building inspection departments have an appeals process, and the chief building official has the discretion to allow some variances. Often no compromise in safety is permitted. If at all possible, spend your time building an acceptable sunspace and enjoying your work, rather than tangling with bureaucracy. However, sunspaces are just enough on the fringe in a few areas to bring you into conflict with the "system."

ZONING

Zoning refers, in your case, to whether you are building a residential structure in a residential zone. This is surely true for a sunspace that serves as a room addition or enclosed porch. Planning, often a function of the zoning department, is concerned with whether the addition fits on your lot legally and conforms to any other adopted community requirements. There are many requirements as to front-, side-, and back-yard *setbacks*—the distance from the lot line to the structure. These requirements are partly to control the appearance and crowding in neighborhoods, and partly to allow room for fire trucks or fire fighters to pass by. Front and back setbacks are wide; side clearance could be as little as 5 feet, but many houses have already been built that close to the line (or closer).

If your layout is tight, you might have extra difficulty or expense. The chances are you do not know exactly where your lot lines are and so cannot leave a margin of safety. In most areas, lot lines are defined by surveyors' pins (with complications if there are curves). Fences or other boundary markers cannot be trusted. Houses themselves are sometimes found to be on or over the line because a poor assumption was made in the past. If you had not checked the requirements on your lot earlier, the process of obtaining the building permit will automatically force you to do so. Sometimes the building inspection department instead of the zoning department regulates clearance and placement of the structure on the lot.

Other aspects to be concerned about are the presence of underground lines through the site itself, either your own sewer, water, telephone, and electrical lines, or public utility lines. A thorough search might not reveal a utility line, and it only turns up when you start digging. Then you note the pipe in the basement wall and say, "Oh, that pipe must go over there where the meter is!" Utility companies will be glad to check if any of their lines run through your lot and mark for you exactly where they go. That is much cheaper to them than having you break one or prevent future access. On the other hand, they might possess the *easement* for that line and you are not permitted to put any structure within a certain distance. There might be other rights attached to your land of which you are not aware. Check all legal papers that go with your lot, examine the courthouse plot of your land, observe what is at the site, and talk to your older neighbors.

If your project must violate setbacks to be built properly, then you have a good case for a "variance". It might cost a fee to petition a zoning committee to examine your case and consider granting the variance that says you may build in a certain place. They might have additional considerations, and they might provide some restrictions. Common zoning problems near lot lines are that the new structure blocks someone's view, drains directly onto public property, or in the case of a sunspace, reflects glare into motorists' eyes on the street. (Even if you build legally to start with, the glare a sunspace can produce under some conditions might involve you in a serious complaint.)

CONTRACTING AND PURCHASING

Do you want to be a contractor—that is, assigning parts of the job to various companies and skilled persons, while retaining part or none of the work for yourself? Would you prefer instead to hire a contractor to take the entire load off your hands? Are you purchasing the sunspace as assembled and delivered by a manufacturer? Will it come as a kit for you or others to assemble?

The relative costs involved deserve another look. The economy model, wood-framed sunspace kit could cost $20 to $30 per square foot. (Floor area will continue to be used for comparison, even if there is no floor.) As a delivered kit, the price surely will not include the foundation. A concrete foundation will cost another $5 to $25 per lineal foot, depending on the depth and who does the work. (That is about $200 to $1,000 for the 40 feet of foundation at the perimeter of a simple 8- x -12-foot sunspace.) As an alternative, you could purchase the materials of the sunspace for as low as $10 per square foot, including the foundation. A factory-completed, aluminum-framed unit might cost $60 to $100 per square foot, plus the foundation.

As a rule of thumb, a local contractor might bid about three times over a somewhat inflated materials cost, thus quoting you about $30 to $40 per square foot to build a sunspace from scratch. To assemble a kit, the cost should be less. If this contractor has built other sunspaces that you like, $30 per square foot for everything might be a "best buy." Otherwise, at this point you know more about certain parts of sunspaces than the contractor does. Despite having theoretical knowledge, if you do not consider yourself a semiskilled builder, you might want to hire a skilled friend or neighbor to work under your supervision, doing what you want but doing it properly and carefully. In such an arrangement, the cost should be a compromise between what you would pay as the solitary builder and what a contractor would cost.

Have you estimated the individual costs of each major materials to build a sunspace which you have sketched? Add 25 percent to cover miscellaneous components, oversights, and wastage, divide by your floor area, and see if you are anywhere near $10 per square foot. If pricing materials is unwelcome labor, take advantage of lumberyards who will do it free. Also take the project to a contractor or two, to see what happens. (By the way, it is not very fair to shop for many quotes, then not engage a company or individual who might have labored many hours to give you an accurate estimate.) The lumberyards might make a package deal on materials. Multiply their estimates by three and compare with the contractors' quotes. Note that there will be some materials a lumberyard cannot obtain—probably the glazing and some miscellaneous components. If careful "costing out" seems unnecessary to you, then just go buy what you need when you need it and start building!

Comparing several quotes might reveal which are more reliable and which are wild guesses. You do not want a contractor to be far wrong any more than you yourself want to be. If an estimate is unusually low, you would need to supervise carefully and watch that that is what you really end up paying. A contractor who underestimates does not want to work at a loss and will find some way to cut corners or raise the payment. If you sign a contract, be certain the stated price is firm and specify a completion date. Do not pay a contractor in full until an official inspection of the work has been successfully made.

If you hire a contractor, you need to keep in mind a few other points. A contractor might be busy and will schedule your project among others. Subcontractors will be brought in, each with new scheduling problems. The fall season is a good time to avoid, when everyone wants their work done before winter comes. Be prepared for delays and watch that they do not result in weather damage. If there are delays, there might seem to be many reasonable excuses:

equipment breakdown, worker illness, temporary shortages, bad weather. You could reach the point that you wished you had control of the project.

Will you have a simple written agreement or contract? Does your contract allow you to take over? Does it penalize the contractor when the completion date has passed? If problems with design and materials develop, your problems might well be greater than if you were the builder. Consider what might go wrong after the contractor has finished. Will you be able to find the person and obtain free corrective action? Be sure your contract states a reasonable time over which the contractor is completely responsible for faulty work. In some states you should try to obtain a lien waiver so that suppliers cannot attach your property if the contractor does not pay bills. Do not assume that the contractor will have complete liability for the job in case someone gets hurt. It might be unfair, but home and lot owners can be sued for injuries they had nothing to do with and could not even imagine happening.

If you are purchasing the sunspace complete, be wary of solar merchandisers who emphasize tax credits, give you the sunspace as a demonstration, provide a large discount, or promise a rebate for each future customer you send to them. If your state has tax credits for solar installations, try to determine how much the price is inflated as a result. If tax credits will not help your particular situation, let the seller know.

DO IT YOURSELF

Let us suppose for the rest of this book that you are going to build it all yourself. The information given here is also of value if you are supervising or checking the work of others. Perhaps you are doing the work for fun, or perhaps it seems the best way to finish the sunspace fast while maintaining high quality. Possibly you need to spend minimum money, cashing in your own labor. You can think of yourself as your own contractor if you wish.

How much you build yourself depends on your skill level and whether you know from experience that your skills in this area will improve as you do the work. Some of the practical skills needed include concrete formwork, concrete pouring and finishing, carpentry, roofing, simple electrical and plumbing work (if any), and finishing. Some of the less tangible skills needed include organizing your time and work, drawing, dealing with suppliers, working carefully (especially near glass), giving attention to details, using imagination in solving unforeseen problems, and being nice to inspectors. A virtue needed is patience. If you have most of these skills already and understand some aspects of the sunspace principles so that you can make informed decisions, then you are as prepared as most in the business.

This book will not go into the basics of general carpentry. For example, I assume you have sufficient general knowledge about nails, screws, bolts, drilling, sawing, and so forth. Where special nailing, bolting, or other fastening techniques are given, however. Likewise, a complete list of needed tools would be long, and would depend on the project and the builder. A sunspace project should not require much investment in power tools, but you might find yourself filling out your selection of hand tools. Essential power tools are: a portable electric drill (a ⅜- or ½-inch chuck with reversing variable speed is strongly recommended) and a portable electric saw with sharp, general-purpose and fine-tooth blades. If you need to make any long, straight cuts, perhaps you can locate a friend with a table saw. The drill doubles as a screw inserter and remover, using a set of screwdriver bits and hex sockets, and will save much time in fastening glazing.

Organized professionals could require a week to build a sunspace. More likely, they will need a month. Guessing how long you would need involves knowing your skill level and efficiency. To make the project go quickly, design carefully, procure all forseeable materials beforehand, then work all day every day until you are done. Finding or ordering materials might be the slowest part.

Having too many helpers, sometimes even one, will make the work go slower as you ponder what to give them to do. If you are paying for help, this is where the majority of the sunspace construction fund might end up going. Sometimes you need help, though, so having one person on hand or within earshot can boost efficiency. When a long tape measure must be held, or boards or plywood fastened, someone must hold while the other measures or nails. Several people should be on hand when concrete is delivered, if glass glazing is to be installed, or if the wind is always blowing.

When you are building your own project, you will be completely responsible for safety—your own and that of anyone else who happens by or works for you. This sounds scary and is. The best approach is to study this and other construction books and try to anticipate most things that could go wrong, then prevent such situations from occurring. A few possibilities follow.

Fence or close the work site to keep out wandering neighborhood children. Close it securely or have someone watching when you are not there. (This step also helps prevents damage and pilferage in unreliable neighborhoods.) Advise adults who visit the site of any present dangers, and watch if they can handle themselves around hazardous footing. Keep far away from excavating machinery.

Glazing roofs is especially tricky. Have plenty of help. Take the time to build sturdy scaffolds and other supports instead of relying on "monkey-climbing" and shaky ladders to reach the unreachable. Do not leave loose sheets of material that can fly in the wind, damaging both the materials and people in the neighborhood. Working while the wind is blowing is especially dangerous. Know your power tools before starting them, especially a saw. Always know whether the electric line is on or not, instead of using the tool to test it. If someone were to be seriously cut, probably by a tool, know where your first-aid supplies are and where you would go for medical help.

If saving money is of utmost importance, there are some more avenues you can explore. Is your project part of a non-profit program, and will it benefit the public? Then suppliers might consider donating some materials, especially those that show and are unique. If the lumberyard is not in position to make donations, go to the manufacturers' representatives. It is better to visit than to call.

Explore the possibilities of recycled glazing, windows, lumber, pipes, bricks, and so forth. Most used lumber is no bargain after you have removed all nails, avoided all holes and cracks, and eliminated all warped beams. Saw blades hate old nails. Window units from old houses are difficult to use and will be difficult to paint and prevent from leaking. There is too much old, rotten wood and not enough glass. Windows from commercial buildings, however, can be a different story. Examine them carefully and see how they would fit your plans. You might find it necessary to design the sunspace around the windows, so consider what happens if you must replace them someday.

If you live near a sawmill, explore whether you can pick up rough-sawn lumber at lower prices. The dimensions will be near actual size—a 2 × 4 measures 2 inches × 4 inches. The surface texture is rough, a virtue to some builders. It would be difficult to paint, but if the lumber is cedar, simple liquid treatment is sufficient, if anything is done to it.

If you plan to use the neighborhood lumberyard, choose one that will let you select your wood at your leisure. In this way you can avoid much waste. Plan to spend a lot of time shopping. Quality control of lumber is dropping steadily, so a load you order by telephone from the yard can be half unusable because of cracks, excessive knots, bark strips, sawmill damage, band marks, curves, twists, wormholes, and numerous other calamities. Worse, some wood looks fine as you load it, but after a night's rain has been dried by the sun it turns into a pile of large hockey sticks. By examining the grain, you can determine which boards will behave best, but that is an art beyond this book.

If you cannot pick through the lumber, then a strategy to reduce waste is to go through the lumber you receive and assign the worst for cutting into small pieces, the bad for concrete forms, the mediocre to be hidden as wall studs, and the best for rafters and glazing framing that show. Generally, it seems that longer lumber has been graded to remain straight better, otherwise it would go crazy before it is sold. Try getting 2 × 4s in 12- to 20-foot lengths and cut them. Problems with quality also occur with plywoods, except that if you pay enough, you can get sheets that are nearly perfect—on one side.

If permanent electrical work in the sunspace or greenhouse will be a major cost overrun for you despite the need for it, consider using heavy extension cords carefully and plugging everything into house circuits. Likewise, a garden hose can provide a water supply, and it can have a shut-off on the end of the hose. Perhaps better installation of utilities can be done another year. Plan for that later work where possible.

FOUNDATIONS OF CONCRETE AND GREENWOOD

Some details of excavation and foundation design have been covered in Chapter 3 to assist with design and cost estimates. Some are repeated here. In order to have room to install wood forms for pouring a concrete foundation, you should excavate a wide trench where the foundation goes. The ground at the bottom should be undisturbed, or packed well. If there is to be an underground heat storage, you should excavate for it at this time. You could pour the concrete (if any) for it at the same time as you do the foundation. Details of preparing the storage system are covered in the next section. Making a concrete-block foundation equivalent to a poured one is in some ways more difficult and was detailed in Chapter 3. Wood foundations are described at the end of this section.

If a building code applies to your sunspace, you should have learned how deep a frostproof foundation must be, whether there must be a footing, and how thick footing and foundation walls must be. If you selected another type of foundation, again you must know its depth and sizes—e.g., the depth and diameter of piers for posts. Pour concrete footings, if any, in the excavated trenches, on firm, moist soil. Footings 6 inches thick and 1 foot wide might be sufficient for a sunspace foundation. The top need not be level or smooth unless you will put concrete blocks on top.

There must be a way to make the foundation wall remain locked to the footing (FIG. 4-2). You should mold or gouge a deep groove into the footing before the concrete sets, for example, by embedding a 2 × 2 into the fresh concrete along the centerline of the footing. Remove this board as soon as the concrete has stiffened a bit. Leaving wood embedded in concrete for whatever purpose is likely to crack fresh, weak concrete because wood swells with moisture. Alternatively, you can insert 1-foot-long steel "rebars" halfway into the footing.

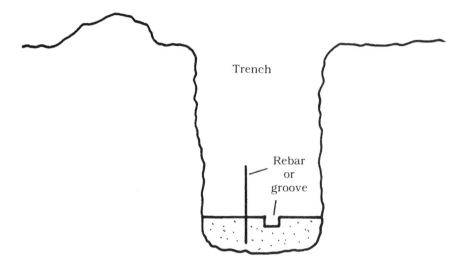

Fig. 4-2. *Excavating for and pouring the footing (if required) prior to building foundation forms (cross-section view).*

Concrete forms are made of low-quality plywood and 2 × 4s. Perhaps you can find a friend or neighbor with used ½-inch plywood forms (¾-inch would be better). If the surface quality of the plywood is poor, obvious imperfections might be cast into a part of the concrete wall that shows. Place foundation forms on top of the footing or on bare, hard ground at the bottom of the trench.

The best way to get your foundation the size you want is to cut the forms to be that size, then assemble them. Be sure to allow for the thickness of the plywood itself. Walls six inches thick might be acceptable. To obtain square corners in laying out square forms, use a long tape measure or string to compare the lengths of the diagonals. A difference of less than ¼ inch is sufficient accuracy for sizes and squareness. You can do leveling with a 6-foot level, a shorter level on a very straight 2 x 4, or a garden hose filled with water, whose level can be seen through clear plastic tubing attached to each end.

The common problem with forms is that they are too weak and sag during pouring. Another problem is that they might change position when someone walks on them or the concrete chute strikes them. More work is put into good forms than into the pour. Plywood gives way easily and needs side reinforcement with 2 x 4s, as shown in FIG. 4-3. Then the 2 x 4s need side bracing, as shown. Hold the top together securely with wood ties nailed on. The corners are a very weak place. Metal reinforcing strap is more effective than nailing in preventing corners from pulling apart during vigorous concrete work. Unless you keep the entire top of the form under control, the poured foundation will not match the intended sunspace size. The bottom also must be secure, since the greatest concrete pressure is there. At the bottom, you can use temporary fill dirt to hold the sides.

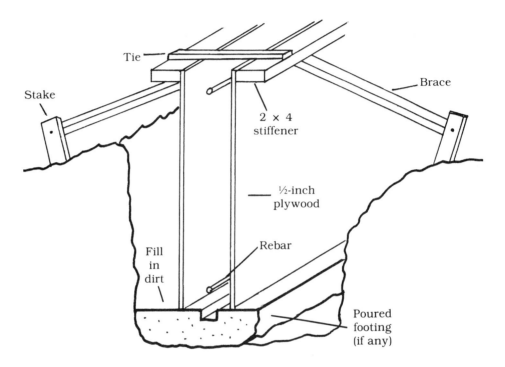

Fig. 4-3. *Building simple wood forms for pouring a concrete foundation wall. (Even if the wall is less than 3 feet high, no effort should be spared on bracing.)*

Sag translates into extra cubic feet of concrete used, which results in running out before the job is poured. Order 5 to 10 percent extra to be sure. Estimate your order from the actual forms built. If your site slopes, the forms will slope at the bottom. Part of the foundation wall might be several feet above final grade. Having a wall with varying height makes estimation of the needed concrete more difficult, and a wall 5 or 6 feet high greatly increases the concrete pressure at the bottom.

Steel reinforcing, or rebars, are best added even if not required. One ½-inch bar near the top and one near the bottom of the foundation wall should be sufficient for a sunspace. Position them so that 3 inches of concrete surround them on all sides (see FIG. 4-3). You can hang them from the ties with old wire. You might need to pull the bottom bars from the ground just as concrete starts pouring around them. Be sure to have sufficient ½-x-8 inch foundation bolts or J-bolts on hand. Insert them about 1 foot from the ends and no farther than every 6 feet between. You might need to mark the form to show where to put them to avoid placing one where a stud or post is to rest.

If you will place posts in or on concrete piers, you might not need forms except for the part of the pier that will show aboveground. Dig the holes to the correct size and let them be the forms. Accuracy is still necessary or you will not estimate the concrete order correctly. If you have or can borrow a good concrete mixer, pouring piers yourself is possibly cost-effective. Each pier will need one or two mixer loads, so the work will be arduous, but you can spread it out over several days. An 8- x -12-foot sunspace with posts every 4 feet would need eight or ten piers, depending on how the roof is held up in the back. No reinforcing is needed. Be sure to place the bolt (FIG. 4-4) or other post hardware in an exact position promptly after pouring. You will need to have tight, level strings around the perimeter for good alignment, but strings always seem to be in the way of concrete pouring. Foundations bring many challenges in preparation and organization.

One such challenge involves concrete. This material is made from water, cement, sand, and rocks of limited size. The sand fits inside the empty spaces among the rocks. The cement fits inside the empty spaces among the sand. The water coats the cement dust particles and should occupy the little remaining space and not a tad more. Thus water content is critical. The resulting substance is very dense, which means it will be laborious to mix and difficult to carry.

Fig. 4-4. *Mounting a wood post on a pier foundation by means of one type of post base hardware. (Use a washer and nut before attaching the post.)*

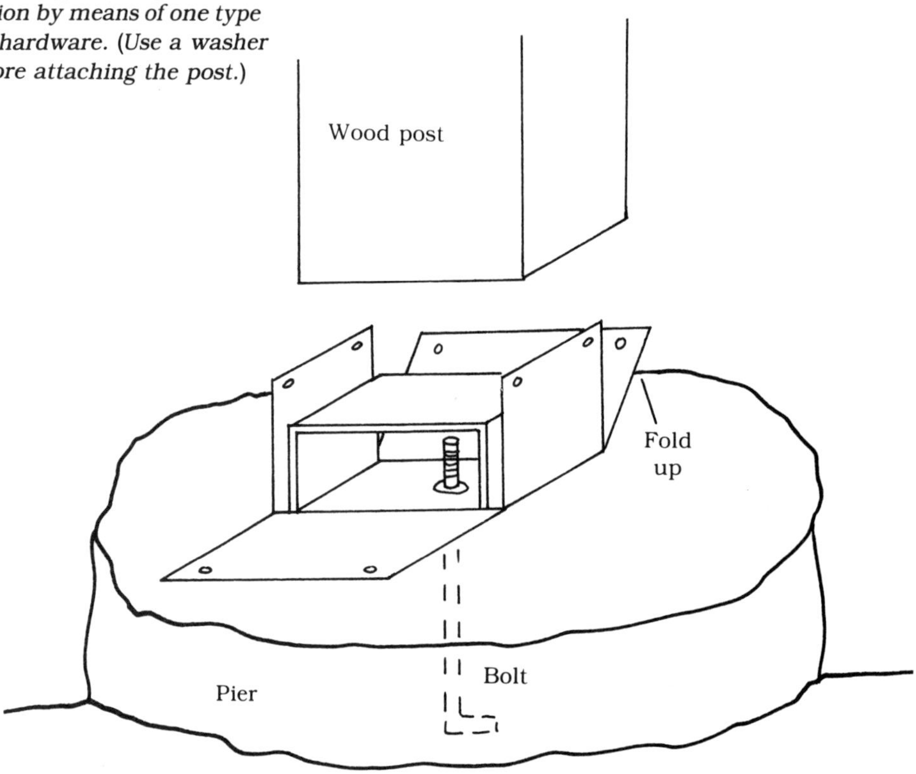

Wood post

Fold up

Pier

Bolt

Concrete is a substance of contradictions. It hardens by setting, not by drying. In fact, drying is fatal to concrete until it has had up to a month to harden. Too much water in freshly mixed concrete weakens it. Twelve hours later you could not get it too wet, and it hardens to the highest strength underwater. Therefore, you should keep concrete covered with a plastic sheet for as long as you can manage. If you cannot obtain white plastic, which reflects the sun's heat, cover the concrete first with clear or black plastic and then with old wood, straw, dirt, or whatever to reduce solar heating. A sunspace hardly needs the highest strength foundation, but the stress the ground can place on the foundation and the need for hardness of the exposed surface call for care in proper curing.

Concrete setting is very dependent on temperature. To make things worse, as it sets it produces its own heat. On a 90° F day, you might have just an hour to smooth concrete after pouring. As soon as it stops wetting its own surface, the time has come for you to do whatever finish work you planned. Keep the surface wet, but avoid washing it and so separating sand from cement. For each 10° lower ambient temperature, you might have another hour to "work" the concrete. Near the freezing point, you need not worry about it freezing before setting, but it is best to cover it with any old insulating material. When the temperature is well below freezing, conditions are difficult, and it is best to wait for a better season.

On pouring day, have everything, including people and back-up people, ready before the concrete arrives. Particularly on delivery of small loads, concrete companies provide very limited free time. There is not much to do to a foundation wall for the sake of appearance, provided that the form is straight and stays that way during pouring. Poke the concrete down, pull any rebars into proper place, tap the sides, smooth the exposed top with a wood block, and insert anchor bolts before it is too late. Have the bolts protrude about 2½ inches for later mounting of 1½ inch-thick wood. Press the concrete around bolts to make certain none are loose. Lastly, remove the ties. By this time the concrete should be so stiff there is no danger of slumping. Smooth the surface again as much as you want and can. Every lump or rock sticking up is an annoyance later, and will need to be chiseled away or the frame will not rest well.

A concrete slab floor should be a separate pouring job. Details of concrete finish work for a floor slab are given in the References. Obtaining a smooth concrete floor is a full chapter in itself. Find experienced help unless you have succeeded before or have practiced on a previous slab. Chapter 5 provides some information about concrete and masonry floors.

Leave the foundation form on as long as possible to keep the sides of the concrete damp. Cover the top with plastic as described, and pour water under it whenever the top dries. Leave the forms on at least a week unless you will place rigid-foam insulation against the concrete. Then you can replace the forms with the insulation the next day while keeping the concrete wet. Fill the dirt back in to hold the foam insulation, tamping the moist dirt as you place it.

One other foundation wall meriting treatment here is the wood foundation. It, too, is placed at the frost line. Various greenwood manufacturers have worked out the design of a wood foundation for residential use. You can consult their sales engineers for free information. The following are general guidelines, in absence of other information, for moderate-load applications. When you are buying greenwood, look it over carefully for quality to accompany its high cost. Be sure it is certified for underground use. Although good lumber is selected for the pressure treatment, some still comes out warped and cracked. When you are cutting greenwood, use a carbide blade because the wood is very dense and tough. Wear a dust mask to avoid breathing or ingesting the dust. It is not dangerous in the small amounts encountered when you are constructing a small foundation. Expect to have a difficult time nailing it, too. You might need to predrill every nail hole. Remember to use double hot-dipped galvanized or better grades of nails.

Excavate 6 inches below the frost line and 12 inches wide. Fill the trench with 6 inches of loose rock, tamping it. In wet areas, install perforated drain pipe outside the rock base. The drain pipe must have a place to carry water to—either a pit or a hillside. You can build the wood foundation in long sections outside on level ground, then lower it in place and connect the sections together. The height should be whatever brings it from the frost line to grade level, plus whatever you want to have aboveground. A typical height would be 3 feet. With green 2 × 6s, build what amounts to a low stud wall, as shown in FIGS. 3-20 and 4-5. You can space the 2-×-6 studs 2 feet o.c. for light loads. Face the outer side with ½-inch green plywood to brace it and lock all parts together.

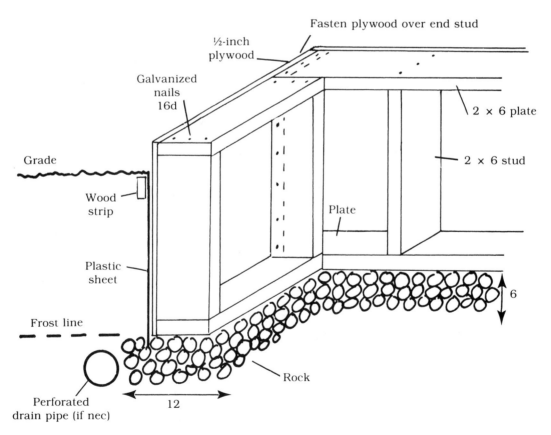

Fig. 4-5. A greenwood foundation. The bottom plate should be held down with rocks, concrete blocks, permanent stakes, or dirt.

If the foundation is longer than the available wood, use the plywood to join adjacent sections, each with its own end studs. At corners you can use plywood to secure the two sections lying at right angles, as shown. Before filling with dirt, attach polyethylene sheet along the outer wall with a nonrotting 1 × 2. This step is done, not to waterproof the foundation, but to control water flow better. Because wood is a much better insulator than concrete, no outside insulation is needed. You can add inside insulation later unless you plan to fill the entire area with dirt now. In that case, add 2 inches of extruded polystyrene between the studs before filling in with dirt.

Because this foundation and the sunspace are low in weight and because there is low friction with the ground, something must be done to keep the foundation from pulling up. The bottom plate is tied securely to the top plate with plywood. In this way, if the bottom plate can be held down, the whole sunspace will stay anchored. Either pile rock about 1 foot deep on the bottom plate or drive permanent, nonrusting rods or pipes laterally into the earth and over the bottom plate. It might be sufficient just to fill dirt all over the inside of the foundation. Another option is to use rustproofed steel augers designed to anchor sheds and mobile homes to the ground.

CONSTRUCTING HEAT STORAGE

The heat-storage methods considered here include the following: a rock bed or bin, concrete blocks used as air ducts, and hot air tubes in a slab floor. A brick floor, a passive concrete slab floor, and a dirt floor involve no special instructions. The rock bed can consist of nominal 2- to 3-inch washed gravel spread about 1 foot deep over an excavation that covers the entire sunspace. Another option is to confine the rock to a tank or bin. In the former case, the foundation wall can serve as the wall of the storage. In the latter case, the expense would be high whether you poured a tank in place at least 5 feet deep or purchased a septic tank, typically 8 feet tall, and had it delivered to a suitable hole.

When you are using the whole foundation to hold a rock bed, place the rock on 2 inches of extruded polystyrene insulation over durable and well-sealed plastic sheeting to keep out moisture from below. The hot air must be ducted uniformly into the rock and returned from it in a similar manner. The ducting must be completely waterproof, and the rock must be kept clean and dry. Poured concrete ducts, concrete blocks set on their side, plastic drain pipe, green-treated plywood, or small concrete culverts are options for forming ducts. None of these methods have been widely studied and written about, but you should be able to create your own system with minimal difficulty. The principle to keep in mind is that air distribution should be uniform. The simple method given here is to leave an open area about 6 inches wide at each end of the storage, from which numerous air passages or tubes branch.

As shown in Fig. 4-6, air ducts can enter at one corner or the center of an air channel at one end of the rock bin. A green plywood or thin poured concrete partition keeps the rock out of the open area. Air is divided through ports about 6 inches in diameter in the partition spaced every 2 feet the width of the rock bed. At the other end, air is picked up through ports and carried to an exit duct at the other corner or the center. For best distribution, place thin green plywood, galvanized metal, or other permanent barriers lengthwise in the bin to encourage air flow from

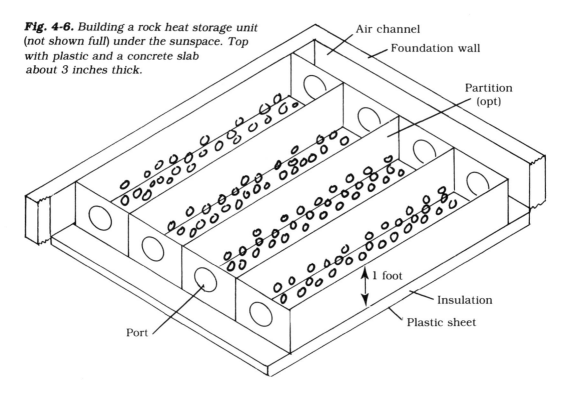

Fig. 4-6. *Building a rock heat storage unit (not shown full) under the sunspace. Top with plastic and a concrete slab about 3 inches thick.*

Labels on figure: Air channel, Foundation wall, Partition (opt), 1 foot, Insulation, Plastic sheet, Port

one port to the corresponding port. Fill the bin level to the height of the final floor less the thickness of a slab. To cover the bin, place a layer of durable plastic on top, then pour and finish a slab of about 3 inches in thickness. Concrete costs more than rock, but the slab could be thicker since it can absorb heat from both above and below in this case.

Instead of using rock, you can fill the excavated floor of the sunspace with concrete blocks on their sides so that the cores form air ducts. Be sure all the blocks have the same core structure. Choosing between two- and three-cored block is a minor point, but you might prefer two-cored blocks for the larger duct cross section, giving less air resistance in long runs. The incoming air is distributed among block cores through placement of an open channel at each end, as in FIG. 4-7. Again, the input duct should enter at one corner or center, and the return exit from the other corner or center. You can install the blocks two deep for more storage, although one layer should be enough. If you place the blocks carefully in sand (over insulation and plastic sheet) to form a smooth subfloor, you can pave them with decorative brick, or pour a concrete cover slab on top. You must cover the end channels with concrete or other durable material such as ¾-inch green plywood. Unless the floor is well sealed, you should put a plastic layer on the blocks to prevent air flow through the floor and dust penetration.

You can pour a slab floor 6 or more inches thick with hot air tubes embedded in it. The average spacing of 4-inch pipe must be about 6 inches to have enough, so you can stagger the pipe vertically in a thick slab. You can partly bury the lower tubes in sand beneath. Poking wet concrete among all these tubes will be difficult. Galvanized metal tubing, such as 4-inch flue pipe, is a better choice than thin plastic

Fig. 4-7. *A concrete-block heat storage unit. Top with plastic and a concrete slab or bricks.*

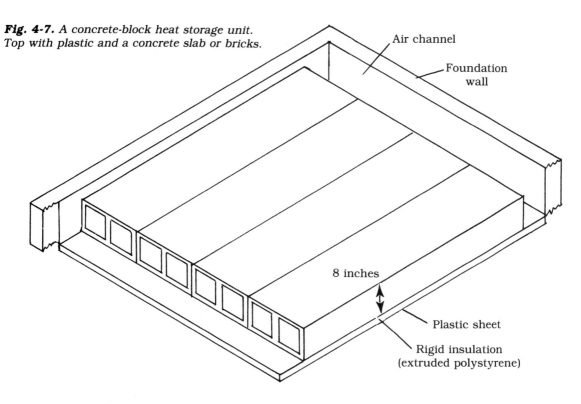

Air channel

Foundation wall

8 inches

Plastic sheet

Rigid insulation (extruded polystyrene)

drain pipe, but more costly. It is difficult to find inexpensive but suitable tubing. Smaller diameters raise the air resistance. The air tubes should be connected in parallel. Rather than embedding many tee connections in the slab and having the entering and exiting tubing too small, leave an open channel at each end of the slab, as for concrete blocks. This large end duct provides a low-resistance, pressure-equalizing connection to all the tubes. You can cover it with green plywood or a few sections of thin, removable concrete slab.

If the sunspace has a raised floor, then the foundation wall and ground beneath can serve as a partial storage. You can even cover the ground with loose rock of almost any large size, among which air would circulate. Duct arrangements to pump heat under the floor, as well as to serve the various types of storage, were discussed in Chapter 3 and will be discussed later in this Chapter.

FRAMING DETAILS

This section gives details of conventional stud-wall construction, along with some variations pertaining to post-and-beam methods. Depending on anticipated moisture levels, the framing might require cedar or redwood. These are weaker woods but will not decay, even without treatment. Some details of wood selection have been discussed, and they pertain even more so to cedar and redwood. Redwood lumber in large sizes is becoming scarce and expensive. Avoid "finger-joint" wood except for trim pieces. Some of the wood methods can be generalized to steel or aluminum structures, with steel members scaled down from the sizes of required wood members. Unusual framing, such as plastic PVC pipe, should be 2 inches or larger in diameter and painted or otherwise protected from the sun. Probably no codes discuss it, so you might need perseverance to work out details, obtain the requisite structural strength, and satisfy building inspectors.

You should have measured the house carefully before designing the sunspace frame to locate variations in height, levelness, wall flatness, and straightness. You cannot assume that the house has been built square, level, uniform, flat in the vertical plane, or geometrically correct in any other way. You should lay out, assemble, and raise the sunspace frame straight and square on its foundation, regardless of variations in the house structure. Imperfections that you could not check before will become apparent as you place the new structure against the house. Keep the sunspace structure as correct as you can, but add whatever pieces are needed to fill in misfits with the house.

Wood framing is described well in many books and in building codes, and your building inspectors might be able to furnish simple diagrams of the procedures required. Basic framing structure was discussed in Chapter 3 and shown in FIG. 3-21. You can hold together stud walls such as the endwalls with nails; use noncorroding nails with redwood or cedar. The wall for the glazing will not have plywood to hold plates to studs, but there should be a positive method of keeping the frame together other than depending on nails not to pull or creep out. To survive wind uplift, the positive method should extend from the foundation to the roof rafters. If studs are to serve as the framing for glazing, you can nail or screw on metal ties or straps to hold the studs to the bottom and top plates (FIG. 4-8). Batten strips will hide them on the outside and simple trim can cover them inside. If you are using glass, be certain that no metal ties extend into the clearance space for the glass.

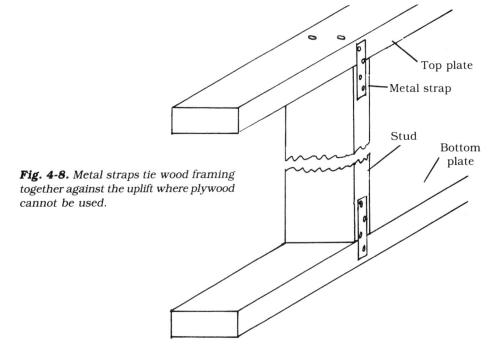

Fig. 4-8. *Metal straps tie wood framing together against the uplift where plywood cannot be used.*

You should solve the details of holding the glazing and of shedding water before you build the south glazing wall. You can mount all glazings, except possibly tempered glass, on the outside of the studs. Some glazings require studs or posts 4 feet o.c. This spacing is twice too wide for conventional strength and might not pass code. Using headers on jack studs is undesirable because a thick stack of three studs (4½ inches) would occur every 4 feet and block the sun. Solutions include using double 2- x -4 studs (two studs fastened together to form a post), 4- x -4 posts, 2- x -6 studs (called posts or mullions in this application), or 2- x -2 (true size) steel tubes. Using a 2- x -6 bottom and top plate (together with headers) to hold 2- x -6 studs is one of the better solutions (FIG. 4-9). You might want to select very straight and possibly attractive 2- x -6 studs. The foundation is wide enough to carry 2- x -6 construction. Another good choice is 4- x -4 posts, and they are more likely to remain straight over time if you have chosen straight ones. If there is a kneewall, build it between glazing posts as a small stud wall. It can be of 2- x -4 or 2- x -6 construction.

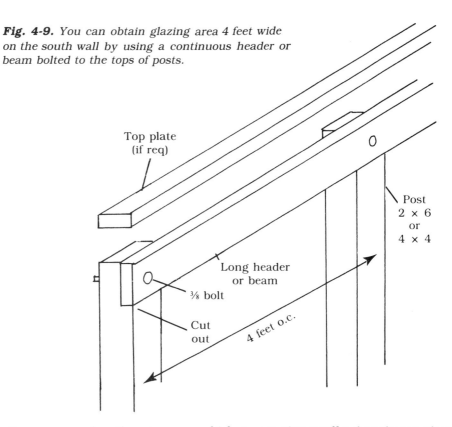

Fig. 4-9. *You can obtain glazing area 4 feet wide on the south wall by using a continuous header or beam bolted to the tops of posts.*

Top plate (if req)

Post 2 × 6 or 4 × 4

Long header or beam

⅜ bolt

Cut out

4 feet o.c.

In any case, when there is a span of 4 feet, something stiffer than the top plate must cross the span and carry the roof load. You can set a single 2- x -6 continuous header or beam as long as the sunspace (boards 20 feet or more are available) on edge and let it into the posts, as shown in FIG. 4-9. If you want more shade control at the top, use a 2 × 8 or larger board. In this sort of post and beam construction, ⅜-inch bolts are much better than nailing to hold posts and beams together. You then can nail the top plate on top. If for some reason, you have planned a larger span, then increase the beam size as discussed in Chapter 3.

In 2- x -4 construction, the bottom plate might better be a 2 x 6 set to protrude at the bottom (FIG. 4-10). You should cut the front edge with a bevel (only a table saw can do this sort of thing neatly) to help shed water from the plate and over the foundation. Cut the bevel back to wherever your particular glazing can rest, leaving battens to hang over the bevel. If you have chosen 2- x -6 construction, then you need a 2- x -8 beveled bottom plate. It would be best to obtain a greenwood bottom plate, or apply the proper treatment to the bottom plate yourself. The treatment will prevent rotting resulting from moisture that seeps under it, comes up through the concrete, or falls on it. Treated wood is necessary if the wood is not cedar or redwood.

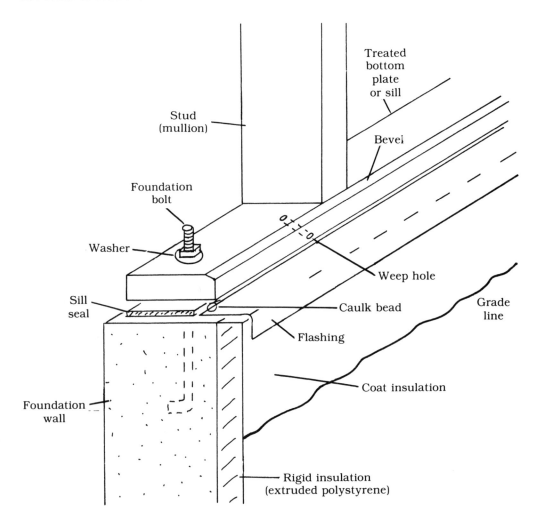

Fig. 4-10. *Attaching and sealing the frame to the foundation, with attention to special details pertaining to the control of water flow and heat loss.*

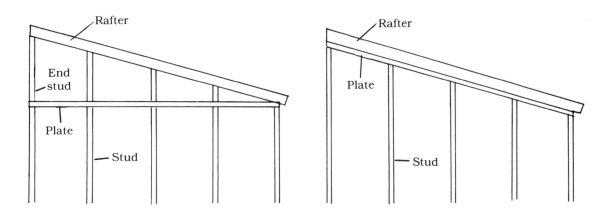

Fig. 4-11. *Two ways to frame a sidewall in its connection to the roof (face view).*

Rather than having their top and bottom plates parallel, the sidewalls could have a sloping top plate to match the roof rafters. Making the angle cuts is no more difficult than cutting end studs later to fit between a level top plate and a sloping end rafter (FIG. 4-11). Door and window framing (FIG. 3-21). should preserve a regular spacing of 2 feet o.c. for studs wherever possible, so that you can nail 4- x -8-foot sheets to frame members. The bottom piece in the window opening, a framing sill, should slope downward 5 to 10 degrees so you can attach a water-shedding finish sill later. Any auxiliary stud beneath it needs a matching angle cut.

The arrangement of studs and posts at the ends of the glazing wall depends on the type of corner you want (FIG. 3-24). The way you handle the corners of the structure depends on what sort of interior finish and appearance you select. Unless you plan an inside south glazing, you do not need any interior fastening surface on the south wall. In one simple arrangement (FIG. 3-24B), the end posts for the glazing are set back behind the sidewalls. This arrangement might look awkward and it might be difficult to reach into the corner to attach any components there. A better solution is to fill the corner with a 4- x -4 or 4- x -6 post or to block in an additional stud as shown. The method you choose depends on whether glazing posts are set 2 or 4 feet o.c. and what extra distance is designed at the ends of the south framing, as discussed in Chapter 3.

You can build stud walls flat on the ground first and then raise them as a unit. This method permits nailing through the bottom plate as well as the top, and avoids unsightly and weaker toenailing into the bottom. Remember that once the wall is up, it is not easy to change your mind or correct an error and move a stud to a new position. You would need to yank it off, then toenail it in place. Do not put any plywood on at this time; instead use temporary braces, such as 10-foot 1 x 4s nailed diagonally across the frame. When several helpers place a heavy stud wall into position, it must slip over the foundation bolts and land in the proper place, regardless of irregular bolt placement or wavy foundations. An easy procedure is to place the bottom plate(s) on the bolts before construction and to premark holes with a hammer. Otherwise, you must drill the holes while helpers hold the whole framed wall above its correct position.

Before final placement, you can place a flashing to cap the whole foundation top to prevent water damage and termite attacks of ordinary woods (FIG. 4-10). Another choice is to use an L-shaped piece of flashing about 2 × 4 inches that rests on the foundation wall lip and covers the rigid foam insulation. The weight of the wall and perhaps a bead of caulk will keep it there. You can place a "sill seal" of fiberglass or flexible foam under the bottom plate to get a better air and water seal to the foundation. Again, fill very uneven places with caulk. The goal is to prevent any water entry at this point, whether from runoff or from sideways spray by sprinklers. If water is excluded, air infiltration also will be stopped at this vital point.

After you have done all preparation and sill sealing, put the framed walls in place and connect the corners together temporarily. Also attach the walls to the house. Only after the walls are lined up exactly and well braced should the washers and nuts be put on the foundation bolts and tightened. The bolts cannot prevent a wall from falling and severe damage could result. The building code for your area might require that you nail on a second top plate, overlapping the first top plate to hold corners together. Otherwise, the best solution is to nail or bolt the corner studs together and to nail metal plates over the top joints. Do not put on any plywood sheathing yet.

If the sunspace foundation is frostproof like that under the house, then you can bolt the sidewalls directly into studs in the house walls. Use ⅜-inch or larger "lag bolts" with washers; these are large screws with hex heads that are turned with a wrench. You should predrill the holes to accept the "body" of the bolt without splitting the wood. If there are no house studs where you want your sunspace connections, then attachment depends on what sort of sheathing or siding is on the house wall. If the sidewall frame fits right up to the rafters, then you should be able to bolt into the house frame there and at the bottom (the house sill). If the sunspace will not be tied to the house structurally, then you can pour a rear foundation and connect the sidewalls to a rear stud wall.

If the walls, whether stud-framed or something else, are to be hung from posts, the attachment methods are different. As shown in FIG. 4-12, 2-×-6 beams (2-×-8, or larger for an 8-foot span) are bolted to the faces of round or square posts of steel or wood. No top plate is necessary, but a beveled 2-×-4 sill is desirable to control runoff from glazing. Fasten the sill to the top of the bottom beam between posts. Fasten 2-×-4 studs for glazing posts to the top beam with bolts and to the top of the sill with lag bolts. If a beam must have a joint, then you must bolt both ends to the post. A metal plate would help strengthen the joint.

If the south glazing is to be tilted, then there are no vertical glazing posts. A tilted wall can still be assembled on the ground. Any kneewall is built as a continuous low and strong stud wall. A tilted glazing wall (FIG. 4-13) applies strong outward forces to the kneewall. The kneewall should then be as low as possible and made of 2-×-6 construction. Unless bracing plywood is on the inside as well as the outside of the kneewall, it should be held together with metal straps on the inside. The foundation bolts are strong enough to resist outward movement of the kneewall until the roof rafters are in place and can tie the glazing wall to the house or rear wall.

You can omit the kneewall, or simply reduce it to a beam, and the sloping mullions or glazing supports can rest on the bottom plate or the beam. The glazing supports are cut at the appropriate angle to rest on the level plate. For heavy roof

Fig. C-1. A two-story curved-eave greenhouse glazed with double-tempered glass.

Fig. C-2. A sunspace with double-walled acrylic roof and double-tempered glass walls, large enough to heat the whole house with blown air. Although heat concentrates near the clerestory window vents in this tall structure, reaching them and the rest of the ceiling to work is difficult.

Fig. C-3. This rooftop sunspace is intended more for heat collection than for occupancy.

Fig. C-4. A steel-framed sunspace with redwood-covered steel floor, used for a hot tub. Glazing is double-tempered glass on the walls, with double-walled acrylic filling in to 8 feet high and on the roof (Courtesy of Better Products).

Fig. C-5. A small sunspace built into a partly underground basement must have short windows, but the patio door entrance has full-height glazing accessible to the sun part of the day. The amount of mass underground means this sunspace cannot grow cold.

Fig. C-6. Exterior of an L-shaped sunspace glazed with double-walled acrylic. The sunspace is wrapped around a west corner of the house (Courtesy of Better Products).

Fig. C-7. The interior of the L-shaped sunspace (Courtesy of Better Products).

Fig. C-8. This interior of a white-enameled aluminum-framed sunspace shows quilted shades that draw in tracks in the frame along the roof and around the curved eaves to control overheating (Courtesy of Janco Greenhouses).

Fig. C-9. The exterior of the white-enameled sunspace (Courtesy of Janco Greenhouses).

Fig. C-10. In summer, a nylon screen with nylon roof awning can replace the double plastic glazing on this aluminum-framed kit (Courtesy of Solar Resources Inc.).

Fig. C-11. This wood-framed greenhouse has double-walled acrylic glazing and a steel wire bracing the glazed west wall. Like all plastic glazings, this material catches dirt easily.

Fig. C-12. An adobe house with an adobe sunspace has abundant adobe mass inside to moderate the heat gained through the tilted glazing. A generous overhang and turbine vents also control overheating.

Fig. C-13. A new house with a two-story sunspace incorporated. The dark brick wall on the house proper collects and stores solar heat, releasing it to the house.

Fig. C-14. The exterior of a low-cost, partly underground sunspace with adobe mass in the rear wall. The sunspace features sloping glass.

Fig. C-15. A free-standing sunspace used for a chicken house permits poultry to survive all year in a hostile climate. The glazing is primarily corrugated FRP, lapped with corrugated metal roofing.

loads, they might be required to be 2 × 6s. Pin them to the knee wall or bottom plate with lag bolts or very heavy nails, predrilling to prevent splitting.

Fig. 4-12. *Preparing a post-and-beam frame for glazing or for solid walls. (If the sill is not cut around the posts, you can fill in matching pieces.)*

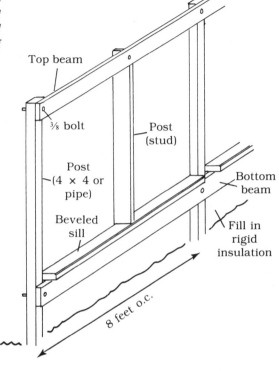

Top beam

⅜ bolt

Post (stud)

Post (4 × 4 or pipe)

Beveled sill

Bottom beam

Fill in rigid insulation

8 feet o.c.

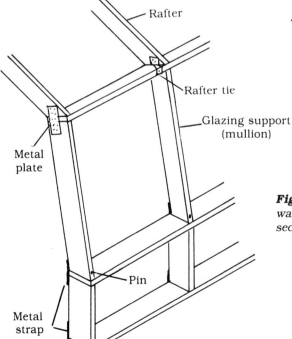

Rafter

Rafter tie

Glazing support (mullion)

Metal plate

Fig. 4-13. *Attaching a tilted glazing wall to rafters. (The structure should be secure against uplift.)*

Pin

Metal strap

ROOFING DETAILS

Roof rafters rest on a rear stud wall or on a rafter support or ledger fastened to the house. The latter is a 2 × 4 securely fastened to the house with ⅜-inch lag bolts into every house stud. Another method would be to use *joist hangers*, U-shaped brackets (FIG. 4-14) that hold the end of a 2 × 4 (or bigger rafter) and fasten to the face of a beam or rafter support. When used with nails, they offer little resistance to the roof pulling away from the house. Therefore, you should screw or bolt the hangers securely to the rafter support. For the best fit, cut a notch in the rafter end just deep enough to give a level place for resting in the hanger.

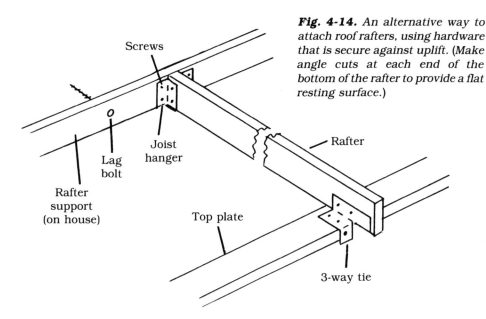

Fig. 4-14. *An alternative way to attach roof rafters, using hardware that is secure against uplift. (Make angle cuts at each end of the bottom of the rafter to provide a flat resting surface.)*

Screws

Joist hanger

Lag bolt

Rafter support (on house)

Rafter

Top plate

3-way tie

At the south end, the rafters can overhang the top plate of the glazing wall as needed for shade control. If they end flush with the wall, there will be less control of water runoff and penetration, as well as no shade. Cut a shallow notch near the end of each rafter to provide a level resting place. Shallow notches near the ends do not weaken the rafter as much as you might think, because most strength is needed in the center where the rafter is subject to the most bending. Thus, you should avoid cuts, notches, large edge knots, and large holes near the middles of rafters and other beams. If the south glazing wall tilts, see FIGS. 3-26 and 4-13 for the connection of rafters to this wall. The rafters can abutt the tilted top plate as shown, or they can be notched to rest on its edge and overhang as before.

Several kinds of steel hardware are available for securing rafters to the top plate to withstand uplift forces. You can use either a twisted strap or three-way angle with a bend-down tab (see FIGS. 4-13 and 4-14). The objective is to put nails through the holes in the hardware sideways into the rafter and sideways into the top plate so that the forces would need to shear thick nails in order to pull the rafter away from the wall. After you have nailed or screwed on all metal straps and ties, you can nail any sheathing plywood (½-inch CDX) over them and over the entire framing so as to connect metal ties, top plate, and studs securely to the bottom plate. Put a nail through the plywood into each metal piece and the wood behind it.

Rafters larger than 2 × 4 inches and longer than 8 feet will tend to lean over under load and must be held vertical with blocks. The roof sheathing will control smaller rafters. If the roof is partly or completely glazed, there is no control of the rafters except blocks. Then blocks are especially needed to keep the rafters in the correct place for the glazing and serve as purlins or supports for the glazing as well (FIG. 3-28). Blocks are also the means for closing the space between rafters at the headwall, if vents are not put there. When the rafters are deep (FIG. 4-15), the purlins will provide much shadowing, and you could use steel braces instead. To install blocks, cut them the size they should be to fit between rafters 2 feet o.c. (22½ inches except for the last ones) and nail into the block ends. You must install them staggered unless you can do careful slantwise nailing.

To sheathe the roof, use ½-inch exterior plywood of the lowest construction grade (CDX). Then lay roofing felt down with its joints glued with roof cement, and install shingles according to the shingle type and package directions. Install flashing (galvanized sheet metal) under the house eaves and over the new roofing to keep blown water from running down the back wall. If there is no house roof overhang, just a bare wall, then the topmost flashing must insert under siding. Fasten a drip edge (type A, an L-shaped 1 × 2 inches) at the lowest end of the sunspace roof.

Fig. 4-15. Mortise-and-tenon joinery connects a redwood rafter, beam, and post in a manufactured sunspace (Courtesy of Creative Structures, Inc.).

It goes over the felt and under the shingles, with the 1-inch side hanging down. Use fibered roof cement to seal all joints. Avoid having any roofing nails exposed, since most kinds rust despite their coating. If you can find double hot-dipped galvanized nails, use them. Water seeps down any nails that must be exposed, so insert them into roof cement.

If you are planning to have vents on the roof, you must provide some means to keep runoff out of the vent. A galvanized metal roof "jack" for a fixed or turbine vent has a tall stack and flanges. The upstream part of the flange goes under the adjacent shingles, and the downstream part lies over the shingles. They are neater and tighter when installed during roofing rather than afterwards. If you want a homemade pop-up vent, then block in the vented area during rafter construction. Use blocks 2 inches taller than the rafters, as shown in FIG. 4-16. Surround the blocking with galvanized flashing to form a dam or curb and use plenty of roof cement. The vent cover should not only cover this opening, but have drip edge or other flashing fit snugly down over the outside of the blocking. If it is made of wood, the vent cover can be shingled.

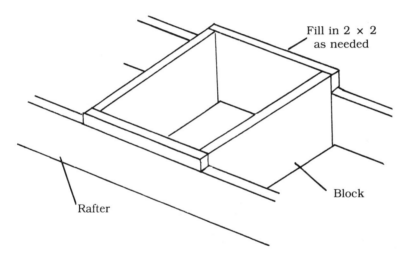

Fig. 4-16. *Blocking in between rafters with extra tall blocks to form a raised vent opening in the roof. (You should wrap flashing around this frame and insert under up-slope roofing.)*

GLAZING DETAILS

Further details of installing glazings are added here to accompany the descriptions of glazing systems given in Chapter 3. The discussion is limited to the glazings most likely to be chosen: tempered glass units, polyethylene film, FRP flat and corrugated sheets, and double-walled acrylic. Another option, using recycled windows, has so many variables that the builder must devise the procedure to suit the windows obtained. Keep in mind the general principles and consult examples given in the References (e.g., Alward in the Books section).

Prior to installing any glazing, examine the framing for its ability to accept components that will shed water, its lack of crevices that would collect water, and the presence of any materials that would deteriorate when wet. If the inside of the sunspace must be kept as dry as your living room, then you should have a backup water rejection system. Water that leaks past the outer glazing should be able to run along a waterproofed sill and out through weep holes drilled at a downward slant to the outside (FIG. 4-10). The moisture that might collect on the inside of the glazing is harder to control. If you cannot drill weep holes from inside to outside, the water must be persuaded to collect in places where it can be mopped up or allowed to fall to a waterproof floor.

Overhead leaks past an outer roof glazing need to be channeled along the rafters rather than allowed to drip to the floor below. This problem is solved in those manufactured sunspaces that use elaborate extruded aluminum rafters with drains or rain channels, but it is not easily solved for wood rafters. You can attach a metal channel beneath the rafter, or form channels in a wood 1 × 4 if you have access to special cutting equipment such as a dado set. Another solution is to buy well-fitting (and costly) neoprene gaskets for the glazing to reduce the possibility of a leak.

Unless otherwise stated in this discussion, a *batten* refers to a nonrotting wood strip (cedar or redwood) in 1 × 2 form (measuring ¾ × 1½ inches). They cannot be purchased over 8 feet, but you can use a table saw to make longer sizes from 1 × 4s or 1 × 6s. Straightness is difficult to obtain, but during the installation process you can remove some bending. Bevel the bottom outside batten downward to help shed water. Battens for some uses can be steel or aluminum strips, channels, or angles, or they can be elaborate extruded aluminum pieces.

Batten down glazing with screws and washers for easy removal and replacement later. Use washers on soft cedar and redwood if you have any doubt that a screw alone will hold. The screws must be noncorroding—either double hot-dipped galvanized or stainless steel. It might be difficult to find sufficiently long thin screws, especially if you are installing double battens on double glazing. Neoprene washers can add extra "grip" and provide a waterseal at the same time. Ordinary plated washers might discolor the batten wood, so you might need to use stainless washers.

It is best to put silicone caulk at the holes on the back of each predrilled batten and under the screw heads. Where battens abut and could hold water, put caulk. Where abutted battens would form a dam that holds water, leave a ¼-inch clearance between them for water to run past. To finish the glazing job, put a bead of the best silicone caulk all around the joint between the glazing and batten. Form the caulk into a bead by pulling a finger or round tool along it. (Watch for splinters.) If the glazing is continuous polyethylene or FRP under the batten, the caulk is unnecessary. Also, silicone caulk will not adhere to polyethylene.

Tempered double-glass units require hard synthetic rubber "setting blocks" underneath (two are sufficient), glazing tape all around, a ¼-inch clearance all around, wood or other soft battens, and protection from injury by nails and screws. The glazing tape should be ⅛ inch thick on both sides, intended to compress to about ¹⁄₁₆ inch on both sides. Therefore, the total mounting thickness of a glass unit is the unit thickness plus ⅛ inch. Rabbets, stops, and other components should match this thickness so that you can screw battens flat against framing and glazing tape, as shown in FIG. 3-5. Use appropriate wood spacers beneath battens to prevent overtightening against the glass.

The time of glass mounting should not be the first time you discover that the frame openings are out of square or out of plane. Glass is unforgiving of misfits, but small errors in squareness can be absorbed into the clearance space, as long as some clearance remains. Push vigorously on the frame first to check if high wind load could distort the frame enough to bear on the glass. If you need more clearance, carefully use an electric saw or chisel to remove wood where the fit is tightest. If the frame is not quite a flat plane, tempered glass will bend slightly to fit it. If the frame is worse, you will need to do some rebuilding first.

Glazing walls that have 2-×-6 posts should have the clearance between posts to accept 46-inch-wide units between the posts (FIG. 3-23). They can be held from the outside by extra wide wood battens about 3 inches wide. On the inside, the glass is held by 1-×-2 stops pressed against the glazing tape. Like the battens, these stops should bear against ¼ to ½ inch of glass. If you are putting glass against wide posts, such as 4 × 4s without rabbeting, then there are no inside stops; however a wood strip should lie between adjacent units to prevent them from ever moving so far that they touch batten screws or each other.

You can mount the glass units from either outside or inside. Put either the stops or the battens on first, then insert the glass. Place battens all around the outside and stops all around the inside. Predrill the holes for batten screws into the posts to prevent any danger of the long screws going at a slant. When you are mounting glass from the inside, it helps to place the glass on two hard ¼-inch fiberboard (hardboard) strips, then slide it into position. Each strip can serve as a lever to raise the glass slightly to insert the synthetic rubber block. The rubber blocks should be no thicker than the glass unit. Use a sheet of wood against the glass to prevent accidental striking of the glass when you hammer nails or insert screws into stops.

For tempered glass units on roofs or sloping walls, you must pay more attention to how the weight is supported at the bottom edge while maintaining a rain seal. A secure method is to use an aluminum angle, channel, or tube as a stop against which the setting blocks and glass rest (FIG. 4-17). Screw the stop to blocks between the rafter ends (or a fascia on the rafter ends), and recess its mounting screws. The stop should be no taller than the thickness of the glass unit plus about ⅛ inch for the glazing tapes. To avoid damming up rain flow, the bottom batten can be a thin (⅛ inch) aluminum strip screwed down against the glazing tape. Place plenty of silicone caulk between the glass and batten strip. Since this batten provides a poor drip edge, you also should insert flashing under it, to lap over the wall below. Be careful that steel flashing does not come near the edge of the glass.

Double-tempered glass units usually come with a tiny metal tube inserted through the seal to equalize pressures between inside and outside. After the glass is in and at ambient temperature, pinch off the tube. Do not forget to join glass and battens with silicone caulk as the first line of defense against rain penetration.

Once a year, you can cover a low-cost sunspace or greenhouse with a large sheet of 6-mil polyethylene film as glazing, or use other, more durable thin film. If the roof is to be glazed, then run the plastic continuously from the top of the roof to the kneewall or foundation, as shown in FIG. 4-18. Round the rafter ends and sand them smooth in this case. Hold the plastic down every 2 feet with battens on rafters and studs. The only need for silicone caulk is between layers of plastic at battened seams and under battens at screw holes. No caulk sticks well to polyethylene.

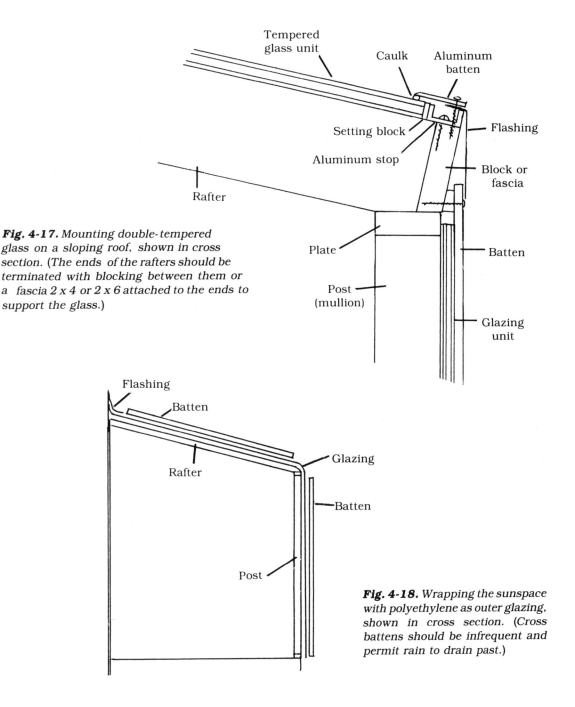

Fig. 4-17. *Mounting double-tempered glass on a sloping roof, shown in cross section. (The ends of the rafters should be terminated with blocking between them or a fascia 2 x 4 or 2 x 6 attached to the ends to support the glass.)*

Fig. 4-18. *Wrapping the sunspace with polyethylene as outer glazing, shown in cross section. (Cross battens should be infrequent and permit rain to drain past.)*

Stretch the plastic tight during battening, unless it is a hot day. Use a minimum of cross battens, and only where they will rest on a backup frame member. Polyethylene will sag part of the time no matter what, so do not attempt to eliminate summertime sag. The plastic will only stretch more or tear when it becomes cold.

The roof pitch must be steep so that rain runs out of sags. Install a smooth-edged metal or other flashing or gasketing over the plastic at the top. Unfortunately, it is during winter that the plastic is tightest and brittle, so the deteriorated plastic will fail suddenly in winter winds, shredding everywhere.

You can run durable sheets of flat fiberglass-reinforced polyester (FRP) 2, 3, or 4 feet wide down rafters or the glazing wall (FIG.3-8). You must support FRP sheet every 2 feet on roofs, and every 2 or 3 feet on walls. You can bend it into a gentle curve of 1 foot or more in radius to form a curved eave. (Making the curved supports, probably from plywood, is a challenge left to the ambitious builder.) Cut FRP with sharp, metal shears. The material should come with a label telling which side is to face the sun (that side has the ultraviolet coating). If in doubt, the concave side of the material, once the inside on the roll, is the outside for sun exposure. Put silicone caulk between layers at each joint of FRP. Batten and apply flashing as usual. If possible, overdrill the holes in the FRP only, so that it can shrink and expand without pulling at and tearing itself on the screws. You can lap this sheet plastic over flashing at the base of the wall. (The flashing, in turn, laps over the foundation insulation.)

As with all sheet plastics, it is impossible to prevent sagging and bowing of FRP as the temperature changes. Snow loads will cause more sag, and you should control its extent by locating support bars (purlins) about ½ inch under roof glazing. The blocking could serve this function. You can control sag on roofs by allowing the FRP sheets to dip downward between rafters to form naturally concave rain channels. To control the dip, blocking with curved edges between rafters, installed about every 4 feet. Use a jigsaw or possibly a saber saw to cut smooth curves about ½ inch deep in 2- x -4 or 2- x -6 blocks. The danger of permitting greater sag is that high wind pressure will pop the roof sags up to convex form. The glazing will be weakened if it snaps back and forth often. If a sidewall has glazing, then you must carefully terminate it at the corner. Cut straight battens of the width needed to lap over the glazing on each side. Have one batten form a corner with the other, as in FIG. 4-19.

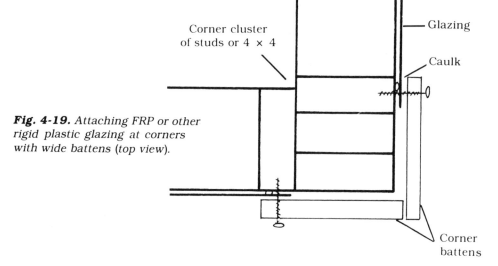

Corner cluster of studs or 4 × 4

Glazing

Caulk

Fig. 4-19. *Attaching FRP or other rigid plastic glazing at corners with wide battens (top view).*

Corner battens

You can assemble sheets of FRP into double glazed units, or you can buy them assembled in standard sizes. Caulk and batten the sheets onto their own cedar or redwood 1-×-2, 2-×-2, or 2-×-4 frames and then place them within, or onto, the sunspace frame. Figure 4-20 shows ways to assemble frames using exterior glue and long screws, angle brackets, or dovetail joints (if you have the machinery). You can encourage flatness by incorporating wood dividers, which also create an interesting window effect. Such units can be removable in summer. You can wrap polyethylene or vinyl around similar frames and batten it, making double-glazed, removable units at a lower cost. Unfortunately, moisture will collect between the glazings and lead to the growth of mold even if the wood does not rot.

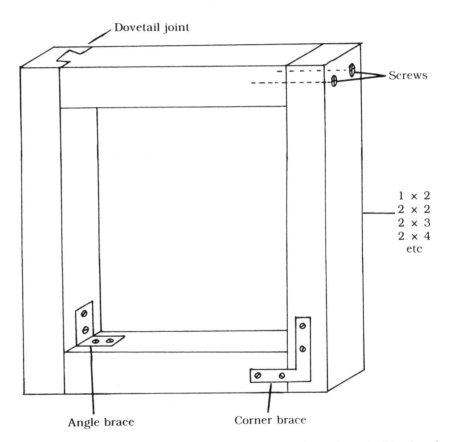

Fig. 4-20. *Four ways to assemble simple wood frames for making double-glazed units, windows, or other components. (Glue all joints with waterproof glue.)*

Corrugated FRP glazing can make attractive walls and roofing if you attach it neatly. You must mount it against corrugated support strips (wiggle strip sawn from redwood, widely available), as in FIG. 4-21. Prefasten the strips with a few small nails at the top and bottom of each run. There must be backup framing. You must use great care in matching up adjacent sections of wiggle strip (matching the "phase"). As provided, wiggle strips are not exactly matched to each other and to the corrugations of the glazing, except in an average sense. Different runs of wiggle strip will start at different places in the sequence of hills and valleys. The one constant factor is that the 26-inch-wide corrugated material is intended to match up every 2 feet o.c.

Install wiggle strips and glazing carefully using the spacing requirement, cutting off pieces of wiggle strip as needed to avoid jogs and obtain a good average match. Overlap the glazing about one full corrugation, or wiggle, with the outside edge pointing downwind according to prevailing wind direction (FIG. 3-9). Corrugated roofing cannot extend much beyond the sides of roofs because it has no stiffness in this direction and will flap, loosening its fasteners or tearing loose from them. To seal the longitudinal edges of corrugated glazing, buy or cut wood strips of the proper thickness to match whatever overlap is left, and caulk and fasten securely. Only about one inch of overhang is suggested, less than one-half corrugation. Corrugated roofing can have more overhang on the eave end, enough to form a good drip edge.

Battens are not necessary with corrugated roofing, and you can fasten noncorroding roofing screws or nails with neoprene washers directly against the roofing. The thin redwood wiggle strip is likely to split, so predrilling through corrugated glazing and backup strips is recommended. Apply silicone caulk between each joint. Caulk between the glazing and wiggle strips only where you need an infiltration seal. On roofs, put the fasteners through the hills (convex part) and all the way into the rafters at joints. You will need fasteners through every third intermediate hill also. At the top of the roof, you can fasten flashing flat onto the corrugated roof only by putting additional wiggle strips upside down on the roof to make a flat surface.

Treat corrugated walls similarly, but put fasteners through the valleys into wall studs, and seal corners (FIG. 4-21). At a corner, the corrugated FRP should overlap onto the stud at least ½ inch and be caulked to it. You can terminate the wiggle

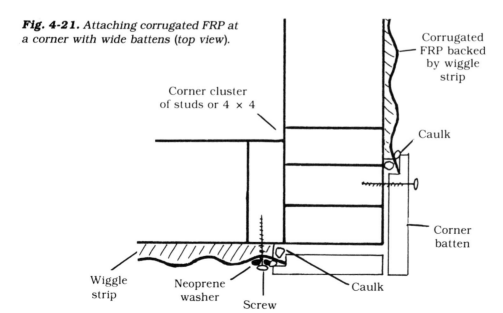

Fig. 4-21. *Attaching corrugated FRP at a corner with wide battens (top view).*

Corrugated FRP backed by wiggle strip

Corner cluster of studs or 4 × 4

Caulk

Corner batten

Wiggle strip

Neoprene washer

Screw

Caulk

strip early and bend the glazing over its thinnest part with caulk filling the small gap. Then you can use caulk to fill a batten with a small rabbet (¼ inch deep, ½ inch or more wide) and place the batten against the edge, pressing it to the frame. (Note that FIG. 4-21 shows only one of several ways to frame a corner. You can use any style of corner with almost any type of glazing.)

You also can use single-thickness or double-walled acrylic or polycarbonate glazing on roof and walls. You cannot add battens, however, because the pressure of the batten cannot be controlled accurately to prevent both binding and leaks. These materials are essentially rigid and will not bow when expanded by heat. Instead they might crack where battened too tightly. Be sure you obtain the descriptive literature on mounting methods for the glazing you purchase.

Care is needed in storing double-walled plastics. Sun shining through stacked layers generates enough heat to melt the protective plastic film and glue it permanently to the glazing. Keep this and all glazings covered until you install it. The protective film on the glazing might be white, a convenience that helps keep sun out of the sunspace during construction when overheating is almost uncontrollable. Remove the white film when you are ready for heat, but be careful not to have it clamped in the mountings. Once the edges are loose, wind might take away the film without warning. The protective film is, of course, intended to prevent damage to the surface during installation since all plastics scratch easily.

Cut acrylic glazing with a fine-toothed saw blade, using a circular saw. A saber saw is slow and causes much cracking. Keep the protective film on during cutting to reduce cracking. The electrostatic behavior of this and most plastic glazings means that dust and chips adhere to it strongly. The only solution is a thorough spraying with clean water just before mounting. Knock the melted chips loose from the edges and flush out every channel in the glazing. Once the glazing is dry inside—blowing with air might be necessary—reinsert the plastic cap strip that should have come with it to seal all the channels. The cap strip should have weep holes at the bottom only. Unsealed channels will degrade the insulating ability of double-walled glazing.

The simplest secure mounting of double-wall acrylic or polycarbonate is to use extruded aluminum T-channels, as was shown in FIG. 3-7. Press a vinyl plastic (PVC) cap strip, usually white, onto the center rib. Its edges clamp the glazing to the channel. Mount the channel 4 feet o.c., so that proper clearance between the 47¼-inch-wide glazing sheets is maintained. Use the channel with cap on all sides of the glazing. Allow an end expansion allowance of about ⅛ to ¼ inch per 8 feet of length when you cut or position the end mountings, or use an allowance as calculated. This is one of the most thermally expansive glazings. Give attention to the temperature at the time of installation and adjust clearances accordingly. On a hot day when the partly glazed sunspace is hot, the material is near maximum size and would not expand more than about ⅛ inch over 8 feet. On a cloudy winter day, it is near minimum size. If you cut the glazing too short, there will be some danger of it pulling past the fastening point, about ½ inch from the center rib.

Fasten the channel to the frame every foot or so, on alternate sides, with rivets or screws with thin heads. When wet, some types of supposedly corrosion-resistant steel screws will interact with the aluminum, leading to deterioration of the fastening. Stainless steel screws are the safest to try. A one-sided type of channel is available (FIG. 4-22A) for mounting the last sheet of glazing, where there are not two pieces to abut. An alternative is to screw on an aluminum or galvanized steel angle ⅝ inch high in place of the absent glazing to simulate the method in FIG. 4-22A.

You will need a rubber hammer to pound the cap strip onto the T-channel. The T-channel doubles as a water drain for rain that leaks past the seal of the cap strip to the glazing. No caulking is needed in this system, nor will it help. The vinyl caps have a shorter life than the glazing and must be replaced after they deform in the sun. If the T-channel is mounted to metal framing, the heat conducted from the frame further shortens the life of the cap strips.

A more expensive mounting method is shown in FIG. 4-22B. Heavy aluminum extrusions (glazing bars) with neoprene gasket inserts clamp the glazing on both sides. The clamping is controlled by having the clamping bolts reach a stop before the gaskets are excessively compressed. This is the only method employing gaskets that has been found to be satisfactory for this type of glazing. The shape of the gaskets permits the glazing to move without losing the seal. These gaskets, and full instructions for their use, are included with glass in many aluminum-framed kits.

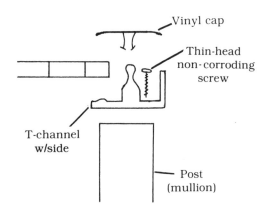

Fig. 4-22. *Special mountings for double-walled acrylic glazing.*

A. One-sided channel for end of wall

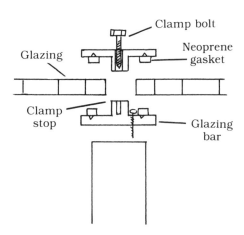

B. Heavier clamping system

If you are not using double-tempered glass or double-walled acrylic, you can add an inner glazing, consisting of polyethylene, vinyl, or flat FRP mounted inside the framing. You can batten the glazing directly to the inside surfaces of studs or between each pair of studs and closer to the outer glazing (see FIG. 4-23). Widths of 4 feet are possible since there will be little disturbance of the film. The air between glazings will not remain dry, so you must accept condensation between them and make provision for its runoff to either the inside or outside. The main purpose of an inner glazing is to provide a still air blanket. Small weep holes in the frame, and small leaks from not caulking will not reduce the insulating capability unless changes in air or wind pressure regularly pump the flexible glazing in and out.

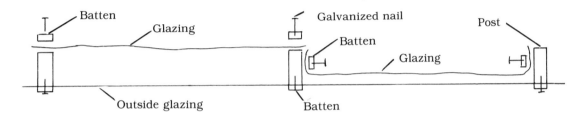

Fig. 4-23. *Attaching thin sheet plastic as inner glazing—two methods are shown in cross section.*

If the roof is partly glazed, then the solid roofing must overhang the glazing enough to let rain run onto the glazing, aided by flashing inserted under the shingles and caulked over the glazing (FIG. 4-24). The joint is difficult to seal against blown rain and melting snow, especially when the pitch is low. Unless the glazing overhangs the wall beneath by several inches, you also need flashing under the roof glazing and over the wall covering. If the glazing comes in units of which several are needed for one run down the roof, you need a Z-shaped flashing (aluminum, with glass) at each joint, inserted under the upper glazing and over the lower as in FIG. 4-24. The joint rests on a purlin.

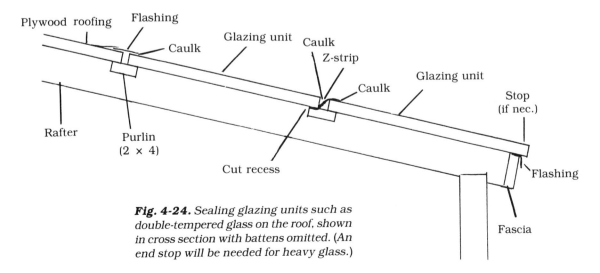

Fig. 4-24. *Sealing glazing units such as double-tempered glass on the roof, shown in cross section with battens omitted. (An end stop will be needed for heavy glass.)*

You should use silicone caulk liberally on such roof joints. Unless the pitch is steep and the glazing thin, this flashing can collect water—not a good idea. Alternatively, you can clamp the glazing units using cross bars or muntins with gaskets over joints. If at all possible, avoid joining several glazing units end to end on roofs.

INSULATION DETAILS

As described earlier, you should put 2 inches of extruded polystyrene insulation against the concrete foundation right after you remove the forms and before you fill in the dirt (FIG. 4-10). Flashing over the top will prevent water penetration and protect the top edge from sun and other damage. The flashing will corrode if it is extended into the ground, so you need some other permanent material between flashing and soil. Best would be a cement, polymer, and sand coating, which will glue itself to the roughened surface of the rigid polystyrene. Mix acrylic polymer with the cement according to the manufacturer's instructions.

You can insulate framed walls and roofs by stapling paper or foil-backed fiberglass between studs, filling every cavity completely. Use R-11 fiberglass with 2-×-4 studs, R-19 with 2-×-6 studs. You can insulate the ceiling similarly before you install the ceiling covering. The backing that comes with this insulation will not form an adequate vapor barrier for moist environments.

Insulating the glazing was discussed in Chapter 3. I leave it to you to consult references or manufacturers and work out methods of putting movable rigid panels over glazing or installing a roll-up or drawstring curtain or shade. (See in the Books section of the References.) You must prevent air movement behind the window insulation, so any panel, quilt, shade, or curtain must have a positive seal to the frame or window at the bottom, sides, and top. Shades can run in tracks, or magnetic strips can attach foam or quilt to walls. The seal is never good enough to prevent moisture from migrating to the glazing, where it condenses and might soak the framing. Any sort of insulation over glazing is likely to require mopping up around the glazing on every cold day.

You can cut blocks of rigid foam to fit snugly into frames around any vents to the outside and to the house. You also can make hinged inside covers for vents by gluing thin plywood or hardboard on both sides of thick rigid foam (FIGS. 4-25 and 4-26). Attach the hinge to a frame glued around the foam block. Water-based latex carpet glue is compatible with most such construction, and silicone caulk is a good glue for many materials. Self-stick gaskets can line openings, although they might need occasional replacement as they fall off. Cabinet hardware, screen hooks, and magnets are among the methods used to hold covers shut. Fans to the outside or to the house also would benefit from insulated doors (FIG. 4-27). The next section discusses exterior covers for vents.

You can press or glue rigid foam, preferably foil-faced, inside wood hot-air ducts to line them. Glues and caulks used around vents and ducts should be able to survive in hot, dry environments. Latex glue, silicone caulks and acrylic caulks hold up well. You should paint exposed wood (except cedar and redwood) with exterior primer, as well as paint or polyurethane.

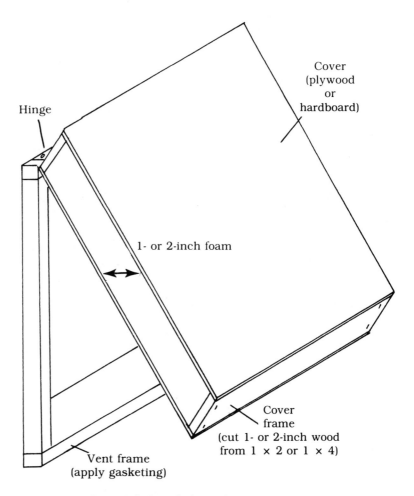

Hinge

Cover
(plywood
or
hardboard)

1- or 2-inch foam

Cover
frame
(cut 1- or 2-inch wood
from 1 × 2 or 1 × 4)

Vent frame
(apply gasketing)

Fig. 4-25. *Simple hinged interior vent cover.*

Fig. 4-26. Screened and louvered vent to outside with hinged inside insulating cover latched with cabinet hardware. (Water stains at these locations are likely to occur over time.)

Fig. 4-27. A fan to force sunspace heat into the house, with an insulated cabinet-style cover on the outside.

DOORS, WINDOWS, AND VENTS

To prepare door, window, and vent frames, line the oversize openings in the frame with 1-x-6 boards (FIG. 4-28). The boards will protrude about 1 inch outside and inside to join with exterior siding and interior finish. Depending on the particular exterior and interior finished thicknesses, you might want to trim them to an exact matching width. For 2-x-6 walls, make the framing boards from 1 × 8s. The finish sill for ordinary windows should slope downward to match the framing sill. It should protrude about 1 inch beyond the exterior finish. Water will not drip from it well unless you cut a shallow, small groove, a *kerf*, in its bottom side. Place flashing under siding and wrap it over the tops of window frames unless there is a good roof overhang at that position. Prime sills and window frames with good oil-based primer or exterior polyurethane, and caulk all crevices with silicone.

You can make your own windows and doors just as you can your own glazing of the sunspace. If you want movable windows, you might need to search for the proper tracks or other guidance system that holds and seals the windows. Obtain this hardware before you make the window, or even before you decide on the window sizes. You can also hinge windows like doors. You can build a simple window frame by cutting a rabbet of a depth compatible with your planned glazing from suitable selected straight 2 × 2, 2 × 3, or 2 × 4. Also consider whether you will match the window to a slanted sill.

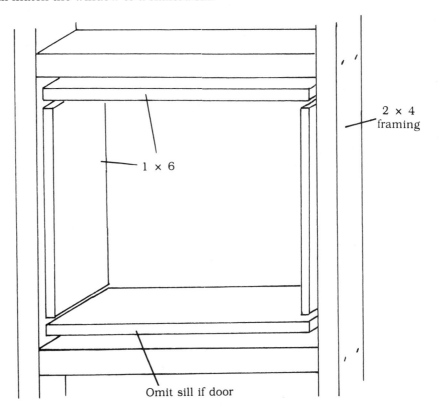

2 × 4 framing

1 × 6

Omit sill if door

Fig. 4-28. *Finish framing around a window, door, or vent. (The sill should slope down toward the outside.)*

Cut and fasten the frames together, being careful to keep them square. You can assemble frames with long screws into the ends, with metal angle brackets, or with more sophisticated methods of cabinetry. Coat the frames thoroughly with exterior polyurethane or exterior oil-based primer. You can order annealed single- or double-glass units in any size, then put them into the frames with glazing tape, caulk, and narrow wood moldings. If you make large windows, keep in mind that they will be heavy. The frames must be very sturdy, and the mounting and control of the window must be very secure.

Frame vent openings with 1 × 6s as if they were small windows. There need not be 2-×-4 rough framing around these openings if you can fasten to the wall material. Otherwise, the vent frame should be between and attached to the framing studs. You can make a simple vent cover from a piece of exterior plywood, sized to cover the vent frame. It should open outward and be hinged to open upward for a hot air exhaust. For cool air inlet, it should be hinged to open downward. Covers hinged to open upward might be controlled by a cord attached to the cover on the inside. See the References for other ways to control an exterior cover from the inside. You might need to walk outside to control the cover. Since intermediate latched positions are difficult to arrange, you might need to be content with two positions: latched shut, and latched fully open.

The vent cover can close against gaskets on the outside of the frame or against stops with gaskets inside the frame. The frame can have an outward sloping sill to shed part of the rain that might enter the vent. Put screen wire over the opening to keep insects out. You can fill the vent frame with a block of insulation in the winter, or you can make the vent cover of a block of foam insulation sandwiched between plywood or hardboard (FIG. 4-25).

If you made roof openings for vents, you can hinge similar foam-sandwiched covers to the blocking around the vents. You will need a rod to push up and hold open the vent since it is not practical to fold the cover onto the roof and latch it there. If you did not use raised blocking with flashing to form a rain curb, then you must take more care to ensure that the resulting "flush" vent does not flush rain into the sunspace. The hinge could consist of a strip of synthetic rubber caulked and clamped under flashing on the upper edge (FIG. 4-29).

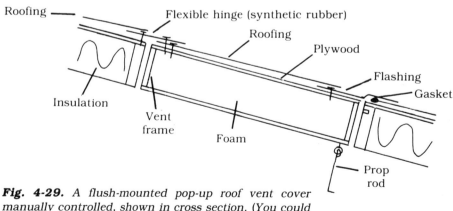

Fig. 4-29. *A flush-mounted pop-up roof vent cover manually controlled, shown in cross section. (You could replace its roofing with glazing to make a skylight, in which case its insulation should be removable.)*

Rain will run over this flexible hinge and run onto the vent cover. Wide flashing sealed to the cover and overlapping the roof on the sides and lower end will shed the rain back onto the roof. Gasketing is needed on the frame where the flashing touches to ensure an air and water seal. There is no reason a roof vent cover cannot double as a skylight and have glazing in its center. Figure 4-30 shows one operated by a thermal vent opener, as well.

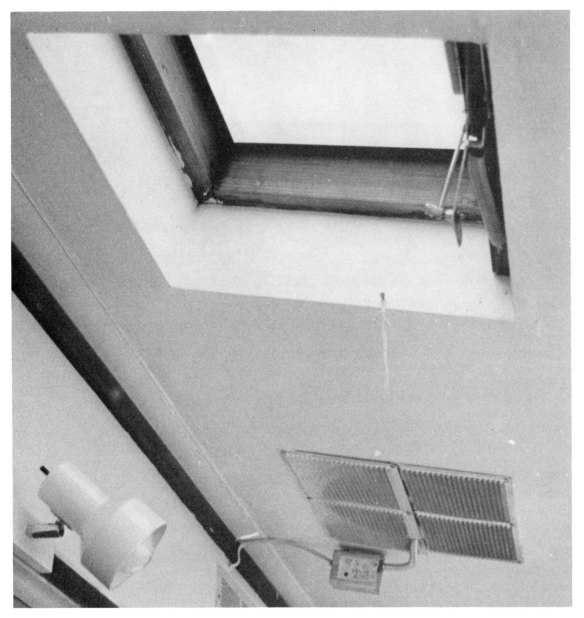

Fig. 4-30. *A glazed roof vent controlled by a thermal vent opener, and a thermostat-controlled vent with fan in the ceiling of a sunspace.*

Fig. 4-31. *Thermostats and blower connected by electric conduit and mounted to force hot air into the house from the sunspace.*

You can obtain metal louvered vent covers to fit some frame sizes. You can install them on the outside (FIG. 3-31) or inside. Obtain the vent cover before you build its frame to be certain you build a frame that it fits. Types with movable louvers have all the louvers connected to one lever. You can use a hand control, thermal vent opener, or motorized control to set the vent opening. An advantage of movable louvered vent covers is that they can seal out rain if installed properly. Their gasketing also prevents most, but not all, infiltration.

FINISHING AND SEALING

Possible interior finishes are gypsum board, paneling, cedar or redwood, plaster, or stucco. Foil-faced insulation with a thick, baked enamel aluminum finish is also available. You also can consider ceramic or clay tiles. Gypsum board might be required for fire protection of the frame. Lumber stores will have instructional brochures on installing most of these materials. Gypsum board and paneling will not withstand high moisture environments. Do not assume that paneling of redwood or cedar is moisture proof. Real redwood and cedar paneling would consist of boards, possibly tongued and grooved. Leave spacing for the boards to swell with moisture. In moist environments, you can use exterior siding with exterior paint or exterior plaster (stucco) on the inside.

The exterior finish can be anything that matches or complements the house. Consult other sources on applying stucco. You can stack adobe or brick against and tied to a wood frame. The weight would rest on an extra wide or a separate foundation.

Final sealing of the structure involves checking how rain, snow, wind, insects, and dust are kept from penetration at every point: at roof, glazing, windows, doors, vents, sill, and special features. The sealing materials should be long-term weatherproof: galvanized and aluminum flashing, silicone caulk, roof cement, neoprene gaskets and washers, stainless or double hot-dipped galvanized fasteners, cement mixtures, aluminum (not plastic) screening, and so forth. Good exterior oil and latex paints are acceptable seals for small cracks that will not flex or enlarge. Marine varnish or boat-grade exterior polyurethane is a good long-term coating for preserving smooth woods from weather and for coating sills (inside and out) beneath glazing that collects condensation. Exterior finishing/preserving compounds are available for protecting rough wood outside.

In addition to silicone caulk, acrylic latex and butyl rubber caulks are suitable crack fillers and sealants. You cannot paint most formulations of silicone, whereas you can apply acrylic latex on at any stage and paint it with anything. Acrylic caulks are not yet available in truly clear form, a consideration in keeping the appearance of glazings simple and neat. You can remove acrylic caulk with water. Silicone is very difficult to remove from glazings if an accidental smear is applied. Only repeated rubbing takes it off; there is no simple solvent for it. Butyl is extremely messy to handle and the solvents to clean up after it are dangerous.

Apply weather stripping where doors and windows are to be sealed when closed. The best types are gaskets made of vinyl, neoprene, or synthetic rubber (EPDM) and inserted in aluminum extrusions, which serve as stiffeners. Adhesive-backed foam strips leak air and water, and neither the foam nor the adhesive lasts in most environments. You could use them in places where the weather stripping or gasket must be removed every spring.

Some flashing cannot be applied as an afterthought. It might need to be attached with one end under previously applied material. Check all parts of the sunspace for flashings needed to control rain flow. Any surface that does not slant downward is a candidate for flashing or extra caulking.

Threaded fasteners (screws, bolts) are a place for water to seep deep into the structure and reach joints, where it can spread and cause deterioration. Caulk, gaskets, neoprene washers, and possibly caps on the fasteners are needed to prevent penetration by water.

Latex paints are not designed to be applied to bare wood, although many people use them this way. Prime clean, dry, bare wood with oil-based primer. A good exterior, flat, white, latex paint would make a long-lasting reflective surface. For black radiation-absorbing surfaces, obtain a "solar" mix paint, usually not latex. It can withstand the high temperatures that develop. Inquire as to the solvent and avoid using a paint formulated with something more volatile than ordinary oil-based paint. The solvent vapors are not only unbearable indoors, but dangerous to your health.

CONTROLS AND OPERATION

For most further details of the parts and methods used in ordinary wiring and plumbing, check the References and consult with building inspectors. Some final words are needed on providing control of air flow and heat in the sunspace. Control is electric, manual, or both. Some sunspaces for some applications require attention several times per day. Frequent handling of movable insulation and operable windows is tedious and demanding. Complete reliability is needed on the closing of vents every night.

Venting and hot-air movement are best controlled by simple thermostats that switch on fans or blowers when the inside air reaches a certain temperature. For both people and plants, locate ventilation controls about 4 feet from the ground. For movement of captured hot air, locate the sensor part of the control, if not the entire thermostat, within a few inches of the ceiling. It should be surrounded by air without touching the wall or ceiling. It also should not be in direct sunlight or receive substantial reflected sun. In a greenhouse, substantial ventilation must start when the plant temperature reaches about 80° F. People also will want ventilation to start by this point, or at a lower temperature in moist environments.

If you do your own wiring of controls and fans, use heavy, well-protected cable. Round plastic-sheathed grounded cable (three wires, type SJ or equivalent) is for exposed interior use in some cases. Size #16 in short runs would be sufficient for operating medium-sized blowers and is much better than #18 "lamp cord" or single wires. Flat Romex interior wiring cable (type NM) is for use inside walls only. Sunlight attacks it. Size #14 Romex run to a 15-amp breaker would be sufficient for permanent wiring of lights and blowers. These and the following wiring suggestions are superseded wherever electrical codes apply.

Avoid wiring where water might be sprayed, or use fixtures that can be sealed against water. When in doubt, steel conduit makes a very secure installation (see FIG. 4-31). Thermostats for 120 volts ac might be intended for use with conduit or cable clamps. Do not leave thin unsecured wires hanging out of them where they can be snagged and pulled loose. The terminal screws should not be the only mechanical means of preventing wiring from being jerked loose. Any wiring underneath a floor or underground should be burial type UG. Where animals might chew on it, protect it by conduit. If you cannot run the sunspace wiring to a breaker in an acceptable manner, provide a remote fuse (simple fuse fixtures that fit outlet boxes are available) and a switch so that the system can be disconnected in a positive manner. Plug this system into a grounded outlet with a sturdy cord and plug.

Once solar heat is available and controls are working, monitor their behavior for an extended period. Does venting or heat storage start when the sunspace is warm? Does it stop soon after sunset? Thermostats have a *differential*, which means that the temperature must fall several degrees below the on-point before it switches off. Some cheaper thermostats have too wide a differential and the room feels cold before it goes off. Put thermometers at the ceiling, midwall, floor, in the house, and in the storage (if any) to help monitor performance. Compare temperature differences wherever air is being used to transfer heat. If hot air is not losing 20° F or 30° F after it is put into the house or storage, some part of the system is not working properly or was not correctly designed.

SPECIAL CONSIDERATIONS & OPTIONS

THIS CHAPTER PROVIDES MORE detail on using and maintaining a sunspace and on variations and options pertaining to sunspace construction and use. Where different construction is indicated, new steps are described briefly, to be combined with previous procedures. If you must adapt a sunspace to an unusual site or application, you might find some special instructions in this chapter.

SAFETY

You must consider sunspace safety in regard to fire, glazing breakage, overheating, high wind, hail, air quality, and—in the case of greenhouses—insect poisons and excessive growth of molds and parasites. Dangers of wood stoves are covered in the section *Auxiliary Heat*.

Unusual fire hazards are plastic glazing, exposed foam insulation, and thick curtains or shades. They will burn readily, and they emit extremely poisonous vapor once ignited. Manufacturers' literature should indicate the conditions needed to ignite these materials. Do not put a wood stove, electric heater, or other radiant heat source near plastic glazings, foam insulation, or curtains. If anyone sleeps in the sunspace, install a fire/smoke alarm. The danger from solar overheating is negligible unless there is overhead glazing. Wood can tolerate 200° F to 250° F temperatures before deteriorating sufficiently to become easier to ignite. However, curved glazing and glass bottles can—if the arrangement is just right—focus solar rays and ignite any readily flammable material that happens to be at the focus.

Glazing breakage can occur as a result of vandals, high winds, hail, shifts in the structure, and long-term deterioration. Place only tempered or other safety glass overhead. Control doors and large vents so that high wind pressure cannot gain access to the inside. Some glazing mountings are more easily released by inside pressure than outside. Roof glazing is more likely to be popped off than wall glazing. A flying sheet of glazing can be very dangerous to the neighborhood. Broken plastic glazings sometimes have very sharp edges and can be as dangerous as glass.

Also consider air quality. High humidity can be bad for many parts of the structure, in addition to promoting mold growth. Solar heating can drive poisonous vapors from woods that have preservatives (except greenwood) or from plywoods and particleboards that have much formaldehyde glue. Herbicides and insecticides inside the closed environment of a greenhouse or sunspace are a serious hazard. Chemical poisons have no way of dissipating—that is, being diluted in the outdoors—and might linger indefinitely in the structure and soil. Do not allow anything to enter a heat-storage system. Once in, particles will recirculate and water will promote growth of mold. A dust filter is advisable somewhere in any large duct system, if only to protect motors.

MAINTENANCE

Regular maintenance centers around the glazing. Glazing should remain clean, dry, secured well, and strong. Some areas have high air pollution, such as soot, which must be washed off. Acid rain attacks some plastic glazings and most hardware. In a rainy area, it would be difficult to keep washing the rain from the glazing.

If you want to clean spots, whether from painting, birds, or whatever, from the glazing, you need to take precautions. Do not try to scrape tempered glass with a razor blade or any other metal object. Use a hard plastic scraper or block of wood. Plastic glazings scratch easily when scraped with almost any object. Ordinary water will leave spots on glazings, so for the greatest clarity use a window cleaner and paper towels. Be cautious using solvents on plastic glazings, since some solvents attack plastics. Paint thinner seems safe for brief cleaning of grease or paint from plastic glazings.

You can pull snow from roof glazing, not only to reduce weight but also to admit light and heat when it is most wanted. A piece of wood 1 x 4 attached to a long handle would do this job. Do not allow snow to pile against wood framing, since melt water will seep in and cause rot. It also will refreeze and injure the structure and seals. Do not let saltwater get on the structure or ground nearby. Inside, wipe up any standing water on the framing as soon as possible. Examine water-stained areas for wood rot. Within limits, it should be possible to replace any damaged component without dismantling the entire sunspace.

Examine the outside caulking twice a year for gaps and loose places. Good silicone caulk (warranted 50 years) will stick to almost everything except polyethylene and Teflon. If the caulk comes loose from materials in a few years, the surfaces were not clean and dry when you applied it. Brush and rub the dirt off and apply fresh silicone where needed. Check all battens for tightness. After the first year, wood battens will have given way somewhat, and screws and nails will seem loose and need tightening. Daily temperature changes will work nails loose, especially near the glazing. Replace loose nails with screws.

Eventually you will need to replace the glazing as part of long-term maintenance. This is the time to inspect fasteners for rust and battens for deterioration. Check if there is water damage in the screw holes. If so, dry the holes, seal them with silicone, and start new holes nearby. At this time, you will need to replace all caulking around the glazing.

Every year, remove vent covers on any ductwork and look for dust, moisture, or even a bird or rodent nest. Examine any mechanical or electric vent controls, looking for loose screws and fatigued metal parts. See if fans and blowers have excessive dust in the blades and coils. Most motor bearings need annual oiling.

AUXILIARY HEAT

Auxiliary heat in the sunspace should be necessary only if the climate is often cold and cloudy, plants must be kept alive, or work must be done in the space day or night. Heat sources have tended to be portable and separate from the house system. They have included kerosene heaters, electric baseboards, portable electric heaters, gas space heaters, and wood stoves. A gas-burning house furnace is the cheapest, safest, and most efficient source of heat, however. Adequate heat might be obtained by holding the door to the house open an amount determined by experience. If there is a vent system to heat the house from the sunspace by day, simply leaving it open at night might let enough heat leak into the sunspace. Tie any backdraft damper into an open position. For more heat, you can run an auxiliary duct from a convenient basement forced-air duct. Be sure to provide a small air-return opening somewhere near the sunspace floor.

The next safest, but most expensive, heat source is a portable or permanent electric convection heater—the baseboard type without exposed electric elements. If you do not have 220 volts ac available, portable ones use 110 volts. You can use a 220-volt baseboard heater on 110 volts ac with only one-fourth the power level provided. There is little advantage to using electric baseboard heaters filled with oil. Kerosene heaters are too dangerous, since they require ventilation to control the level of carbon monoxide. Catalytic heaters, which burn a fuel with a catalyst rather than open flame, are still dangerous because of carbon monoxide emission and other pollutants.

If you use a wood stove, provide it with the proper vent and draft. Wood stoves have been major fire and pollution hazards. You should install one only with full supervision by building inspectors. Try to find a high-efficiency low-pollution model, even if not required by your building code. A wood stove emits much radiation, which is bad for plastic glazings and plants. You must locate a wood stove far from glazings and plants and is not recommended for a greenhouse. The flue pipe should not run through a glazed wall or roof, and you should provide heat protection for any foam insulations.

HUMIDITY CONTROL

If glazing is collecting excessive moisture, you might not be able to do much except build the sunspace/greenhouse moisture-proof and ensure that condensation can run down without damage. Plants will emit much water in a greenhouse, and you cannot remove this water without drying out the plants rapidly. More watering just starts the cycle over. Exposed soil, such as a moist dirt floor, would produce enough moisture to drench cold glazing. If the humidity is too high, there will be mold and rotting of the plants. Wet glazing is not an indication of excessive humidity if the glazing is very cold. No matter how tightly you seal movable insulation to windows or sunspace glazing frames, some moisture will travel behind it and condense on the glazing. Use a vapor-barrier covering on any hot tub or other warm-water tank or pool, even though some moisture will escape the covering.

A solution to consider is to dehumidify the sunspace. This method could work if there is no substantial number of plants or other internal moisture sources and if excess moisture from the house is not entering the sunspace. A dehumidifier would do part of the work of an air-to-air heat exchanger. A fan draws air in and water vapor condenses on refrigerated coils. The water is collected in a pan, which you must empty. You can drain some models outside through a hose. This process can remove several gallons per day, depending on the size of the unit. Unless there is a hot tub or moist air from the house, only a quart per day might be wrung from a sunspace.

Dehumidifiers rarely include air preheaters and so will ice up and cease operating when the air is colder than about 65° F. Thus, they will not work on a cool night. Make sure your dehumidifier has an ice-up shut-off. As it runs, the dehumidifier also provides heat from its use of electricity and from water condensation. Thus, the dehumidifer can be most effective when the air is beginning to cool in the evening. It might only need to run 2 hours per day to keep the sunspace dry.

An air-to-air heat exchanger is a major piece of equipment, probably too expensive to justify installing in a sunspace. Perhaps you need it in the house instead. In this new way of obtaining fresh air without losing heat, heat is removed from warm air before blowing the air outside to remove pollutants. Meanwhile, an equal amount of cold air is pulled in from outside. The cold air is prewarmed with the extracted heat. Moisture condensed from the inside air is drained to the outside.

GLAZING A WALL FOR A SUNSPACE
INSIDE THE HOUSE OR GARAGE

Putting a sunspace inside the house is like putting a solar collector inside. There is no longer a buffer zone to protect from extremes of hot and cold. There is no barrier to high humidity. You cannot use the foundation mass, if any, directly as heat storage unless you also remove the floor—a drastic reconstruction. On the other hand, there is no foundation or roof to build. The costs could be lower. In cold climates, having the house wrapped around the sunspace this well raises the efficiency. The roof losses are less, and more of the solar energy that enters stays inside the house.

It is best to include internal sunspaces when you build the house. As a retrofit, substantial wall modification is needed. First study the available south wall and decide whether the amount of glazing you want is compatible with modifying the south wall's frame. Perhaps you must remove some old windows and doors, together with the framing around them. Examine the electrical outlets and other electrical installations on the wall and form a plan for dealing with them. You probably will need to move or remove outlets. Determine if there is a main service line in the wall or on the outside. Moving it will be expensive. Make the same study for plumbing. If a sewer vent or stack is in the wall, moving it could be very difficult.

You probably will need to remove both inside finish and outside siding. A temporary weathertight barrier made of sheet plastic and studs will be needed around the whole site. You could place this barrier inside the house, so that you work outside of it. If an internal wall occurs where you want the sunspace, you might not be able to remove it and must build two sunspaces instead. The course of action depends on what is holding up the ceiling, the second floor, if any, and the roof. Arrange the glazing to leave places for vents, unless the glazing is operable and can be opened at top and bottom. These vents will go to the outside to control summer heating and should have screens, rain protection, and insulated covers.

You should reconstruct a wall bit by bit after the siding is off. You need to convert the wall to one with studs or posts on a regular spacing, probably 2 or 4 feet. You must accomplish this task without letting the roof sag during the conversion. If you open a span longer than 4 feet, even temporarily, jack the top plate slightly and install a sturdy post as prop. You must toenail in the new posts. Using metal hardware such as angles would fasten them better. Cut the posts to the correct height and do not fasten them permanently until the weight is back on them. If the glazing is 4 feet wide (or 6 feet in the case of patio doors), you must install a header over the glazing to carry the ceiling, second floor (if any), and roof loads. Use a header made of two 2 × 8s on edge if there is a second-floor load. If the span is 6 feet, you might need a header as large as a double 2 × 12.

While you are replacing a house wall is the time to consider making part of the wall into a heat-storing Trombe wall. As described in Chapter 2 and FIG. 2-14, a Trombe wall consists of thick (1½ feet or so) masonry painted black on the outside. Poured concrete or concrete blocks with the cores well filled are common approaches. Laid brick or adobe are also possible. You will need a new and thick foundation to support this weight. Add glazing a few inches in front of the wall to trap heat radiation. There should be no air gaps in the wall to prevent heat conduction. Vents near the top and bottom of the wall are optional. At night the wall radiates heat into the house and back to the outdoors, so you could add movable outside insulation. Arrange outside shade to keep the Trombe wall from functioning in the summer.

The benefits of making your garage into a sunspace are rarely considered, yet the construction problems are minimal. Probably all you need to do is knock the siding off the south wall and put up plastic glazing—polyethylene, corrugated FRP, or whatever one you prefer and can afford. Instead of dark, cold gloom all winter you have instant heat and light. You also can perform many moisture-producing and otherwise unpleasant, but necessary, winter activities there— out of the house and out of the way—for example, hanging wet clothes or sanding and painting bookshelves. Also, if the garage has a slab with perimeter insulation (easily added), you can collect and store sufficient heat under most conditions to make car starting easy on cold mornings. You might want to insulate the garage walls minimally. A solar-heated garage is a good winter workshop, and when you must repair your car on a cold windy day the benefits are obvious even if the sun does not shine.

One major caution about using a garage sunspace concerns carbon-monoxide emissions and other fumes. Do not let the existence of this sunspace cause members of your family to move into it while other members use it to tune car engines. Venting car exhaust outside with a hose is a necessary, but probably not a sufficient, precaution. Professional garages require active ventilation in winter.

CONVERTING A PORCH OR DECK TO A SUNSPACE

If your south-, east-, or west-facing porch has a good roof well connected to the house and no other virtues, you probably can jack the roof up 1 or 2 inches beyond its final position and temporarily prop it up with a strong post every 4 feet or so. Then you can rebuild everything else. Be sure to fasten each prop to a stake at the bottom and with a metal tie at the top so that it cannot fall out as you jack up and install the next one. Arrange each prop to splay out so that there is room to excavate and work. Prop the sides if the roof seems shaky. (If you plan tilted south glazing, propping up the old roof will require much more ingenuity since the props want to rest where the new foundation must be.) Next remove the old posts and walls if any, then tear out the rotted wood foundation. Examine the exposed parts of the house for damage, rot, termites, or whatever needs fixing before you proceed.

If the porch already has a floor and posts that fit your plans, then it is ready to glaze. Measure every post spacing and be sure you can obtain glazing that fits. Usually existing porch posts are not suitable, but are easily replaced with new posts or studs at the proper spacing. If you want a kneewall, construct it between the posts. Otherwise, fasten a sill or plate on top of the floor and under the posts. Caulk it well so rain will not run under it. Prepare a fastening surface at the top and put on the chosen glazing. If you live in a warmer climate, you might want some or all of the glazing to be removable, leaving a screen porch in summer.

Avoid glazing any wall that does not face south. Cover and insulate it instead. Chances are the porch has a large overhang, and running the glazing to the roof provides no extra sun. Put a headwall and some vents above the line where the winter sun will shine. Whether or not the roof has a ceiling, you will want to insulate beneath the roof. You can blow insulation above the old ceiling, but it is better to remove the ceiling and see what is going on with the house there. You might want to add a vapor barrier. Then cover the insulation and old rafters with gypsum board, paneling, or whatever is appropriate.

If you use an existing porch floor, you will likely have plenty of cold air leaks from below. If a wood porch floor is compatible with your sunspace plans and is in good condition, then consider insulating around its perimeter and fastening a tight skirt all around. You can use an appropriate combination of plywood, concrete, or green plywood (in the ground), and flashing. Caulk all joints. You might need to place plastic sheet on the ground to prevent moisture buildup once the sides are well-sealed. If your porch floor is solid concrete, consider yourself lucky and insulate the sides as described earlier. The chances are that your porch has an old and simple foundation, not immune to frost heave, and the porch has been moving—rising or sagging. This is a good time to obtain a good poured concrete foundation, then put in the posts and wall framing for a sunspace.

New and old housing with decks is becoming common. You could cover a deck with a sunspace, but you might have some problems. Often the deck was not designed to carry more than a nominal floor load. Adding the sunspace would require the perimeter foundation of the deck to carry a roof snow load as well. Examine, by digging if necessary, whether the thickness and depth of the deck foundation is of the same quality as the house or is much less robust. For example, 4 × 4 posts in a few inches of concrete will not serve as the foundation of a permanent sunspace. If the deck is tall and has a wood post-and-beam framework for the decking, it might not be braced sufficiently to carry a sunspace. The wind pressure on the deck would be much increased with the large glazed sunspace aboard. Another consideration is the open structure of the decking. Unless the floor is covered solid and insulated beneath, the air leaks into the sunspace will eliminate its heat-gathering ability, and there still will not be any floor heat-storage mass.

There are pros and cons to adding a sunspace to a concrete-slab patio. The best procedure would be to excavate around the slab and install a proper frostproof concrete foundation. If the slab is the wrong size, perhaps you could knock off a part or add an extra section. An old slab, which could be replaced for a couple of hundred dollars if you do the work, might not be worth saving to mismatch to a more costly sunspace. A simple slab might amplify the movement of certain soils and be an unstable place to build. There are probably no bolts embedded in it, so you would need to drill deep holes in it to place adequate anchors. Also, its edges might not be strong enough to support the sunspace without cracking off.

USING THE NORTH SIDE OF THE HOUSE

Sometimes there is no choice but to try to build a sunspace on the north side of the house. It might not be truly a sunspace, but you might want a sunspacelike structure on the north side of a house for several reasons. A permanent glazed structure will provide much light for working in cloudy, rainy weather. Some artists prefer "north" light, whether or not the sun is shining, for the best seeing. Heating a glazed structure on the north will be much more expensive than heating a multiwindowed north room of a house, however, and is to be avoided. A glazed north roof can understandably provide a pleasant environment. Even if you do not want special north light, the feel of the sky overhead is of aesthetic value, especially with the disturbance of wind and rain eliminated. North-side glazed structures can have a purpose in the summer in northern climates and in the winter in southern climates.

A sunspace built tall enough on the north side can "see" over a one-story house roof and collect sun for use on the north (FIG. 5-1). Its glazing functions as a large

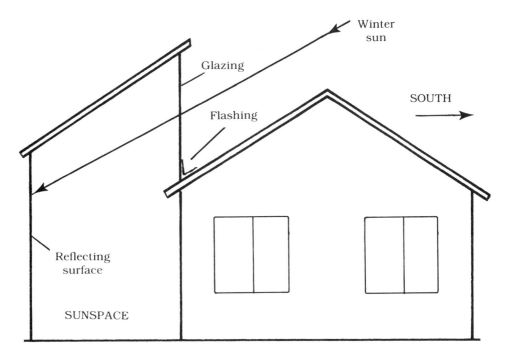

Fig. 5-1. Putting a true sunspace on the north side, sufficiently tall to look over the house roof (shown in profile view). The roof and north wall should be heavily insulated, and rain runoff must be well controlled at the connection to the house roof.

clerestory, a high window under the roof intended to bring sunlight to a room that has no south windows. The glazing must be tall to receive sufficient winter sun over the roof peak, so the sunspace is very tall—over two stories. White paint on the north interior wall will help reflect the light downward. The heat collected in a tall sunspace might not reach the ground floor unless a large duct system brings it down.

You can build the tall north sunspace freestanding behind the house, or you can build it to overlap some fraction of the roof. You can even bring the south wall of the sunspace to the peak of the roof if the roof slopes that way. Most residential roofs are not built to carry additional structural loads, however. Also, you must well-seal and insulate the north wall and roof of the sunspace, since there is no other protection from winter wind. This sunspace is very exposed, and 2 × 6 walls with R-19 insulation are the minimum recommended.

With careful design, you can match the sunspace to any sort of roof shape. Whenever a sunspace rests on the house structure, its foundation must be as good as that of the house. Where the sunspace joins the house roof, you must use extra care to control rain. You must bring flashing at least 1 foot up on the sunspace and under the roof shingles so that heavy rain has a channel in which to flow around the sunspace instead of seeping into the roof. Heavy snow will cause special problems here, and you might need to remove it. The V-shaped notch between a sunspace wall and a house roof that slopes down toward it is a large rain and snow trap, and is not easily drained.

SUNSPACE FLOORS

The choices for floor material for a sunspace are many and varied: concrete slab, loose brick, mortared brick, tile on concrete, earth, gravel, sand, wood, or carpet. Some special ideas for floors are given here. Whether a concrete slab is to be finished or to serve as substrate, do not pour it directly against the foundation wall. It could expand later when hot and crack the foundation. Provide ½ to 1 inch of spacing using strips of extruded polystyrene or other crushable but durable material (not wood). For instructions on pouring and finishing a slab, see the References for concrete work.

You can color and stamp concrete into almost any pattern before it sets. Add the coloring to the whole slab batch, or to a cement-sand mixture about ¼ to ½ inch thick poured on fresh, wet, level concrete. Since the coloring agents are expensive, the latter procedure is preferred, but you might need your own mixer, sand pile, and crew to do the work quickly. Surface colorants are also available. You can dust them onto wet concrete, then trowel them in. Uniform color will be more difficult to achieve. You can brighten and lighten colors by using white cement for the top layer. Again, the cost is greater. Before you make a colored slab, make test pieces of concrete and keep careful record of the formula you used in the mixes. It takes several days of wet curing, then drying, before the final color is revealed.

To stamp a pattern into the floor, pour the slab on a cool day so there is time to work. The sunspace should not be in place yet to make the area hot. A simple pattern would consist of making regular shallow grooves in the surface to simulate tile joints. The resulting floor looks nice, but costs much less than tile. To form the pattern, press a square or rectangular wood frame into the concrete to the desired depth, then move to the next position and repeat. Wrap very thin plastic sheet around the frame to prevent concrete from sticking to it. The frame should make a whole-number multiple of tiles across the slab unless you want fractional tiles. The edges of the frame should be rounded to the degree you want. A straight edge across the unstamped part of the slab will ensure that the pattern remains straight. Work neatly since there is little time to repair mistakes. If you want to make a negative mold with a more complex shape and pattern, there is no limit to the creativity possible with stamped floors. (See ''Sizzling Slabs,'' in the Articles Section of the References for a fact sheet on colored and stamped concrete, naming suppliers.)

Thick or paving brick must be set in sand. No mortar is necessary, and you can dust sand on later to fill all joints. You must pack the bricks tightly or they will start moving around. Brick floors are a large topic in itself. A heat-storing example is shown below in FIG. 5-2.

Fig. 5-2. A mortared brick floor for heat storage, and an awning vent window for summer cooling in a sunspace.

Bricks of uniform size are much more costly than bricks that vary too much to fit together tightly. Thin bricks (Z-brick) need a substrate, either a wood floor or concrete, on which to rest. You can glue them down with cement-based compounds or with actual glue such as carpet cement. You should grout thin brick and tile, not necessarily with cement, to prevent rubbing and abrading when used. You can use thin bricks, or clay or ceramic tiles on raised wood floors to add a little heat-storage mass without overloading the floor joists. Brick or tile also does not deteriorate when exposed to the high insolation levels under glazing and will protect an existing wood floor. You can rent a hand-operated brick cutter to make the fractional bricks needed to fill in a floor. Do not expect exact cutting, however.

You can build a wood floor in a sunspace, as anywhere else, by bolting treated wood sills (possibly just 2 × 6) to the foundation before you build the sunspace walls. Then fasten floor joists on the sills. The thickness (height) of the joists depends on the span, and the spacing could be 2 feet o.c. Your building inspectors can tell you the thickness you need. You must brace and block joists, and add a header joist on the ends. After you nail a ¾-inch plywood subfloor over the joists, you are ready to erect the sunspace as if you were starting on a foundation. You need plenty of headroom for the sunspace, since the floor structure occupies nearly a foot of height. Cover the subfloor later with a finish floor of redwood, tile, exterior carpet, brick, or whatever you want. The raised floor has, of course, decoupled the sunspace from any heat storage in the foundation or ground. You can use ducts and blowers to move the heat to such storage.

Chances are, your sunspace floor is a foot or two lower than your house floor. You will need poured concrete steps or wooden steps to provide easy access as a finishing touch to the sunspace. For sturdy wood steps, use only 2 x 12s in construction.

THE SUNSPACE AS A GREENHOUSE

Most discussion of using the sunspace as a greenhouse is best left to the many references dedicated to greenhouses and horticulture. Of special interest is the possibility of growing food fish, since the temperature required by plants matches that for fish, and the fish tanks serve as heat-storage mass. A few introductory remarks are given here: relevant comments were given in preceding chapters.

Using the sunspace to grow food or ornamental plants requires a change in basic approach and design, as discussed in Chapter 1. A sunspace not intended for plants can be difficult to convert. The general needs of most plants are high light levels, moderate and controlled temperature levels (60° F to 80° F), and moderately high, but controlled humidity (40 to 60 percent). A new set of problems will appear, such as maintaining soil quality, safely controlling pests, and watering consistently.

The greenhouse might need auxiliary light in winter even if there are roof glazing and wall reflections. Some ornamental plants can "rest" at winter light levels, but food and flower growing requires light almost as strong as natural summer light. Some growers believe special-spectrum plant-growing fluorescent bulbs are needed. Others find regular and cheaper fluorescents adequate. In some cases, you must add incandescent lights to provide more red light. You can use artificial light at the beginning or end of the day, if the length of the day is more important than the midday light level. You can lower the lights very close to the plants, to increase the light intensity while decreasing the power costs. Most plants do not want light all night, although the heat from the large number of lights needed is probably sufficient as auxiliary heat to maintain minimum temperatures.

If the site or size requires it, a freestanding greenhouse in cold climates is best built similar to the Brace design (FIG. 1-1). The south glazed roof slopes more steeply, depending on latitude, and joins a south kneewall 2 to 3 feet high, which might or might not be glazed. If the ground slopes toward the south, or the greenhouse is dug in to the depth of the kneewall, so much the better. The north roof slopes steeply (60 to 70 degrees) and is also the north wall. Its interior surface should be white for maximum light reflection to plants. *The Solar Greenhouse* (see McCullagh in the Books section of the References) mainly concerns the Brace design, but recommends (as I do) that you determine the pitch of the glazed roof by adding 20° to your latitude, rather than using the 35° in the original Brace design. In summer, you must use thermostat-controlled power venting to remove the excess heat.

A special place to put a greenhouse when the house will not serve is the south side of a garage, shed, or barn. Any sturdy permanent building that provides north protection is a viable candidate. A detached greenhouse or sunspace is not limited to plant or human use. Chickens or other farm animals have been raised in solar-heated sheds built like sunspaces.

A greenhouse can enable insects to survive that otherwise would hibernate or die each winter. They include ants, wasps, fleas, and mosquitoes, as well as many other possibilities. In addition, most plants have their own pests and parasites which, once introduced, are difficult to eradicate. Insecticides and most other chemical controls are hazardous in enclosed areas, especially in spaces attached to a house. You can introduce some natural predators, and some "natural" chemical methods of controlling pests are reasonably safe. The References provide much detail on possible solutions, but experimentation is still occurring on the best ways to make the closed environment of a greenhouse stable in the long term.

Watering plants in a crowded greenhouse can be tedious. A drip irrigation system is recommended. Relatively low-cost kits are available which provide a water-pressure regulator, a water filter, lengths of large and small tubing, connectors, and small watering devices called *emitters.* One type emits a drop at a time in the soil near a plant, and another type sprays a very fine mist on selected plants. You can control the drip system by a timer, or by hand as needed. In some cases, you can leave them on continuously. The alternative is to carry many pitchers or cans of water to plants every day, or to drag a cumbersome hose around. Attaching a faucet at the end of the hose would be an interim solution to the watering problem.

VERY SMALL SUNSPACES

A pleasant addition to a house can be a *window box,* sometimes misleadingly called an *atrium window.* This new window box is not just a box for plants, but a glazed enclosure over a window (FIG. 5-3). The area of glazing can be twice the window size, so that twice as much heat can be gathered while a broader view of the world is provided. Usually, the window box is installed over an existing window, so that when the window is open, heat gathered in the box can enter the house.

Fig. 5-3. *A window box, a tiny sunspace mounted on a window.*

At night the window box performs an insulating function as a good storm window over the existing window.

If you need a small greenhouse to start or grow plants on a small scale, then the *cold frame*—better called a *hotbed*—might be the low-cost structure to build. A cold frame is a low box with a glazed roof built in or on the ground in a sheltered area. Placed on the southside near a sunspace and the house for warmth, it could be the solution to the question of how to have a sunspace without the problems of a greenhouse while also growing some plants. Some of the references show simple, clever, and inexpensive ways to construct such structures. These are only large enough to reach into. If you want a walk-in structure, then you need a true greenhouse.

VERY LOW COST AND UNUSUAL SUNSPACES

If you have a north- or south-facing old porch and want to do something to improve your energy balance at very low cost, then wrap the porch in polyethylene sheet. With this procedure, the north porch will be converted to a buffer, keeping cold winter wind away from the house wall itself. The south porch so treated will gain some solar energy, which can be let into the house through windows.

You can fasten the polyethylene by nailing on the simplest battens. You must replace it every year, however. Over the years, you can gradually upgrade the porch by replacing its components as your budget permits. Eventually, you can install permanent glazing.

You can build a lean-to sunspace at very low cost, while obtaining heat fasten and floor space, by eliminating roof, foundation, and frills. As shown in FIG. 5-4, 2 × 4s spaced 2 feet o.c. to the upper wall or near the end of house roof rafters (if accessible). At the bottom fasten them to a new or old wood plank that rests on the ground. The angle is set by the angle with which a piece of 4-× -8-foot siding is cut, as shown for end walls. Keep the plank in place by driving a few metal stakes in the ground. This lean-to should face south if possible. You can fill in little gaps with scrap wood. If there is no house entrance, you can hinge a small door in one wall. The glazing can be sheet polyethylene nailed onto the 2 × 4s with vertical battens, or the lowest grade of corrugated FRP battened both vertically and horizontally. You can let a backup 1 × 2 into the center by notching the 2 × 4s.

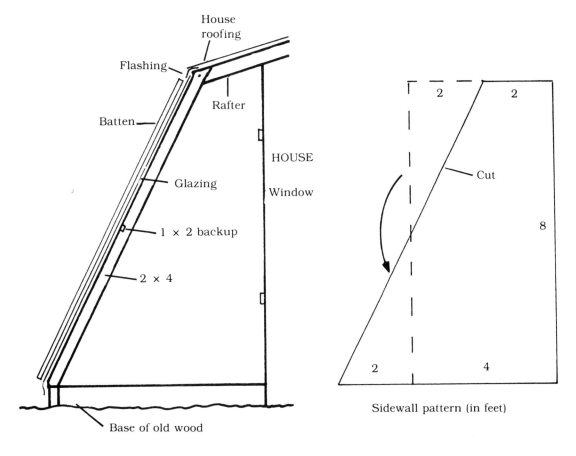

Fig. 5-4. *A very low cost lean-to style sunspace, shown in profile.*

If the house wall is uninsulated and can be painted black inside the lean-to sunspace, the entire structure could pay for itself in 2 months of heat savings. You also can introduce heat by opening windows, if any. A window fan on its lowest setting will move heat in rapidly. For a house or site where no sun is otherwise available in winter, this bottom-of-the-line sunspace provides usable warmth whenever the sun shines in, despite zero temperatures outside. You can paint the side walls and make other improvements, but the lifetime is limited to a few years. Be careful that frost heave does not cause the lean-to to damage the house wall or roof.

Inflated glazings are another way to use low-cost polyethylene. Batten two layers of polyethylene to a sunspace frame as usual. Then use a small blower, one intended for constant use to produce pressure at low flow, to inflate the spaces between the glazings. Leave gaps in vertical battens somewhere so that the two sheets can form one continuous tube. At least one manufacturer sells this sunspace as a kit at low cost. (See Chapter 6.) You can also dispense with the frame and inflate the sunspace from one closed sheet of plastic, like a balloon.

WATER HEATING

Rather than putting expensive (but high-efficiency) water-heating solar collectors on "stilts" on the house roof, you can use the heat of the sunspace to preheat water. The maximum water temperature might be lower, but the quantity can be greater and as much money saved. Raising winter water temperature from, say, 45° F to 90° F before it reaches the indoor water heater should cut your water heating bills in half. The main difficulties with solar water systems, resulting in high costs, have been the prevention of freezing and the provision of extra plumbing and pumping to collect and store the hot water until needed. You can solve both of these problems by using the sunspace for the job and letting the city's water pump provide the flow. A water preheater could need no control at all.

One approach is to put the flat-plate solar collectors inside the sunspace near the always warm rear wall, but where sun shines on them. If you cannot afford selective-surface copper collectors, then try copper tubing painted black. City water pressure can drive water directly through the collector to the water heater, but the capacity of the collector is low, so only a few gallons are heated at one time. At night no extra heat is picked up, but probably none is lost either. Situated next to a slightly warm wall, the system should not freeze, but this method does not collect as much heat from the sun as is possible.

Another approach is to put one or more water tanks in a sunny part of the sunspace. If painted black and not too large (10 to 20 gallons each), they will become hot during a day of normal use. If surrounded by extra glazing and insulation (a breadbox approach), they will not cool as much at night. You can even close the breadbox with a sheet of insulation at night. Such small tanks are difficult to find, however, and might rust out in a few years. The best source is to disassemble old water heaters and use tanks not damaged by rust. Plan on replacing them every few years.

It would be nice to find fiberglass or stainless steel tanks sufficiently strong for city water pressure. The pressure buildup in a water heater as it heats would not be relieved until it reaches 125 pounds per square inch, according to the conventional required safety valve. All plumbing must withstand this pressure unless lower relief is provided. If you wish to explore solar water heating beyond these introductory guidelines, check the References, such as those from the Department of Energy.

Whatever glazing area is devoted to water heating is not available for space heating. Therefore, if the water system is large, you must design the sunspace bigger. This might be the case if you plan to heat water for a tub, pool, or laundry.

HOT TUBS AND WARM POOLS

One of the most popular reasons for acquiring a sunspace is to have a place to put a hot tub or spa (FIG. 5-5). Sometimes the tub is acquired first, then the sunspace added later; sometimes the other way around. As will be seen, a hot tub almost demands a sunspace to enclose it.

Traditionally, a *hot tub* was a wood tub outdoors, and a *spa* was an oversized bathtub indoors with bubbly or circulating water. Now the terms are interchanged. A hot tub is generally kept filled with several hundred gallons of water.

Fig. 5-5. *A hot tub installed at floor level in a small raised sunspace. The floor is covered with durable heat-storing ceramic tiles.*

You must chemically treat the water in a hot tub, filter it, and circulate it to prevent bacteria and algae growth. The chemicals release chlorine, bromine, and other noxious materials into the air. Because you can insulate the tub, you can keep the water hot continuously. A built-in heater is used. You should keep a water-vapor cover and a heat insulating cover on the tub when not in use, since the warm-to-hot water (about 100° F) emits substantial vapor.

The high humidity a tub can cause, especially when in use with air jets and rapid circulation, is a principal reason for providing a special enclosure that can withstand high humidity. A tub in a basement would make the walls wet enough to mold the concrete and rot the house frame. The cost of keeping the water warm also suggests a sunspace as a warm place to keep the tub. The tub is usually not well insulated, and the costs of electric heating are substantial. On the other hand, neither the cover nor the basic material of the tub—usually acrylic with fiberglass—can stand long-term exposure to sunlight. The partial solution is to make sure that the wood frame and an easily replaceable cover keep all sunlight off the tub when it is not in use.

The tub itself weighs several hundred pounds, but when filled with water the total weight is over a ton. Although theoretically this weight might be spread over enough area to just meet the modern floor load requirement of 40 pounds per square foot, you are asking for trouble if you put the tub in the middle of a large room. Other furnishings might be heavy, some floor joists might have defects, or the house might not have been built as strongly as assumed. The floor is likely to acquire a sag. Also, the humidity of the tub will attack the finish on walls of rooms not built to withstand high moisture exposure.

Thus, a new room or location is often needed for a hot tub, and the sunspace is perfectly matched to the job. The sunspace is warm and can be built to withstand high humidity while keeping it out of the house, and its floor can take the weight. If the floor is a raised one, be certain that the floor joists are oversized. The sunspace also can provide the setting for using a solar water heater to take care of the entire tub-heating job. You might need to hire a solar water heating specialist to ensure that you get a working system, as discussed earlier.

Most electrical codes and plumbing codes are now regulating hot tub installations. Thus, you usually need a permit to install one, which the dealer should take care of unless you are getting the tub cash and carry. Building officials are particularly concerned with the presence of electrical outlets near the tub and with tub water siphoning back into the water line during the process of filling. These concerns might seem finicky, but people have died in a tub because they came in contact with faulty electric equipment plugged into an outlet not protected by a GFI. The tub's own electric system requires heavy wiring with GFI protection and a good grounding. If you want to install a hot tub in an existing sunspace, you might need to do some reworking of the existing electrical outlets to provide shock protection.

The situation with water in which people have bathed is also of concern. Even if members of a family cannot contaminate each other, neighbors on the same water line could be affected if contaminated water reached them through a failure of both treatment and filling technique. The local health department can explain the problem further. In addition to controlling sanitation, you will want a handy means of filling and draining the tub, so plumbing is a likely part of the sunspace.

A freestanding sunspace is appropriate if you want a bigger pool of water than a hot tub provides—perhaps the long, narrow swimming pool called a *lap pool* is suitable. The sunspace can easily straddle the narrow pool without needing excessively heavy roof rafters and can provide most or all of its heat, depending on climate and insulation. A swimming pool, although slow to warm, is a very stable heat storage, just as slow to cool. It can be heated two ways: one active and one passive.

The passive method is to let sunlight penetrate into the water. Unfortunately, a substantial negative temperature difference is needed between surface and bottom before the water will turn over, or start convection currents to distribute the heat. If you use a plastic pool cover on the water, little sunlight penetrates it, and only a tiny depth of water is warmed. You need a circulating pump to distribute heat throughout the pool, and filtering requires that a pump be used daily anyway. Do not omit the pool cover, because of the problems of excess humidity in the building. Construct the sunspace pool building to withstand the highest humidity.

To actively heat the pool, pull hot air down through a duct from the ceiling of the sunspace pool building and circulate it around the pool itself under the floor (FIG. 5-6). This process is aided with modern shallow pool construction by the fact that the pool sides are heavy steel, instead of thick masonry. The space around the pool is open, obstructed only by steel braces. Although you can use heat from the pool building to heat the house, you must remember that warm moist chlorinated air will be a very undesirable heat source. You would need some sort of heat-exchange system to isolate pool air from house air. One possibility that has been developed is to divide the chamber around the pool into two separate parts: one for pool heating and one for extracting heat from the pool.

Other uses for pools have been found in sunspaces and greenhouses. Tanks of water or pools in the ground have been used for growing fish, often for food. A greenhouse and a fish pond have been shown to be ecologically complementary by the New Alchemy Institute on Cape Cod, Massachusetts, and others (see, e.g., McCullagh, in the Books Section of the References). The dark, fertile water absorbs solar heat readily from direct radiation, and the large mass of the pond keeps the greenhouse warm overnight or longer.

TAX CREDITS AND INSURANCE

Tax credits have been available federally (not at present) and in many states for installing a solar heating system. Many states have recognized passive heating systems and sunspaces/greenhouses as sources of solar heat. The rules change every year, and the availability of credits has been decreasing in recent years. You should be able to obtain a complete description of your state's allowances from your state tax office, legislator, energy office, or similar source. In regard to sunspaces, the requirements have been especially complex. Some states disallow them and others might not let them be used for any purpose but heat. You might be able to claim for credit that fraction of the structure devoted to heat collection and storage. Some states require a storage or an active heat transfer system.

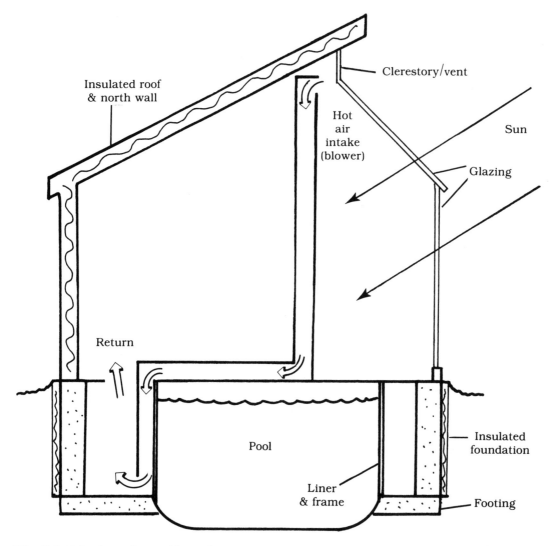

Insulated roof
& north wall

Clerestory/vent

Hot
air
intake
(blower)

Sun

Glazing

Return

Pool

Liner
& frame

Insulated
foundation

Footing

Fig. 5-6. Solar-heated air is blown down into storage to heat a ''lap'' swimming pool installed in its own free-standing sunspace built for high humidity (shown in profile; design courtesy of Better Products Inc.).

In addition to tax credits, other forms of financial encouragement or relief exist in some areas for the purposes of promoting solar development. Your sunspace might be exempt from property taxes for a certain period, or forever. You might qualify for a lower utility rate. Your utility might loan you the money at low interest to build the sunspace. If your income is sufficiently low, you might qualify for a public program that installs sunspaces for heat. Ask what forms of energy assistance are available. Check if some other, perhaps obscure, benefit has been adopted in your area. It might not be well publicized. Locate the little-known Solar Energy & Energy Conservation Bank, which makes grants and subsidizes loans.

Ordinarily a standard homeowner's insurance policy will cover almost any sort of room addition, including a sunspace, without a special request. Ask your agent to be certain. Problems with glazing have not yet resulted in excessive claims, so insurance companies have not yet increased premiums for sunspaces or solar systems. Weather damage to glazing is treated just as roof damage would be. A freestanding greenhouse might not be covered automatically, since policies usually cover just one extra structure, such as a garage.

EXAMPLES

PHOTOGRAPHS OF A WIDE variety of sunspaces at all cost levels are provided in this chapter so that you can find inspiration for deciding upon a design. Many people have tried many designs to fit many applications. This selection presents many ideas to consider, including some that might not suit your particular requirements. You can learn what you want from seeing the desirable and from discovering what seems undesirable.

The arrangement of the photographs cannot be ordered simply, so browsing is suggested. The captions point out some of the special features of each sunspace. The type of glazing and framing is usually identified. The photographs include sunspaces built by homeowners of various economic means and skill levels, contractor-built ones from local designs, installed kits, and factory-built sunspaces. Some features to watch for are roof glazing (if any), type of frame, foundation or anchoring against wind loads, heat-storage mass, means of moving heat, vents, movable insulation, and shading. Particular photographs might not provide the answer you seek on particular aspects. You might want to see if you can determine from the photograph alone whether the sunspace is owner-built or manufactured.

Fig. 6-1. *An old style of sunspaces is the conservatory, glazed with small panes in many operable windows. Curtains were used for sun control—and probably too often to gain much heat.*

Fig. 6-2. *Two identical houses, one with a low-cost sunspace and one with a conventional concrete slab porch.*

Fig. 6-3. *A long porch or veranda converted to a sunspace on an older house. The sun is controlled by inside roll-down shades.*

Fig. 6-4. *A potential site for a sunspace: an old screened porch facing south. The floor is an old, thick slab, readily insulated on the outside.*

Fig. 6-5. *A modest sunspace double glazed with FRP and having small side windows for ventilation. The triangular glass is probably not tempered.*

Fig. 6-6. *The interior of the same sunspace, showing the pleasant effect of lattice spacers between the glazings and the thick bricks for heat storage.*

Fig. 6-7. *A sunspace created on a long, rambling side porch by framing in four sets of sliding patio doors two sets of which are in active use. Ventilation control is excellent since all sets are screened.*

Fig. 6-8. *This sunspace built for $500, including labor has a standard three-part sliding window and serves as a heat-gathering airlock for the house. The net heat gain is worth the investment.*

Fig. 6-9. *The front porch on this small older house was converted with double tempered glass to a sunspace with substantial heat-collecting ability. The cost was kept low through bartered labor.*

Fig. 6-10. *A steel-framed sunspace with double-tempered glass sides and a double-walled acrylic roof, used for a hot tub and other relaxations. Although it faces east and has north glazing, collecting and pumping heat to the basement results in substantial net gain (Courtesy of Better Products, Inc.).*

Fig. 6-11. *Longer-lived polyethylene sheet is stretched in a double layer over the anodized aluminum frame of this sunspace. A small blower inflates and keeps the two glazing layers separate. In the summer, the glazing can be pulled off as one sheet and replaced with a sheet of nylon screening with awning on top. The simplicity makes this one of the lowest cost sunspace kits (Courtesy of Solar Resources Inc.).*

Fig. 6-12. *A low-cost sunspace built on the old porch by a trained local contractor for a needy family to reduce their heating bill. The glazing is double-tempered glass, and a massive old slab was insulated for heat storage.*

Fig. 6-13. *A sunspace glazed with double-walled acrylic intended purely as an airlock with moderate heat-gathering potential.*

Fig. 6-14. *When a sunspace is needed on the second floor, two posts and the house frame can hold it up. Glass is used outside and plastic film inside the redwood frame (Courtesy of Sturdi-built Manufacturing Co.).*

Fig. 6-15. *A full-length, but narrow, front porch with a gable roof was rebuilt and extended to obtain this spacious sunspace. Glazing is double-tempered glass, and the foundation is insulated.*

Fig. 6-16. *The interior of the same, showing the extra width beyond the original front steps. The height of the old foundation permitted a high-ceiling sunspace resting at grade level. The roll-down blinds are needed to control sun mainly on warm fall and spring days since the glazing is vertical.*

Fig. 6-17. *A sunspace consisting of all tempered glass, with curved eaves and a bronze aluminum frame.*

Fig. 6-18. *A tall sunspace that can collect sufficient heat to cover most of the house's need. Intended as a possible greenhouse, this steel-framed structure is roofed partly with bronzed overhead tempered glass units to provide more summer light while reducing overheating (Courtesy of Better Products Inc.).*

Fig. 6-19. *Owner-built at $10 per square foot, this sunspace is partly underground and has never needed auxiliary heat. A turbine vent and operable side window help remove summer heat.*

Fig. 6-20. *The interior of the same sunspace shows overhead double-walled acrylic glazing for more light, a massive plastered adobe back wall for more heat storage, and a window fan to push warm air into the house. White surfaces spread the sunlight around.*

Fig. 6-21. This bronze aluminum-framed sunspace made from one of the lowest cost kits of this type is designed for direct on-ground placement next to the house. The double-glazed walls and roof use two layers of clear, sheet acrylic or translucent FRP, and the panels can be replaced with screens in the summer (Courtesy of Vegetable Factory Inc.).

Fig. 6-22. A redwood-framed double-tempered glass kit sunspace with abundant awning-style vent windows. The hinged glazed mahogany door is a pleasant touch (Courtesy of Creative Structures Inc.).

Fig. 6-23. *This sunspace rises two stories to match the house and illustrates the variety of designs that can be built from a kit. Framing is bronzed aluminum and glazing is double-tempered glass, including the curved eaves (Courtesy of Janco Greenhouses.).*

Fig. 6-24. *A different way to incorporate a slant in the design of a sunspace without tilting the south glazing is shown in this redwood-framed unit built from a kit. Double-tempered glass is used. Awning vents near the ground and a narrow ridge vent at the top of the roof help with summer cooling (Courtesy of Sun Room Co.).*

Fig. 6-25. *This large old house now gains much of its heat from the sun since the entire south wall was covered with a two-story wood-framed sunspace that uses tempered glass.*

Fig. 6-26. *An unusually long overhang protects this post-and-beam framed sunspace from overheating. Railings trim this unique design, blinds also control solar heating, and storage mass is replaced by a carport underneath.*

Fig. 6-27. *A sunspace intended for maximum heat gain with its double-walled acrylic-glazed tilted south wall and roof. A special concrete foundation design has permitted this structure to adapt to terrain that slopes steeply to the west.*

Fig. 6-28. *This greenhouse has a painted redwood frame, tempered glass on the outside, and plastic sheet on the inside. The glazed roof has hinged vents on this kit (Courtesy Sturdi-built Manufacturing Co.).*

Fig. 6-29. *A white-enameled, aluminum-framed, double-tempered glass sunspace matched to the house and built from a custom kit. Banks of awning vents help provide cooling necessary at times for the glazed roof (Courtesy of Janco Greenhouses.).*

Fig. 6-30. *An old-fashioned wood hot tub occupies part of this massive redwood post-and-beam sunspace with double-tempered glass and abundant awning vents. The special roof glass units can be nearly 10 or 13 feet long (Courtesy of Creative Structures Inc.).*

Fig. 6-31. *This size sunspace is needed to heat a large old house. Corrugated FRP is battened to a wood frame. The distinction between a sunspace and a large walk-in solar collector is blurred in this owner design.*

Fig. 6-32. *Steeply pitched roof glazing matches the house roof for this redwood-framed sunspace which comes with preassembled wall units. Glazing can be double- or triple-tempered glass, and there is a continuous ridge vent at the top (Courtesy of Sun Room Co.).*

Fig. 6-33. *Braced steel posts hold up this second-story sunspace independently of the house. White-backed drawstring curtains all around control solar heating and privacy, and abundant heat is pumped into the house with a blower. Roof and wall glazing is double-walled acrylic with a few tempered-glass units included for clearer views.*

Fig. 6-34. *A long sunspace with double-tempered glass, vents, straight eaves, and bronzed aluminum frame in 38-inch modules (Courtesy of Sunplace, Inc.)*

Fig. 6-35. *This new house includes a sunporch. Glazing is tall, narrow, French glass doors, each framed separately.*

Fig. 6-36. *A built-in sunspace incorporated in the second floor of a multisided house. The wood framing is covered with cedar, the glazing is double-tempered glass, and the hopper-style vents open outward. White panels across the lower half of the southeast and southwest glazing reduce solar penetration in morning and afternoon. Because there is little mass upstairs, excess heat is pumped from the ceiling to the slab floor below.*

Fig. 6-37. *A freestanding sunspace for heating a swimming pool. The steel-framed structure is glazed with double-walled acrylic and designed to be moistureproof inside (Courtesy of Better Products Inc.).*

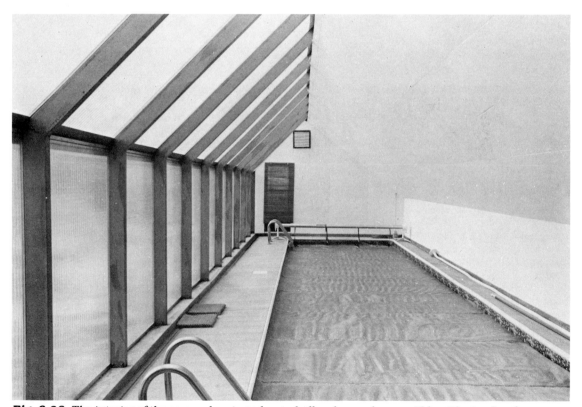

Fig. 6-38. *The interior of the same, showing a long, shallow lap pool compatible with simple rafter spans. The foundation is insulated so that the concrete deck is as warm as the pool, which reaches over 80° F in the winter without auxiliary heat (Courtesy of Better Products Inc.).*

Additional Information

TABLE 1.

Solar Position and Clear Day Insolation, by Latitude

Notes:

Insolation is solar radiation flux or energy per unit area per time, measured in Btus per square foot per hour.

Positions of the sun are given for the 21st day of the month shown, at the solar hour shown. Altitude (ALT) is in degrees above the horizon; azimuth (AZM) is in degrees from true solar south. Solar time is defined so that the sun is most overhead (highest altitude) exactly at noon. For each morning hour, there is a corresponding afternoon hour when the sun is at the same altitude, and therefore the insolation is the same.

Daily and monthly total insolations are given in Btus per square foot; 28, 30, and 31 days are used for calculation of the monthly totals as appropriate. Insolation data pertains to the 21st day of the month and is assumed to be the average insolation for the entire month. The small bias introduced nearly cancels over the year. Months are arranged to run continuously through the heating season.

Insolation data given is the sum of direct and diffuse insolation on an average clear day at zero altitude, without ground reflection. Cloudy days will lower the table values; a higher altitude will raise them (at the rate of about 10 percent per mile of altitude); polluted or dusty skies will lower them; unusually clean air will raise them; and ground reflection will raise them. Do not assume that the given values are as accurate as implied by the number of digits shown.

Insolation is given for three useful surfaces: horizontal (simulating a roof), tilted at latitude plus 20 degrees (a steep tilt for maximum fall-spring collection), and vertical (90 degrees). Insolation is also given for a "normal" surface: a surface that is always aimed at the sun and receives the maximum possible insolation. The normal surface data is useful for theoretical purposes or tracking collection only.

Table data is adapted from ASHRAE *Handbook of Fundamentals*, 1972. A later edition (1985) provides insolation data for vertical windows facing various compass directions, but not for tilted surfaces. It is used by permission of the American Society of Heating, Refrigerating, and Air-Conditioning Engineers.

BTU/HR.SQ.FT. SOLAR POSITION AND INSOLATION, 32° N LATITUDE

MONTH	SOLAR TIME AM	PM	SOLAR POSITION ALT°	AZM°	HORIZONTAL	TILT 52°	VERTICAL	NORMAL
MAR 21	7	5	12.7	81.9	54	56	32	185
	8	4	25.1	73.0	129	137	78	260
	9	3	36.8	62.1	194	209	119	290
	10	2	47.3	47.5	245	265	150	304
	11	1	55.0	26.8	277	300	170	311
		12	58.0	0.0	287	312	177	313
	DAILY TOTALS				2084	2246	1276	3012
	MONTH TOTALS				64600	69600	39600	93400
APR 21	6	6	6.1	99.9	14	5	3	66
	7	5	18.8	92.2	86	51	10	206
	8	4	31.5	84.0	158	120	35	255
	9	3	43.9	74.2	220	183	68	278
	10	2	55.7	60.3	267	234	95	290
	11	1	65.4	37.5	297	265	112	295
		12	69.6	0.0	307	276	118	297
	DAILY TOTALS				2390	1994	764	3076
	MONTH TOTALS				71700	59800	22900	92300
MAY 21	6	6	10.4	107.2	36	12	7	119
	7	5	22.8	100.1	107	44	13	211
	8	4	35.4	92.9	175	105	15	250
	9	3	48.1	84.7	233	163	33	269
	10	2	60.6	73.3	277	208	56	280
	11	1	72.0	51.9	305	237	72	285
		12	78.0	0.0	315	247	77	286
	DAILY TOTALS				2582	1788	469	3112
	MONTH TOTALS				80000	55400	14500	96500
JUN 21	6	6	12.2	110.2	45	14	9	131
	7	5	24.3	103.4	115	41	14	210
	8	4	36.9	96.8	180	99	16	245
	9	3	49.6	89.4	236	153	19	264
	10	2	62.2	79.7	279	197	41	274
	11	1	74.2	60.9	306	224	56	279
		12	81.5	0.0	315	234	60	280
	DAILY TOTALS				2634	1690	370	3084
	MONTH TOTALS				79000	50700	11100	92500
JUL 21	6	6	10.7	107.7	37	12	8	113
	7	5	23.1	100.6	107	44	14	203
	8	4	35.7	93.6	174	104	16	241
	9	3	48.4	85.5	231	159	31	261
	10	2	60.9	74.3	274	204	54	271
	11	1	72.4	53.3	302	232	69	277
		12	78.6	0.0	311	242	74	279
	DAILY TOTALS				2558	1754	458	3012
	MONTH TOTALS				79300	54400	14200	93400
AUG 21	6	6	6.5	100.5	14	6	4	59
	7	5	19.1	92.8	85	50	12	190
	8	4	31.8	84.7	156	116	33	240
	9	3	44.3	75.0	216	178	65	263
	10	2	56.1	61.3	262	226	91	276
	11	1	66.0	38.4	292	257	107	282
		12	70.3	0.0	302	268	113	284
	DAILY TOTALS				2352	1934	736	2902
	MONTH TOTALS				72900	60000	22800	90000

MONTH	SOLAR TIME AM	PM	SOLAR POSITION ALT°	AZM°	HORIZONTAL	TILT 52°	VERTICAL	NORMAL
SEP 21	7	5	12.7	81.9	51	52	30	163
	8	4	25.1	73.0	124	131	75	240
	9	3	36.8	62.1	188	201	114	272
	10	2	47.3	47.5	237	255	145	287
	11	1	55.0	26.8	268	289	164	294
		12	58.0	0.0	278	300	171	296
	DAILY TOTALS				2014	2154	1226	2808
	MONTH TOTALS				60400	64600	36800	84200
OCT 21	7	5	6.8	73.1	19	36	32	99
	8	4	18.7	64.0	90	134	104	229
	9	3	29.5	53.0	155	212	153	273
	10	2	38.7	39.1	204	270	188	293
	11	1	45.1	21.1	236	306	209	302
		12	47.5	0.0	247	318	217	304
	DAILY TOTALS				1654	2232	1588	2696
	MONTH TOTALS				51300	69200	49200	83600
NOV 21	7	5	1.5	65.4	0	1	1	2
	8	4	12.7	56.6	55	119	111	196
	9	3	22.6	46.1	118	208	176	263
	10	2	30.8	33.2	166	270	217	289
	11	1	36.2	17.6	197	307	241	301
		12	38.2	0.0	207	320	249	304
	DAILY TOTALS				1280	2130	1742	2406
	MONTH TOTALS				38400	63900	52300	72200
DEC 21	8	4	10.3	53.8	41	108	107	176
	9	3	19.8	43.6	102	204	183	257
	10	2	27.6	31.2	150	267	226	288
	11	1	32.7	16.4	180	305	251	301
		12	34.6	0.0	190	318	259	304
	DAILY TOTALS				1136	2086	1794	2348
	MONTH TOTALS				35200	64700	55600	72800
JAN 21	7	5	1.4	65.2	0	1	1	1
	8	4	12.5	56.5	56	123	115	203
	9	3	22.5	46.0	118	212	181	269
	10	2	30.6	33.1	167	274	221	295
	11	1	36.1	17.5	198	312	245	306
		12	38.0	0.0	209	324	253	310
	DAILY TOTALS				1288	2166	1779	2458
	MONTH TOTALS				39900	67100	55100	76200
FEB 21	7	5	7.1	73.5	22	42	38	121
	8	4	19.0	64.4	95	141	108	247
	9	3	29.9	53.4	161	220	158	288
	10	2	39.1	39.4	212	279	193	306
	11	1	45.6	21.4	244	315	214	315
		12	48.0	0.0	255	328	222	317
	DAILY TOTALS				1724	2322	1644	2872
	MONTH TOTALS				48300	65000	46000	80400

MONTH	SOLAR TIME AM	PM	SOLAR POSITION ALT	AZM	HORIZONTAL	TILT 60°	VERTICAL	NORMAL
MAR 21	7	5	11.4	80.2	46	51	35	171
	8	4	22.5	69.6	114	131	89	250
	9	3	32.8	57.3	173	202	138	282
	10	2	41.6	41.9	218	258	176	297
	11	1	47.7	22.6	247	293	200	305
		12	50.0	0.0	257	305	208	307
	DAILY TOTALS				1852	2174	1484	2916
	MONTH TOTALS				57400	67400	46000	90400
APR 21	6	6	7.4	98.9	20	7	4	89
	7	5	18.9	89.5	87	50	12	206
	8	4	30.3	79.3	152	117	53	252
	9	3	41.3	67.2	207	179	93	274
	10	2	51.2	51.4	250	229	126	286
	11	1	58.7	29.2	277	260	147	292
		12	61.6	0.0	287	271	154	293
	DAILY TOTALS				2274	1956	1022	3092
	MONTH TOTALS				68200	58700	30700	92800
MAY 21	5	7	1.9	114.7	0	0	0	1
	6	6	12.7	105.6	49	13	9	144
	7	5	24.0	96.6	214	44	13	216
	8	4	35.4	87.2	175	104	25	250
	9	3	46.8	76.0	227	160	60	267
	10	2	57.5	60.9	267	205	89	277
	11	1	66.2	37.1	293	234	108	283
		12	70.0	0.0	301	243	114	284
	DAILY TOTALS				2552	1760	724	3160
	MONTH TOTALS				79100	54600	22400	98000
JUN 21	5	7	4.2	117.3	4	2	1	22
	6	6	14.8	108.4	60	16	10	155
	7	5	26.0	99.7	123	41	14	216
	8	4	37.4	90.7	182	97	16	246
	9	3	48.8	80.2	233	151	47	263
	10	2	59.8	65.8	272	194	74	272
	11	1	69.2	41.9	296	221	92	277
		12	73.5	0.0	304	230	98	279
	DAILY TOTALS				2648	1670	610	3180
	MONTH TOTALS				79400	50100	18300	95400
JUL 21	5	7	2.3	115.2	0	0	0	2
	6	6	13.1	106.1	50	14	9	138
	7	5	24.3	97.2	114	44	14	208
	8	4	35.8	87.8	174	102	24	241
	9	3	47.2	76.7	225	157	58	259
	10	2	57.9	61.7	265	200	86	269
	11	1	66.7	37.9	290	228	104	275
		12	70.6	0.0	298	238	111	276
	DAILY TOTALS				2534	1728	702	3062
	MONTH TOTALS				78600	53600	21800	94900
AUG 21	6	6	7.9	99.5	21	7	5	81
	7	5	19.3	90.0	87	49	12	191
	8	4	30.7	79.9	150	113	50	237
	9	3	41.8	67.9	205	173	89	260
	10	2	51.7	52.1	246	221	120	272
	11	1	59.3	29.7	273	252	140	278
		12	62.3	0.0	282	262	147	280
	DAILY TOTALS				2244	1894	978	2916
	MONTH TOTALS				69600	58700	30300	90400

SOLAR POSITION AND INSOLATION, 40° N LATITUDE

MONTH	SOLAR TIME AM	PM	SOLAR POSITION ALT	AZM	HORIZONTAL	TILT 60°	VERTICAL	NORMAL
SEP 21	7	5	11.4	80.2	43	47	32	149
	8	4	22.5	69.6	109	124	84	230
	9	3	32.8	57.3	167	193	132	263
	10	2	41.6	41.9	211	247	168	280
	11	1	47.7	22.6	239	281	192	287
		12	50.0	0.0	249	292	200	290
	DAILY TOTALS				1788	2074	1416	2708
	MONTH TOTALS				53600	62200	42500	81200
OCT 21	7	5	4.5	72.3	7	17	16	48
	8	4	15.0	61.9	68	118	100	204
	9	3	24.5	49.8	126	198	160	257
	10	2	32.4	35.6	170	257	203	280
	11	1	37.6	18.7	199	294	229	291
		12	39.5	0.0	208	306	238	294
	DAILY TOTALS				1348	2074	1654	2454
	MONTH TOTALS				41800	64300	51300	76100
NOV 21	8	4	8.2	55.4	28	82	81	136
	9	3	17.0	44.1	82	183	167	232
	10	2	24.0	31.0	126	249	219	268
	11	1	28.6	16.1	153	288	248	283
		12	30.2	0.0	163	301	258	288
	DAILY TOTALS				942	1908	1686	2128
	MONTH TOTALS				28300	57200	50600	63800
DEC	8	4	5.5	53.0	14	54	56	89
	9	3	14.0	41.9	65	171	163	217
	10	2	20.7	29.4	107	242	221	261
	11	1	25.0	15.2	134	283	252	280
		12	26.6	0.0	143	296	263	285
	DAILY TOTALS				782	1796	1646	1978
	MONTH TOTALS				24200	55700	51000	61300
JAN 21	8	4	8.1	55.3	28	85	84	142
	9	3	16.8	44.0	83	187	171	239
	10	2	23.8	30.9	127	254	223	274
	11	1	28.4	16.0	154	293	253	289
		12	30.0	0.0	164	306	263	294
	DAILY TOTALS				948	1944	1726	2182
	MONTH TOTALS				29400	60300	53500	67600
FEB 21	7	5	4.8	72.7	10	24	22	69
	8	4	15.4	62.2	73	127	107	224
	9	3	25.0	50.2	132	208	167	274
	10	2	32.8	35.9	178	267	210	295
	11	1	38.1	18.9	206	304	236	305
		12	40.0	0.0	216	317	245	308
	DAILY TOTALS				1414	2176	1730	2640
	MONTH TOTALS				39600	00609	48400	73900

SOLAR POSITION AND INSOLATION, 48° N LATITUDE

MONTH	SOLAR TIME AM	PM	SOLAR POSITION ALT	AZM	TOTAL INSOLATION ON SURFACES BTUH/SQ.FT. HORIZONTAL	TILT 68°	VERTICAL	NORMAL
MAR 21	7	5	10.0	78.7	37	45	35	153
	8	4	19.5	66.8	96	122	96	236
	9	3	28.2	53.4	147	193	152	270
	10	2	35.4	37.8	187	248	195	287
	11	1	40.3	19.8	212	283	223	295
		12	42.0	0.0	220	294	232	298
		DAILY TOTALS			1578	2074	1632	2780
		MONTH TOTALS			48900	64300	50600	86200
APR 21	6	6	8.6	97.8	27	7	5	108
	7	5	18.6	86.7	85	48	21	205
	8	4	28.5	74.9	142	113	69	247
	9	3	37.8	61.2	191	174	115	268
	10	2	45.8	44.6	228	223	152	280
	11	1	51.5	24.0	252	254	177	286
		12	53.6	0.0	260	264	185	288
		DAILY TOTALS			2106	1902	1262	3076
		MONTH TOTALS			63200	57100	37900	92300
MAY 21	5	7	5.2	114.3	9	3	2	41
	6	6	14.7	103.7	61	13	10	162
	7	5	24.6	93.0	118	43	13	219
	8	4	34.7	81.6	171	101	45	248
	9	3	44.3	68.3	217	156	86	264
	10	2	53.0	51.3	252	200	120	274
	11	1	59.5	28.6	274	228	141	279
		12	62.0	0.0	281	238	149	280
		DAILY TOTALS			2482	1728	982	3254
		MONTH TOTALS			76900	53600	30400	100900
JUN 21	5	7	7.9	116.5	21	7	5	77
	6	6	17.2	106.2	74	16	12	172
	7	5	27.0	95.8	129	39	15	220
	8	4	37.1	84.6	181	95	35	246
	9	3	46.9	71.6	225	147	74	261
	10	2	55.8	54.8	259	189	105	269
	11	1	62.7	31.2	280	216	126	274
		12	65.5	0.0	287	225	133	275
		DAILY TOTALS			2626	1644	874	3312
		MONTH TOTALS			78800	49300	26200	99400
JUL 21	5	7	5.7	114.7	10	4	3	43
	6	6	15.2	104.1	62	15	11	156
	7	5	25.1	93.5	118	42	14	211
	8	4	35.1	82.1	171	99	43	240
	9	3	44.8	68.8	215	153	83	256
	10	2	53.5	51.9	250	195	116	266
	11	1	60.1	29.0	272	223	137	271
		12	62.6	0.0	279	232	144	272
		DAILY TOTALS			2474	1694	956	3158
		MONTH TOTALS			76700	52500	29600	97900
AUG 21	6	6	9.1	98.3	28	8	6	99
	7	5	19.1	87.2	85	47	20	190
	8	4	29.0	75.4	141	109	65	232
	9	3	38.4	61.8	189	168	110	254
	10	2	46.4	45.1	225	214	146	266
	11	1	52.2	24.3	248	244	169	272
		12	54.3	0.0	256	255	177	274
		DAILY TOTALS			2086	1836	1208	2898
		MONTH TOTALS			64700	56900	37400	89800

MONTH	SOLAR TIME AM	PM	SOLAR POSITION ALT	AZM	TOTAL INSOLATION ON SURFACES BTUH/SQ.FT. HORIZONTAL	TILT 68°	VERTICAL	NORMAL
SEP 21	7	5	10.0	78.7	35	40	35	131
	8	4	19.5	66.8	92	115	90	215
	9	3	28.2	53.4	142	183	143	251
	10	2	35.4	37.8	181	236	185	269
	11	1	40.3	19.8	205	269	212	278
		12	42.0	0.0	213	281	221	280
		DAILY TOTALS			1522	1966	1546	2568
		MONTH TOTALS			45700	59000	46400	77000
OCT 21	7	5	2.0	71.9	0	1	1	4
	8	4	11.2	60.2	44	95	87	165
	9	3	19.3	47.4	94	178	157	233
	10	2	25.7	33.1	133	239	207	262
	11	1	30.0	17.1	157	276	237	274
		12	31.5	0.0	166	288	247	278
		DAILY TOTALS			1022	1866	1626	2154
		MONTH TOTALS			31700	57800	50400	66800
NOV 21	8	4	3.6	54.7	5	22	22	36
	9	3	11.2	42.7	46	141	135	179
	10	2	17.1	29.5	83	215	201	233
	11	1	20.9	15.1	105	258	238	255
		12	22.2	0.0	115	272	250	261
		DAILY TOTALS			596	1544	1442	1668
		MONTH TOTALS			17900	46300	43300	50000
DEC 21	9	3	8.0	40.9	27	140	109	140
	10	2	13.6	28.2	63	214	190	214
	11	1	17.3	14.4	86	242	231	242
		12	18.6	0.0	94	250	244	250
		DAILY TOTALS			446	1444	1304	1444
		MONTH TOTALS			13800	44800	40400	44800
JAN 21	8	4	3.5	54.6	4	22	4	37
	9	3	11.0	42.6	46	145	139	185
	10	2	16.9	29.4	83	206	206	239
	11	1	20.7	15.1	107	243	243	261
		12	22.0	0.0	115	255	255	267
		DAILY TOTALS			596	1578	1478	1710
		MONTH TOTALS			18500	48900	45800	53000
FEB 21	7	5	2.4	72.2	1	4	1	12
	8	4	11.6	60.5	49	106	96	188
	9	3	19.7	47.7	100	190	167	251
	10	2	26.2	33.3	139	251	217	278
	11	1	30.5	17.2	165	288	247	290
		12	32.0	0.0	173	301	258	293
		DAILY TOTALS			1080	1978	1720	2330
		MONTH TOTALS			30200	55400	48200	65200

TABLE 2.

R-Values of Common Building Materials

MATERIAL	R-VALUE	REMARKS
Concrete	0.20	
Rock/sand	~0.1	solid or packed, dry, without air spaces
Brick	0.20	
Adobe	~0.40	dry
Aluminum	0.00071	
Steel	0.0029	
Copper	0.0037	
Glass	0.2	
Plastic	~1	for almost any common plastic
Softwoods	~1.2	
Hardwoods	~0.9	
Air space	~1	almost independent of thickness from ¼ to 4 inches
Air film	~0.7	for still air; very dependent on orientation and air speed

Notes:

R-values are given for a 1-inch thickness of the material. Materials commonly used as thin sheets will have proportionately lower R-values. Because the air film on each side contributes much more insulating capability than the thin material itself, the effective R-value is about 1 as determined by the air film(s). A reflective surface can more than double this R-value. Some values are approximate because of variation in materials (shown by the symbol ~ for the most uncertain cases).

Values are adapted from many sources. R-values of insulations are in TABLE 6. The units of R-value are: hours, square feet,, of, per Btu inch.

TABLE 3.

Coefficients of Thermal Expansion for Selected Building Materials

MATERIAL	COEFFICIENT
Aluminum	0.000012
Iron & steel	0.000006
Copper	0.000009
Concrete	0.000006
Wood	0.000005 to 0.0000010
Glass	0.000005
Acrylic	0.000041

Notes:

Units are per degree Fahrenheit. The coefficient for wood depends on moisture, species, and particular growth and curing history of each piece. See TABLE 5 for coefficients for more plastic glazings.

To obtain the length change, multiply the coefficient by the change in temperature in degrees Fahrenheit and by the total length of the material. Use the total length in inches to obtain a result in inches.

TABLE 4.

Heat Capacities and Densities of Selected Building and Storage Materials

MATERIAL	HEAT CAPACITY BTU/LB °F	BTU/CU.FT. °F	DENSITY LB/CU.FT.
Concrete	0.22	32	145
Rocks (loose)	0.20	20	90
Sand (dry)	0.20	20	100
Brick	0.20	25	120
Adobe	0.25	25	110
Glass	0.18	28	155
Aluminum	0.21	37	170
Steel	0.12	59	490
Copper	0.09	51	570
Softwood	0.65	18	25
Hardwood	0.6	25	40
Water	1.00	62	62
Air	0.24	0.018	0.075

Notes:

The density is a weight density for nonmoving mass calculations. Values vary for some materials, depending on content and structure, especially for woods. Most dry soils have values similar to sand, rocks, bricks, and adobe. Values for rock depend on geological type. Values given are approximate for types of rock commonly mined for building purposes. Values are adapted from many sources and rounded according to working accuracy. Consistency among the columns varies because of rounding. See other sources for a longer list of building materials.

Air density decreases significantly with temperature and altitude. The value given for air is at one atmosphere pressure (zero altitude) and 68° F.

The latent heat capacity for water to ice is 144 Btu/lb. and for water to vapor is 970 Btu/lb.

TABLE 5.

Glazings

MATERIAL	APPROX. COST PER SQ.FT.	CLARITY	SOLAR TRANSMITTANCE	LIFETIME YEARS	STRENGTH	THERMAL EXPANSION COEFFICIENT PER °F
Glass, Annealed, ⅛ inch, Single sheet	$1	Good	86%	20 +	Weak	0.000005
Glass, Tempered, Double unit of two ⅛ inch & air gap	$3	Good	72%	20 +	High	0.000005

MATERIAL	APPROX. COST PER SQ.FT.	CLARITY	SOLAR TRANSMITTANCE	LIFETIME YEARS	STRENGTH	THERMAL EXPANSION COEFFICIENT PER °F
Polyethylene, 6 mil, Generic	$0.02	Poor	87%	½	Weak	~0.0003
Polyethylene, 6 mil, Solar-coated (e.g., Monsanto 602, 603, Visqueen)	$0.06	Poor	87%	2?	Weak	~0.0003
Polyvinyl chloride (vinyl), 6 mil	$0.10	Good	90%?	2?	Fair	~0.0002
Methyl methacrylate (acrylic), (e.g., Plexiglas) Double-walled (e.g., Exolite)	$3 to $4	Fair	83%	10+	Good	0.000041
Polycarbonate (e.g., Lexan), Double-walled (e.g., Exolite)	$6	Fair	74%	10+	High	0.000038
Polyester (e.g., Mylar), 4 mil	$0.10	Good	85%	5?	Fair	0.000015
Fiber reinforced polyester (FRP), Best grade, 40 mil (e.g., Filon, Crystalite, Sun-Lite)	$1 to $1.50	Poor	80% to 85%	10+	Good	~0.00002
Polyvinyl fluoride (e.g., Tedlar), 4 mil	$1	Poor	90%	10+	High	0.000024
Polyfluorocarbon (e.g., Teflon), 1 mil	$1	Good	96%	20+	Fair	0.00009
Composite polyester & acrylic laminate, 7 or 11 mil (e.g., Flexigard)	$1	Good	87%	10+	Good	0.000019

Notes:

These are the commonly available glazings, in use for many years and likely to remain available. See text for available sizes and details on properties.Costs are mid-1980s' prices, retail level. A mil is $1/1000$ inch. Solar transmittance is given for visible plus near-IR solar energy. Glass and only a few plastics (notably vinyl and FRP) have poor transmittance of heat radiation (far-IR), a desirable property.

Using double glazing more than doubles its R-value, from about 1 to between 2 and 3 because of the air layer. The principal limit to glass lifetime is the seal in double units. Single sheets of acrylic and polycarbonate are available in $1/8$ inch and thicker and are clear. Teflon's weakness is partly attributed to the 1-mil thinness. Thicker sheets are available, but the cost increases proportionately. Best-grade FRP has ultraviolet-protected coating. FRP is available in 25- and 60-mil thicknesses also, and in corrugated form.

Many other characteristics of glazings might be of interest, such as maximum service temperature, brittleness when cold, weight density, coloration if any, R-value (all near 1 to 2), refractive ability, and strength measurements. Values are adapted from many sources.

Manufacturers of brand names given as examples are as follows. (Not all currently available brands are listed, and some might now be unavailable):

Visqueen—Ethyl Film Products
Plexiglas—Rohm & Hass Co.
Exolite—CYRO Industries
Lexan—General Electric
Sun-Lite (formerly Kalwall)—Kalwall Corp.
Filon—Vistron Corp.
Lascolite, Crystalite—Lasco Industries
Mylar, Tedlar, Teflon—E.I. duPont de Nemours
Flexigard—3M Co.

TABLE 6.

Common Insulations

MATERIAL	FORMS	SPECIAL PROPERTIES	R-VALUE PER INCH	APPROX.COST PER SQ.FT. PER INCH
Extruded polystyrene	Sheet	Waterproof	5	$0.30
Expanded polystyrene	Sheet, beads	Weak	4	$0.15
Polyisocyanurate	Sheet	Foil-faced	8	$0.40
Fiberglass	Batts, board	Fireproof	3	$0.05

Notes:

Sheets available in 4- x -8-foot and 4- x -9-foot sizes, with thicknesses from $1/2$ inch to 4 inches.

An air space of at least $1/2$ inch raises the effective performance of foil-faced insulation, adding about R-2.

Plastic foams are sensitive to ultraviolet-light degradation.

Fiberglass batts are sometimes available as foil-faced but usually are kraft paper-faced. Kraft paper is paper with a tar layer to reduce moisture flow. Fiberglass board, also known as ductboard, is highly compressed, nearly rigid fiberglass, with usually one side foil-covered.

Examples of brand names are: extruded polystyrene (Styrofoam—Dow Chemical Co.) and polyisocyanurate (Tuff-R & Thermax—Celotex Corp.).

MAP 1.

Average Daily Opaque Sky Cover over 12 Months

Notes:

Contours are shown in terms of the fraction in tenths of sky that is covered by clouds over one day. Thus, along the 5/10 or 0.5 contour, direct radiation from the sun was essentially zero for 0.5, or 50 percent, of the time during the daytime. There might remain significant diffuse radiation if the clouds are thin or the sky is partly cloudy.

These maps should be useful with clear-day insolation tables, but are not needed with the SERI daily insolation maps. The maps will help identify whether a locality is predominantly cloudy or clear in each month of the year.

Maps are from *Solar Radiation Energy Resource Atlas of the United States* prepared by the Solar Energy Research Institute (SERI). This information is in the public domain.

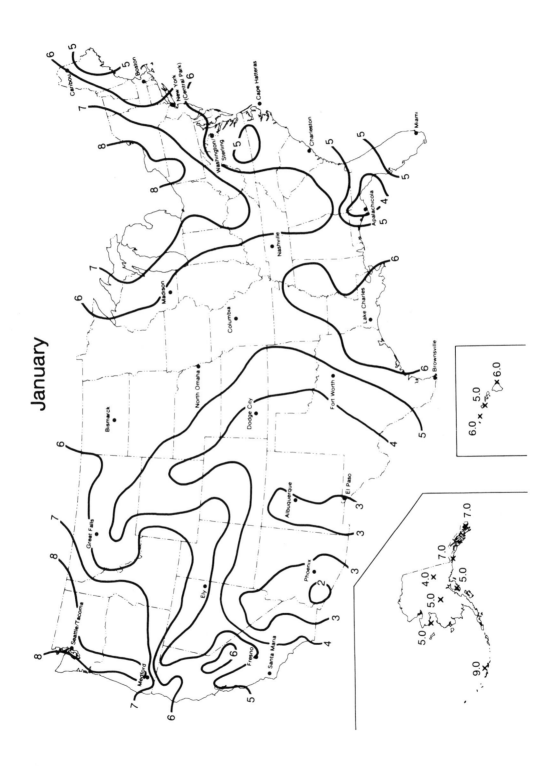

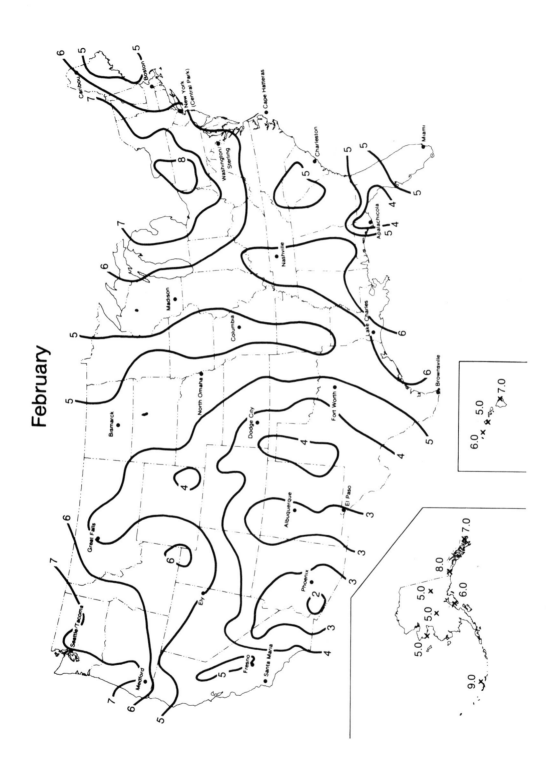

February

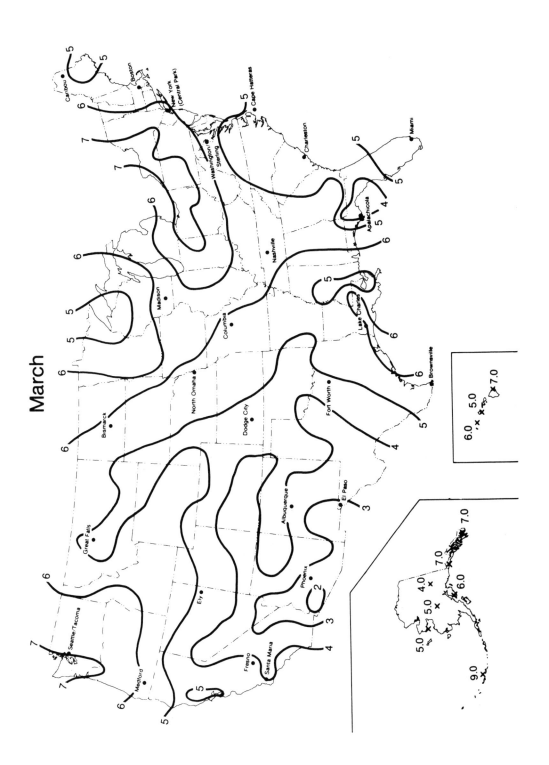

March

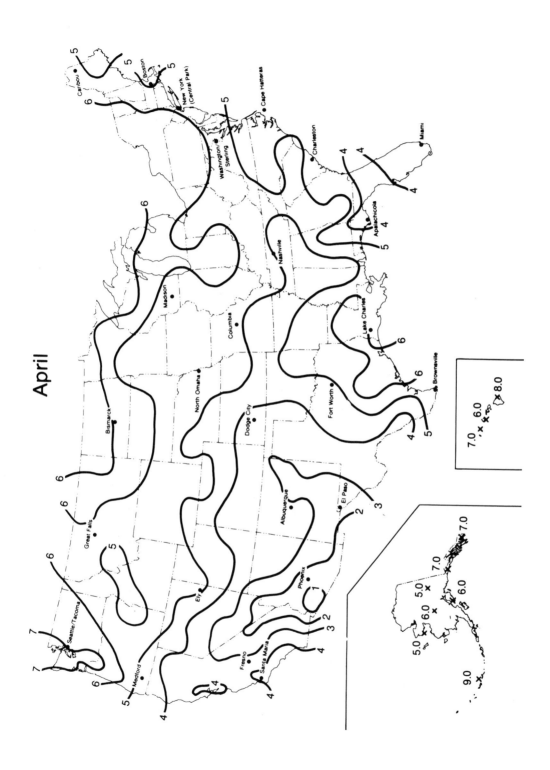

April

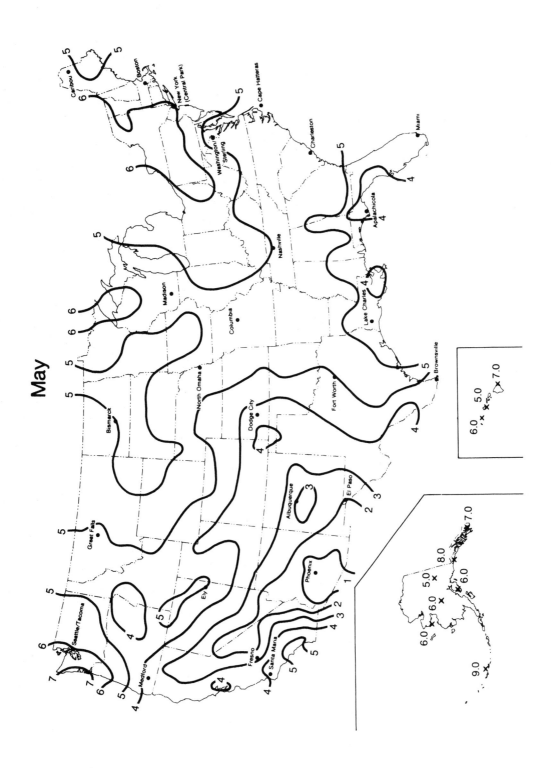

May

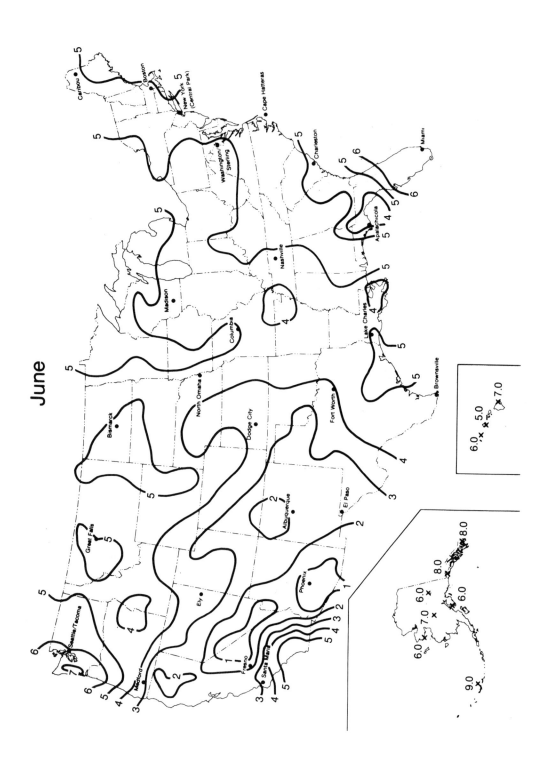

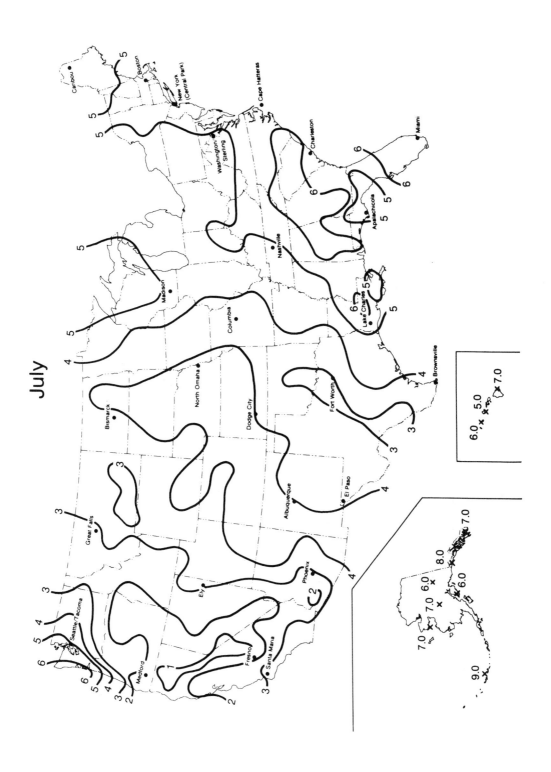

July

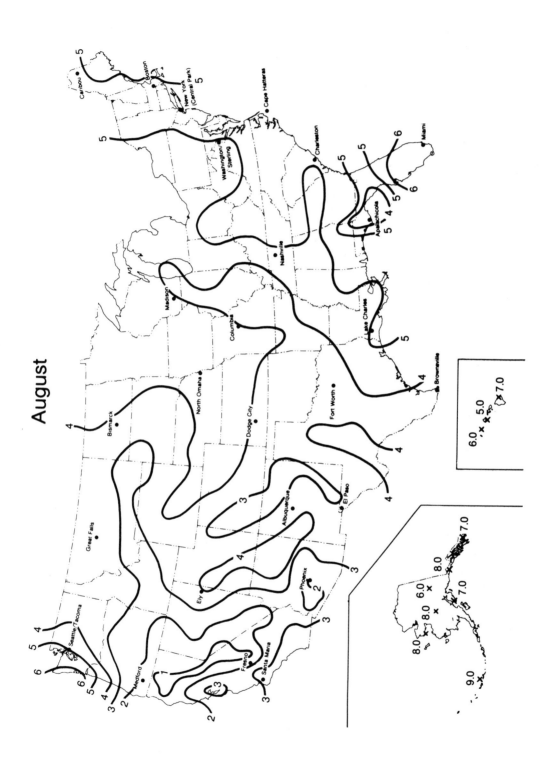

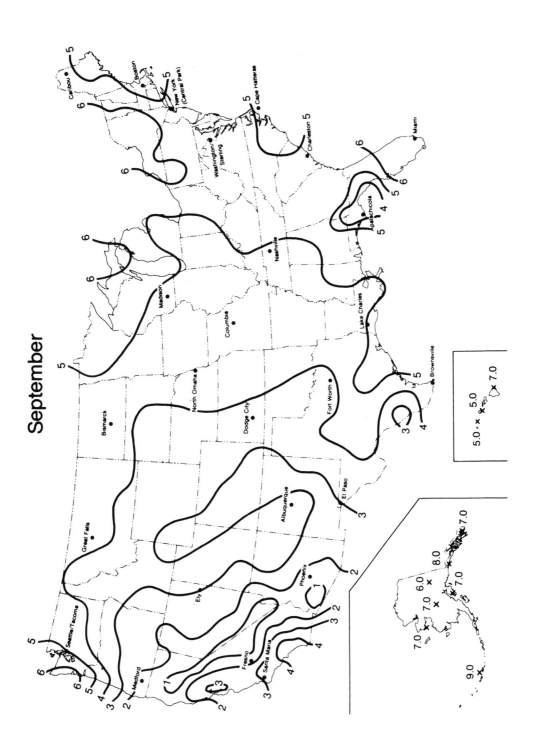

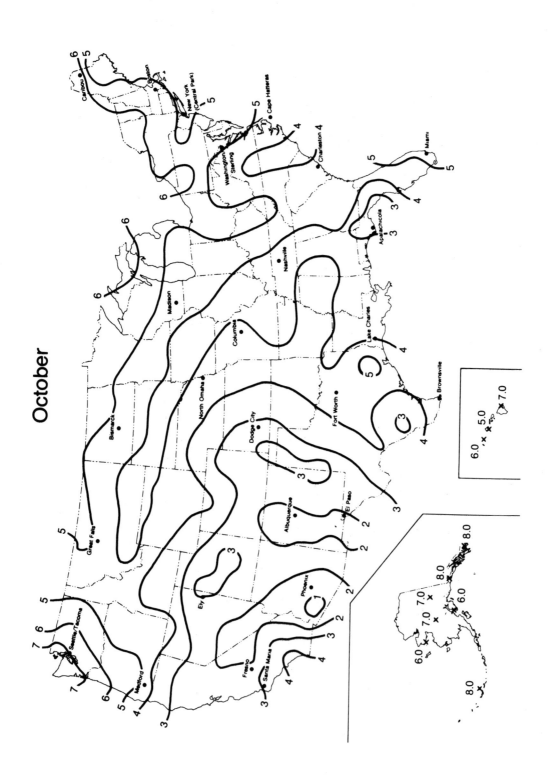

October

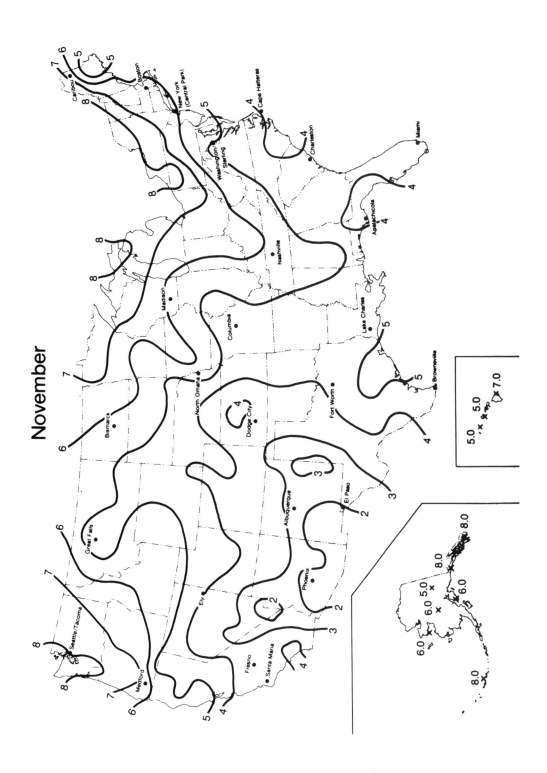

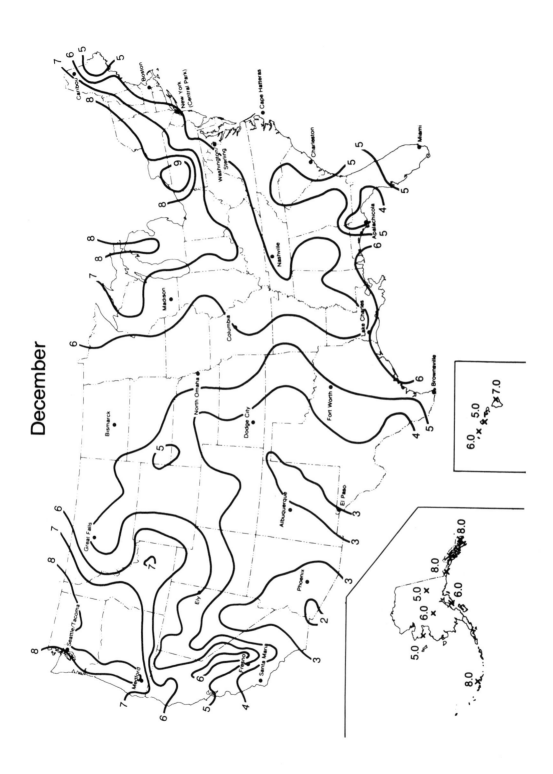

MAP 2.

Average Daily Global Solar Radiation
on a South-Facing Surface with Tilt = Vertical, over 12 Months

Notes:

The global radiation includes direct, diffuse, and ground reflection, and allows for average cloud cover, altitude, and any other major climatic effects prevailing at the stations obtaining the data. Global radiation is most appropriate for calculations for flat surface collectors. The values given constitute the daily total, averaged for the month. Thus, multiplying the daily value by the number of the days in the month will give an accurate monthly total. Daily values were summed from hourly measurements. This data would be useful for glazed walls that are vertical or nearly so. Substantial reductions occur if the wall does not face within 30° of south.

The information in these maps is a recent large-scale compilation of available solar energy measurements and calculations. Good field measurements have been made at only 26 stations for about 23 years. Models have been refined to estimate radiation at 222 more stations with proven accuracy so that the solar resources over the entire United States can be described. Prior tables and maps of insolation are expected to be less accurate and do not take into account many, if any, climatic variables.

The contours in megajoules per square meter (MJ/m^2) can be converted to Btus per square foot by multiplying values by 88.11.

Maps are from *Solar Radiation Energy Resource Atlas of the United States* prepared by the Solar Energy Research Institute.

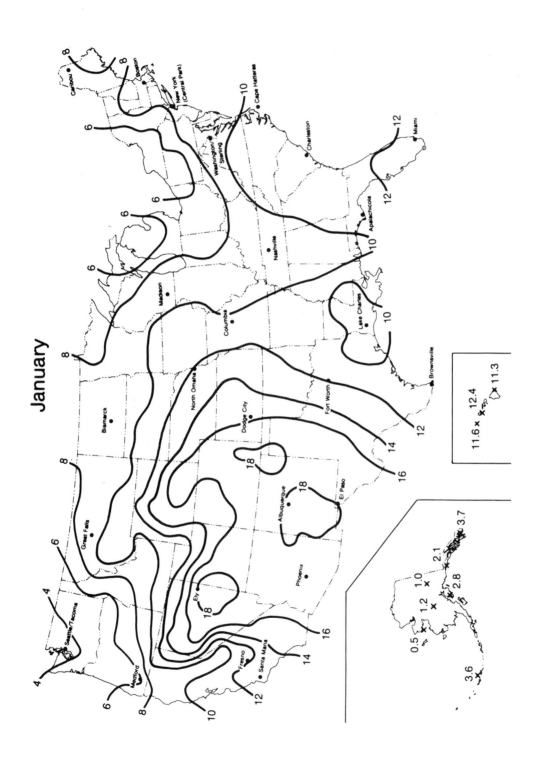

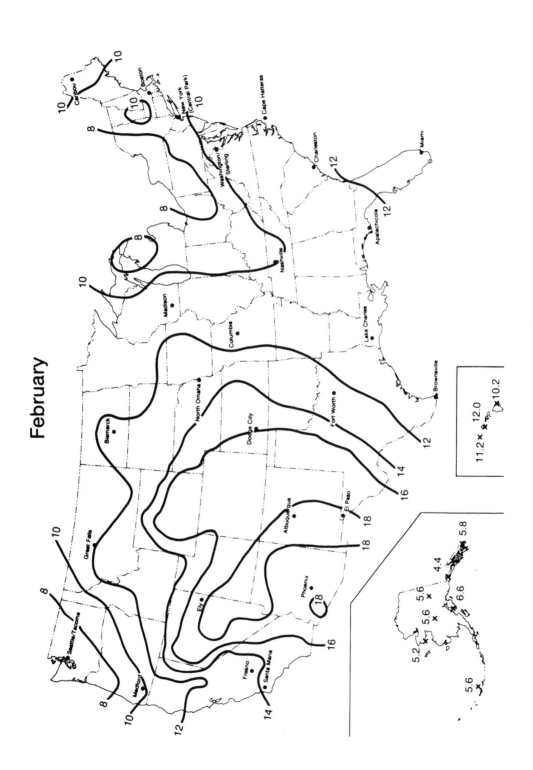

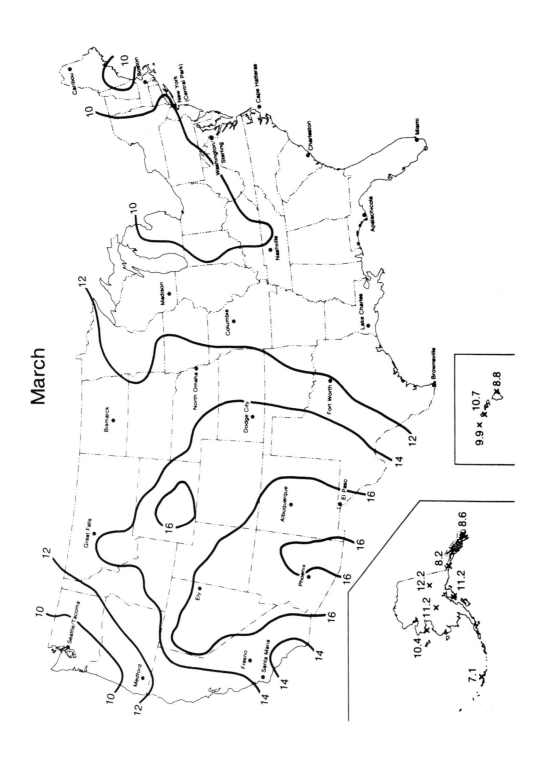

March

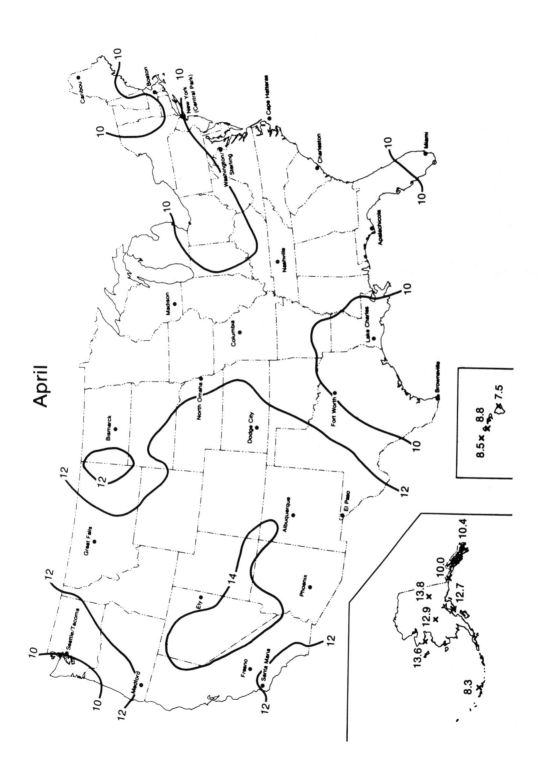

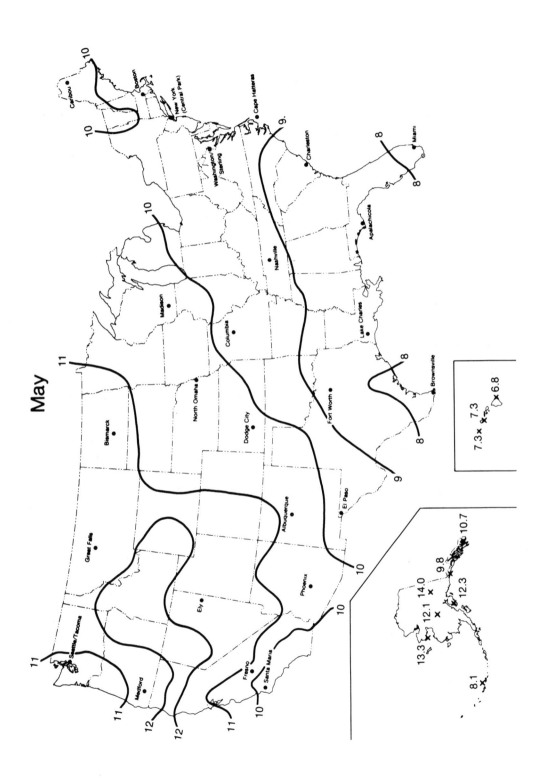

May

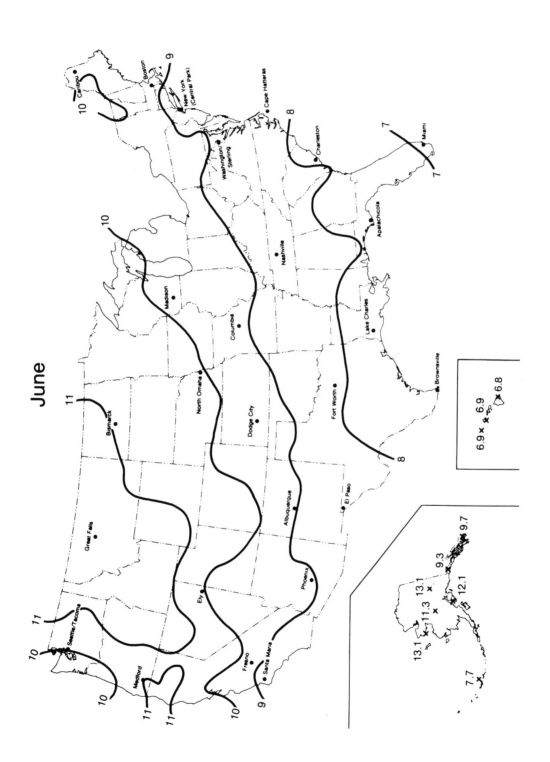

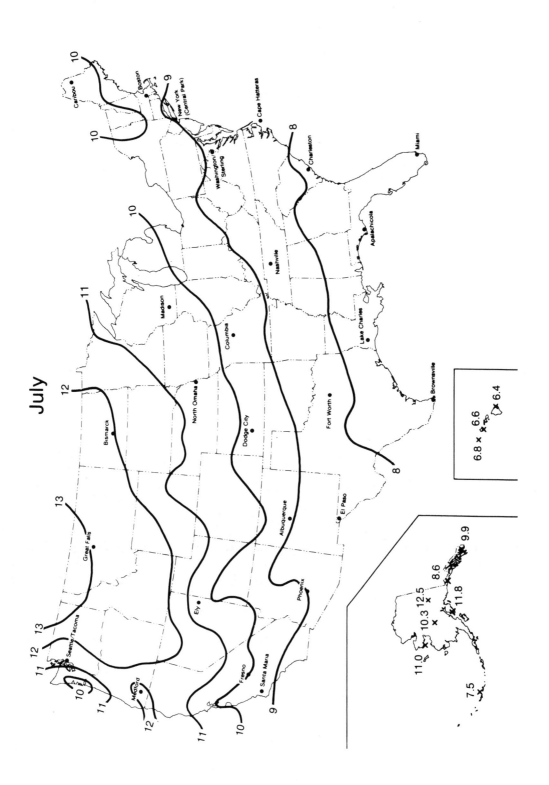

July

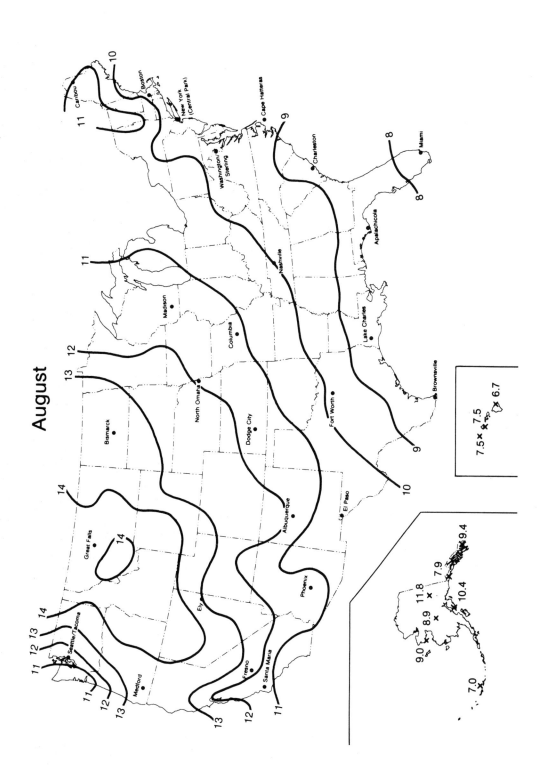

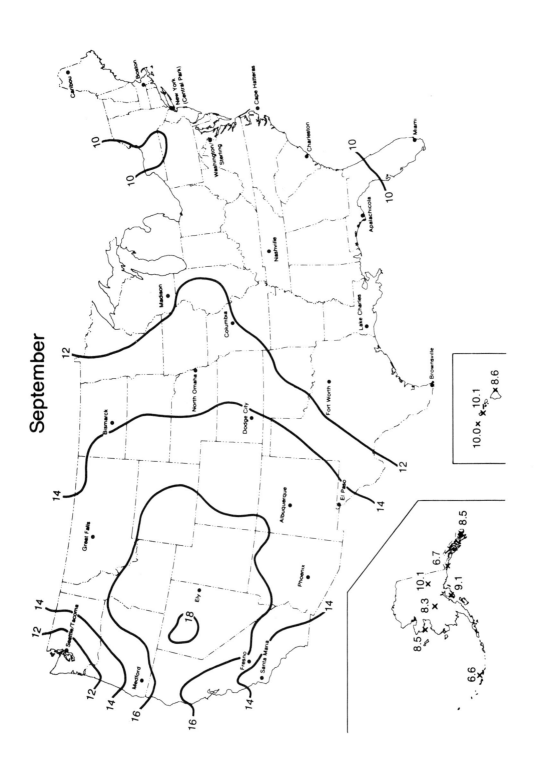

September

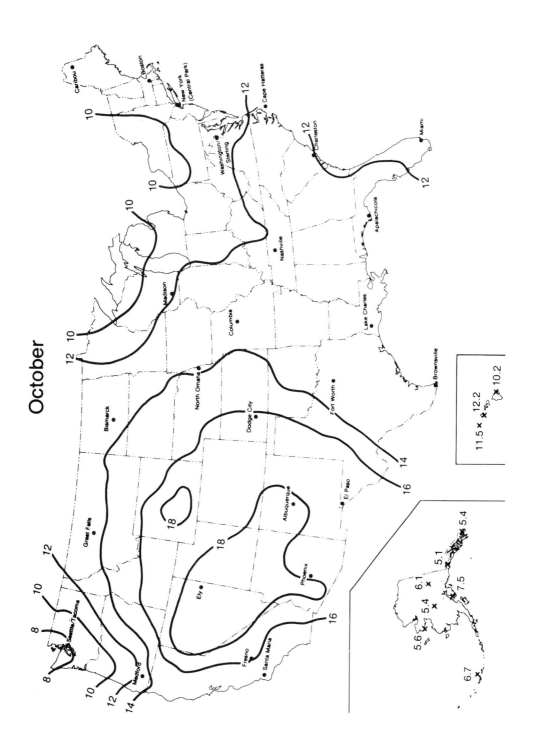

October

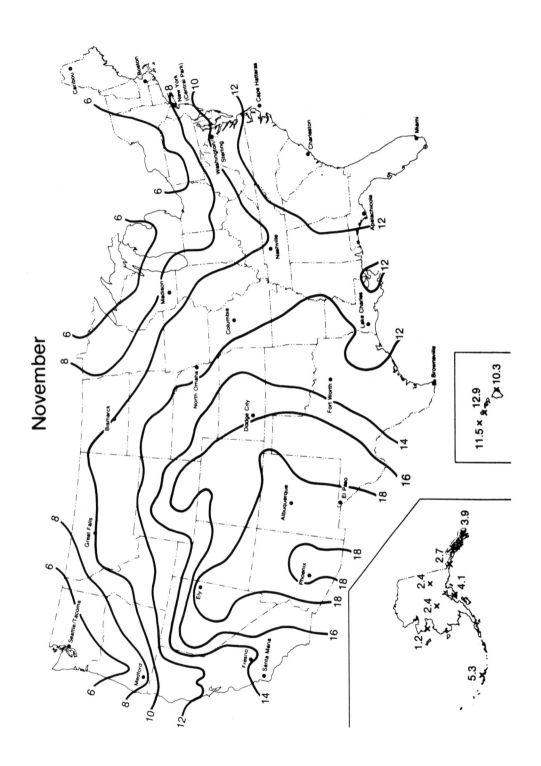

November

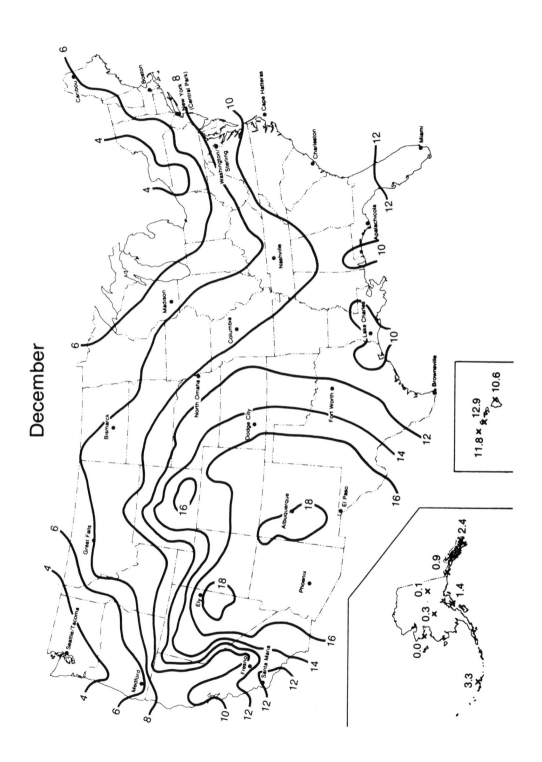

December

MAP 3.

Average Daily Global Solar Radiation
on a Horizontal Surface over 12 Months

Notes:

The global radiation includes direct, diffuse, and ground reflection, and allows for average cloud cover, altitude, and any other major climatic effects prevailing at the stations obtaining the data. Global radiation is most appropriate for calculations for flat surface collectors. The values given constitute the daily total, averaged for the month. Daily values were summed from hourly measurements. This data would be useful for glazed roofs that are nearly horizontal.

The information in these maps is a recent large-scale compilation of available solar energy measurements and calculations. Good field measurements have been made at only 26 stations for about 23 years. Models have been refined to estimate radiation at 222 more stations with proven accuracy so that the solar resources over the entire United States can be described. Prior tables and maps of insolation are expected to be less accurate and do not take into account many, if any, climate variables.

The contours in megajoules per square meter (MJ/m^2) can be converted to Btus per square foot by multiplying values by 88.11.

Maps are from *Solar Radiation Energy Resource Atlas of the United States* prepared by the Solar Energy Research Institute.

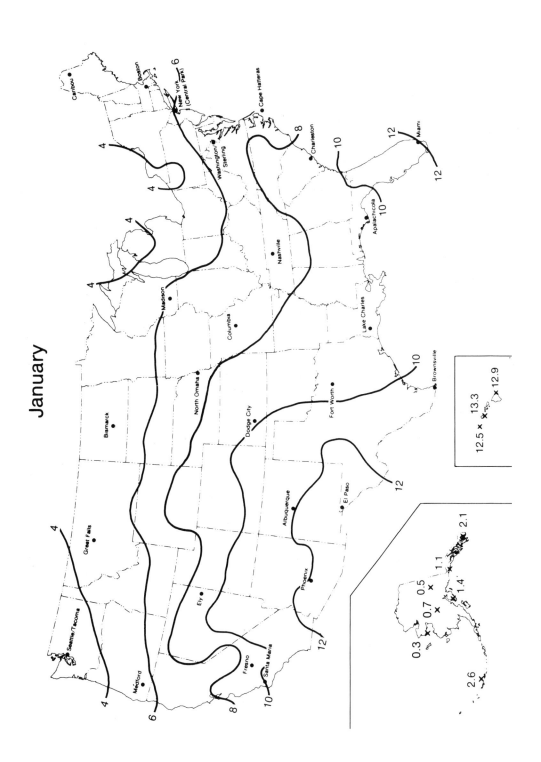

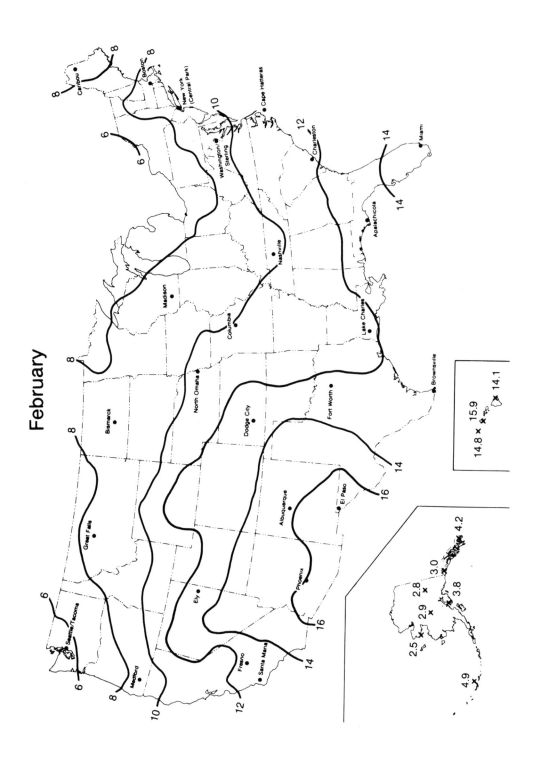

February

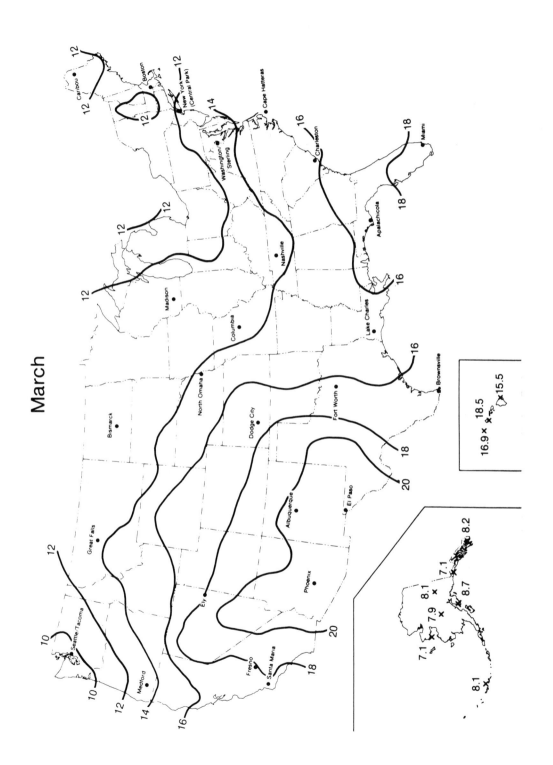

March

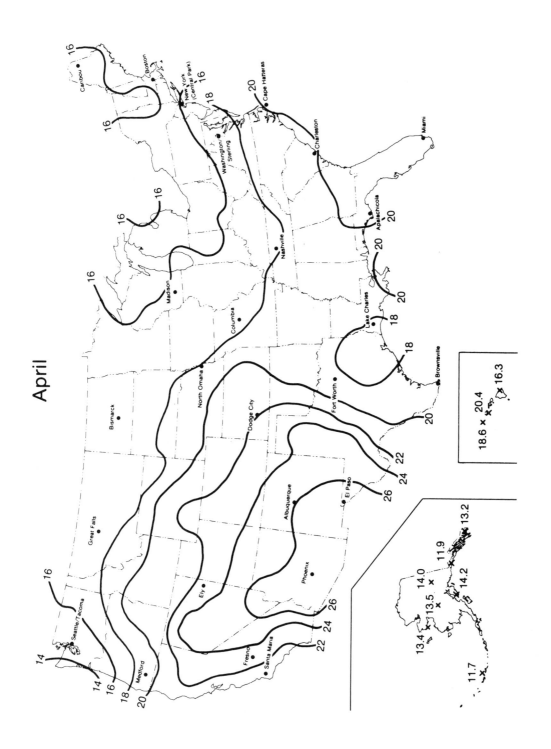

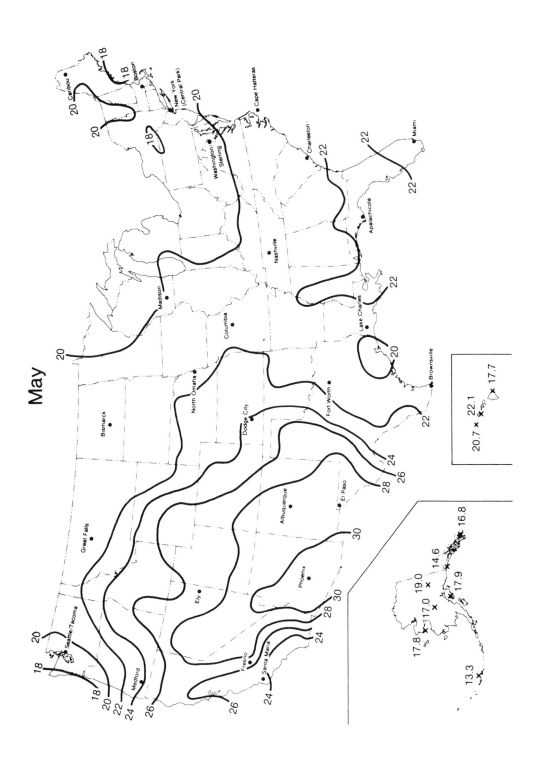

May

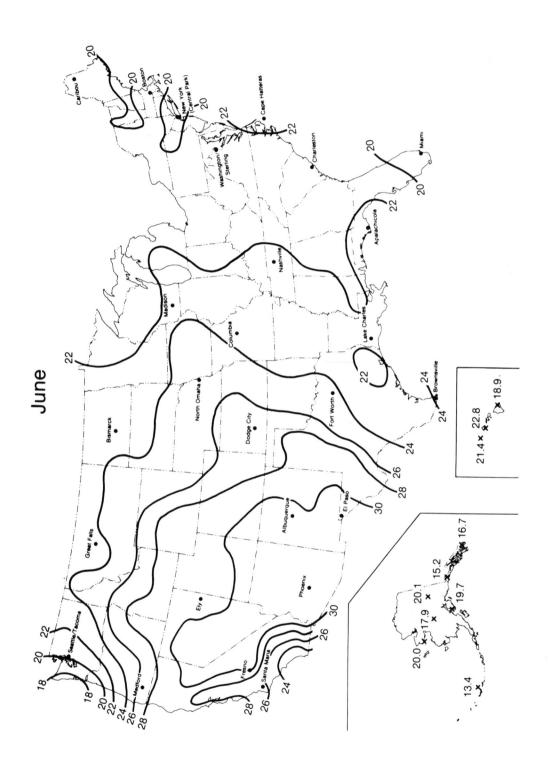

June

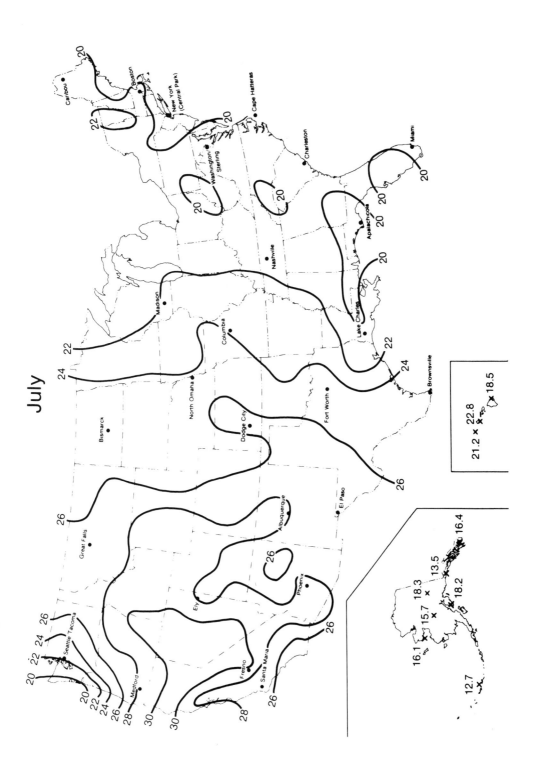

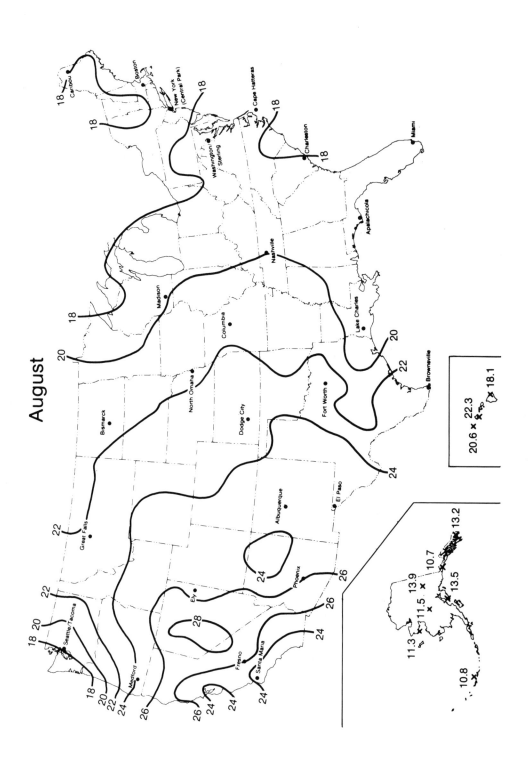

August

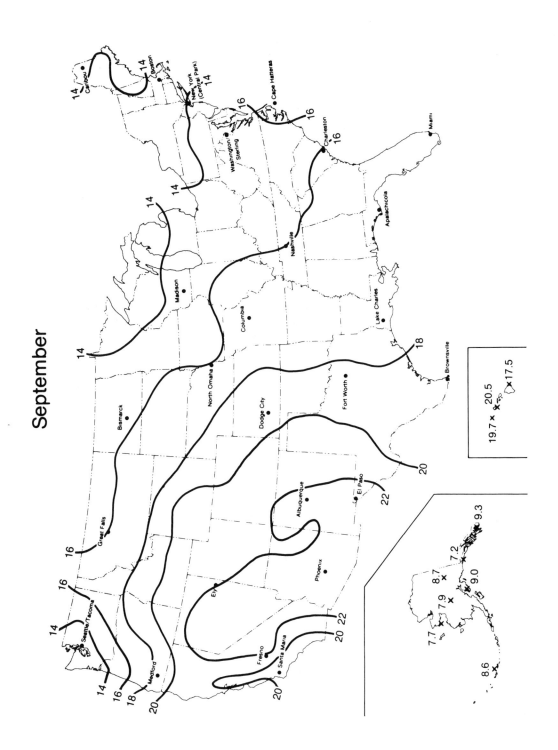

September

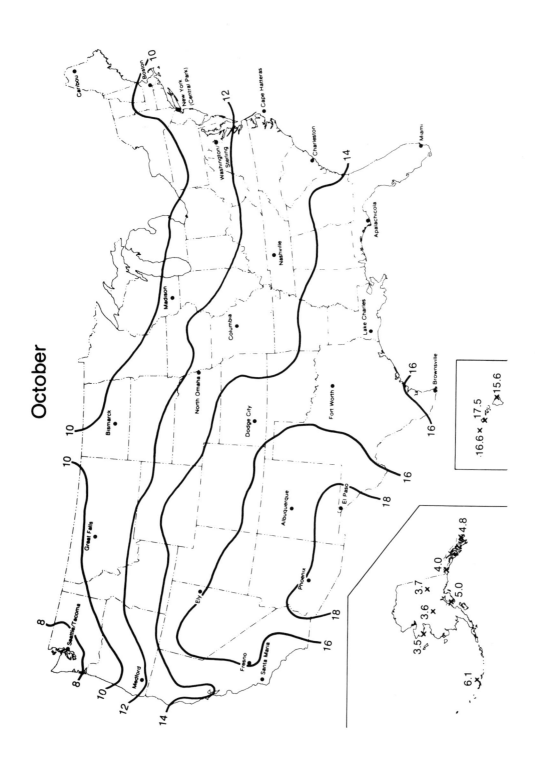

October

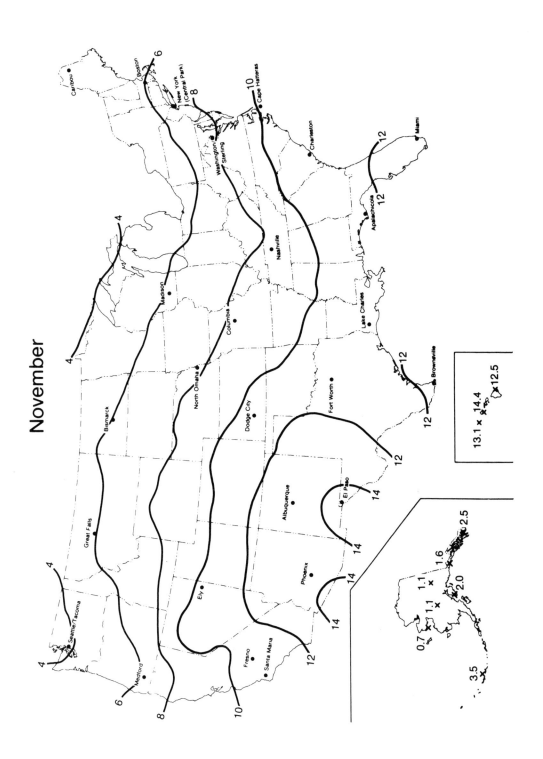

November

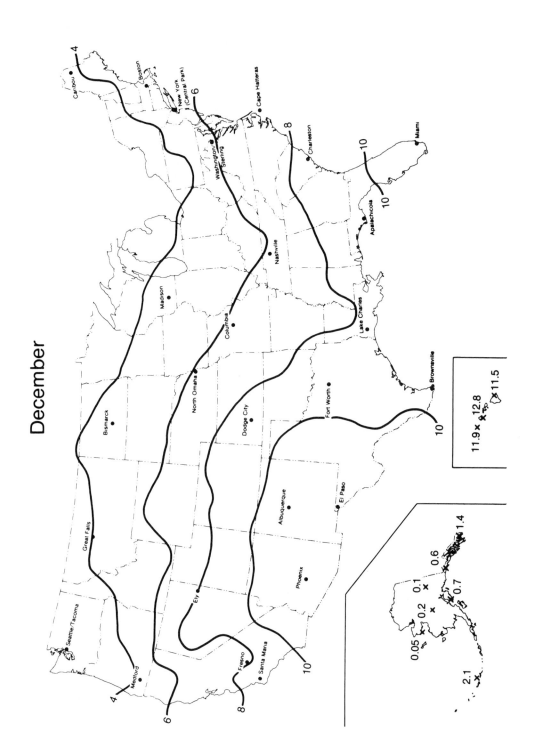

December

MAP 4.

Mean Total Hours of Sun, Annual

Notes:

This map is provided as an alternative means of determining how sunny a particular locality is. Average cloudiness is included in the data. Monthly maps are also available.

This map is from *Climatic Atlas of the United States*, National Oceanic and Atmospheric Administration (former Environmental Science Services Administration). This information is in the public domain.

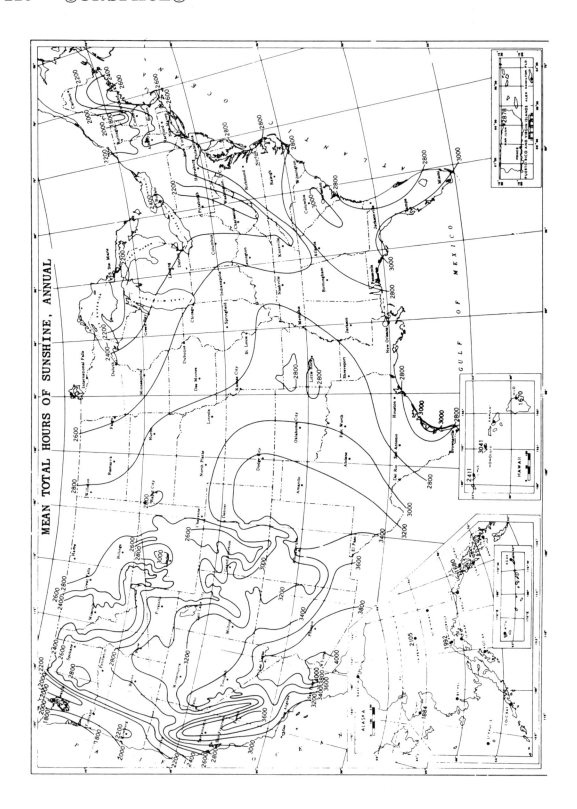

MEAN TOTAL HOURS OF SUNSHINE, ANNUAL

MAP 5.

Normal Total Heating Degree Days, Annual

Notes:

The contour values give the annual total heating-degree days, which is the number of days times the number of degrees below 65° F for each day. Thus, if the indoor temperature were regulated at 65° F, this information would assist in finding how much heat would be needed. (See Chapters 2 and 3.) Monthly maps are also available.

Rough estimates of the requirement for heating-degree days can be made for other indoor temperatures. For example, suppose the indoor temperature is 60° F and there are 100 days when the outdoor temperature averages lower than this. Then there are 5 × 100 = 500 less degree days.

This map is from *Climatic Atlas of the United States*, National Oceanic and Atmospheric Administration (former Environmental Science Services Administration).

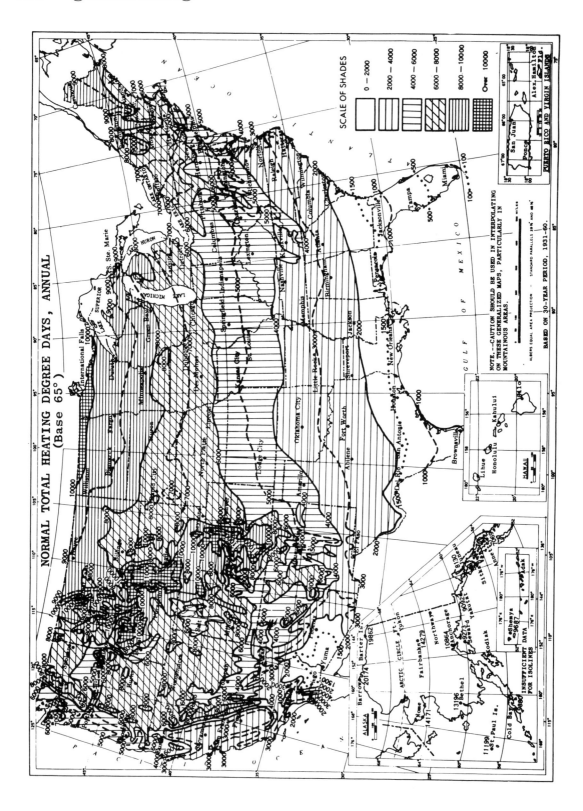

NORMAL TOTAL HEATING DEGREE DAYS, ANNUAL
(Base 65°)

CHART 1

Sunpath Charts for Mid-Latitudes

Notes:

These charts are graphs of the solar position in altitude and azimuth as listed in the insolation tables. They show many aspects of the apparent motion of the sun in the sky over the day and over the year. The exact path is shown for day 21 of each month.

The location and solar time of sunrise and sunset at any time of year is shown along the bottom axis (zero altitude position). The locations vary little with latitude.

The height of the sun at solar noon in winter and summer is easily read. This height varies significantly with latitude, however, as can be seen by comparing the three charts, and would better be calculated from a particular latitude.

The rate at which the sun climbs into the sky and the hours of high and intense sun are shown graphically. The rate at which daytime lengthens and shortens at various times of the year is also indicated. Of particular importance is the substantial number of months over which the sun is very low in northern latitudes.

The sunpath chart can be compared with the view from an actual site to determine where obstacles to winter sun are. Estimating levelness and angles is difficult without instruments, however. Sunpath charts are reprinted by permission of National Center for Appropriate Technology, Butte, MT.

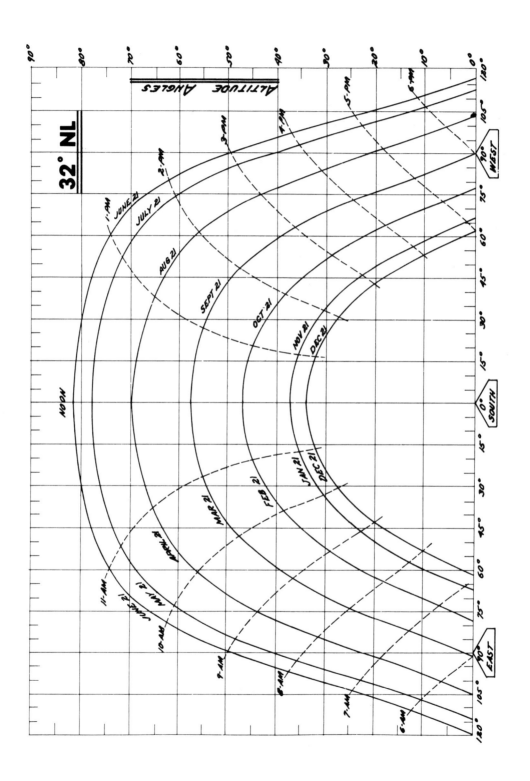

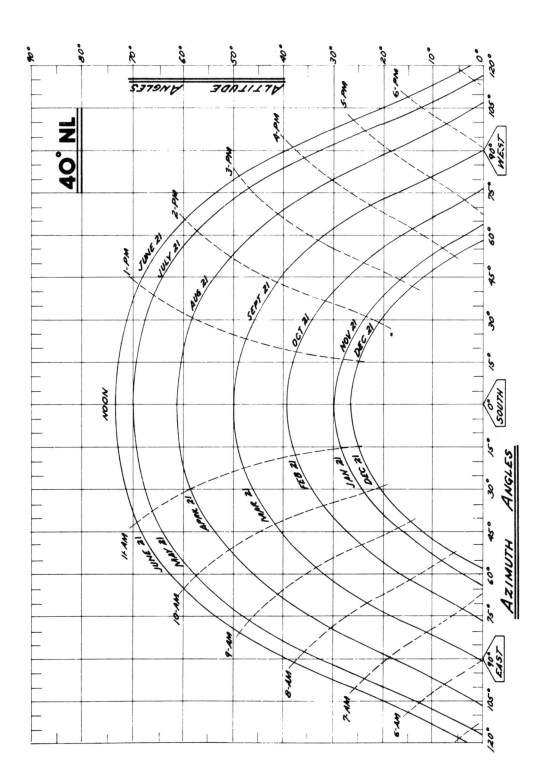

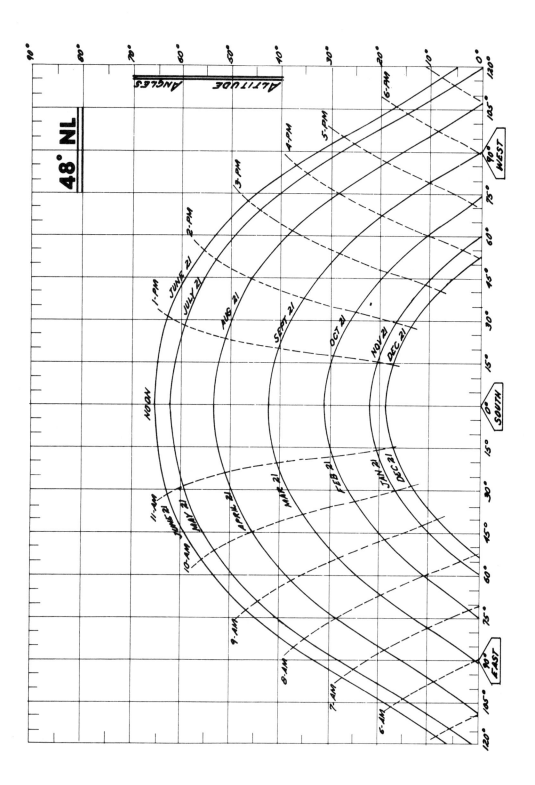

References

YOU ARE URGED TO browse among the book and article titles, manuals, and other resources given here to identify those of interest, then to find which are available in local libraries and stores. In addition to these and other books and publications, you can obtain information from some state and local agencies that assist the public with energy conservation and solar energy utilization. The books and articles also will lead you to more specialized books. Some relevant catalogs also are listed, as well as a toll-free telephone resource on sunspaces.

Magazines and journals such as *Solar Age* (renamed *Progressive Builder* in Aug 1986), *New Shelter* (renamed *Practical Homeowner* in Sep 1986), *Home Mechanix*, *Popular Mechanics*, *Popular Science*, *Handyman*, *Home Resource*, *Home*, *Metropolitan Home*, *House Beautiful*, *House and Garden*, *Better Homes and Gardens*, *Organic Gardening*, *Mother Earth News*, *Fine Homebuilding*, *Harrowsmith*, and *Greenhouses for Living* (annual) have various amounts of coverage on sunspaces, with pictures of sunspace ideas, updated information, descriptions of new materials, recently uncovered problems with methods and materials, and current lists of suppliers.

The general content, emphasis, and level of many books and articles is indicated by code letters at the end of the listing. Other notes are added as needed.

- **d:** design principles
- **c:** practical construction (for the subject matter covered)
- **e:** pictorial examples of sunspaces/greenhouses
- **g:** growing plants
- **t:** technically advanced

BOOKS

Climatic Atlas of the United States, 1968, Environmental Sciences Service Admin./NOAA/Dept. of Commerce. Mostly maps.

Fundamentals of Solar Heating, 1978, DOE/Dept. of Commerce. General principles; active air and water systems. dt

Greenhouse Gardening, 1976, Sunset Books. g

Moisture and Home Energy Conservation: How to Detect, Solve, and Avoid Related Problems, 1983, U.S. Government Printing Office (202-783-3238). dc

Passive Design: It's a Natural, 1980, U.S. Government Printing Office (202-783-3238). d

Passive Solar Construction Handbook, 1981, U.S. Government Printing Office (202-783-3238). dc

Solar Dwelling Concepts, 1976, HUD/U.S. Government Printing Office. Ideas only, including sunspaces. de

Solar Greenhouses and Sunspaces: Lessons Learned, 1984, National Center for Appropriate Technology, Butte, MT. Questions and answers on problems solved from experience. dc

Solar Heating and Cooling of Residential Buildings: Design of Systems, 1980, Dept. of Commerce. General principles; active air and water systems. td

Solar Remodeling: Passive Heating and Cooling, 1982, Sunset Books. de

Solar Radiation Energy Resource Atlas of the United States, 1981, SERI/DOE. All maps and graphs. Technical appendix.

Adams, Robert W. *Adding Solar Heat to Your Home*, 1979, TAB BOOKS #1196. General principles; active air and water systems; no sunspaces. dc

Alward, Ron, and Andy Shapiro. *Low-Cost Passive Solar Greenhouses: A Design and Construction Guide*, 1980, National Center for Appropriate Technology, Butte, MT or Charles Scribners & Sons. dcge

Anderson, Bruce. *The Solar Home Book*, 1976, Cheshire Books. 1986 edition, Brick House. de

Anderson, Bruce, and Malcolm Wells. *Passive Solar Energy*, 1981, Brick House. dce

Antolini, Holly, ed. *Sunset Homeowner's Guide to Solar Heating*, 1978, Lane. Includes sunspaces. dce

Booth, Don, et al. *Sun/Earth Buffering and Superinsulation*, 1983, Community Builders, Canterbury, NH. Includes sunspaces. dce

Butti, Ken, and John Perlin. *A Golden Thread: 2500 Years of Solar Architecture and Technology*, 1980, Van Nostrand Reinhold/Cheshire. Historical only. g

Clegg, Peter, and Derry Watkins. *The Complete Greenhouse Book: Building and Using Greenhouses from Cold Frames to Solar Structures*, 1978, Garden Way. dcg

Cook, Jeffrey. *Award Winning Passive Solar Designs*, 1984, McGraw-Hill. Includes some sunspaces and greenhouses. e

Dezettel, Louis. *Masonry: Vol. 1 Concrete*, 1972, Audel.

Fontanetta, John, and Al Heller. *Building and Using a Solar Heated Geodesic Greenhouse*, 1979, Garden Way. Very low cost project. dc

Geery, Daniel. *Solar Greenhouses: Underground*, 1982, TAB BOOKS #1272. dcg

Gropp, Louis. *Solar Houses: 48 Energy Saving Designs*, 1978, Random House. Includes some sunspaces and greenhouses. e

Hibschman, Dan. *Your Affordable Solar Home*, 1983, Sierra Club. Six houses, some with sunspaces. de

Hotton, Peter. *So You Want to Build an Energy-Efficient Addition*, 1983, Little Brown. Sunspaces. c

Kohlmeier, Georg, and Barna von Sartory. *House of Glass: A Nineteenth Century Building Type*. 1986, MIT Press. Many large European greenhouses.

Langdon, William K. *Movable Insulation: A Guide to Reducing Heating and Cooling Losses Through the Windows in Your Home*, 1980, Rodale Press. Very thorough and applicable to any sunspace/greenhouse. dc

Mazria, Edward. *The Passive Solar Energy Book*, 1979, Rodale Press. Mostly sunspaces and greenhouses. dcg

McCullagh, James, ed. *The Solar Greenhouse*, 1978, Rodale Press. dceg

Mohr, Merily. *Sunwings: The Harrowsmith Guide to Solar Addition Architecture*, 1985, Camden House, Ontario. de

Olkowski, Helga, Bill Olkowski, et al. *The Integral Urban House*, 1979, Sierra Club. Much broader than greenhouses.

Schepp, Brad, and Stephen M., Hastie. *The Complete Passive Solar Home Book*, 1985, TAB BOOKS #1657. Includes sunspaces and a large recent resource list. dce

Shurcliff, William. *Solar Heated Buildings*, 1978, Brick House. e

———. *Thermal Shutters and Shades*, 1977, Brick House. For windows and applicable to sunspaces. c

Skurka, Norma and Jon, Naar. *Design for a Limited Planet*, 1976, Ballantine. e

Smith, Charles. *Third Annual Conference on Solar Energy for Heating of Greenhouses and Greenhouse-Residential Combinations*, 1978, DOE/USGPO. tdcg

Smith, Shane. *The Bountiful Solar Greenhouse: A Guide to Year-Round Food Production*, 1982, John Muir, Santa Fe, NM. g

Tamami, Kusuda, and K. Ishii. *Hourly Solar Radiation Data for Vertical and Horizontal Surfaces on Average Days in the U.S. and Canada*, 1977, Dept. of Commerce. Tables for selected cities only.

Twitchell, Mary. *Solar Projects for Under $500*, 1985, Garden Way. Includes a greenhouse. dce

Watson, Donald. *Designing and Building a Solar House*, 1985, Garden Way. dce

Wolfe, Delores. *Growing Food in Solar Greenhouses*, 1981, Doubleday. Very complete.

Wolfe, R., ed. *Rodale's Solar Growing Frame*, 1980, Rodale Press. Variety of cold frames/hotbeds.

Yanda, Bill, and Rick Fisher. *The Food and Heat Producing Solar Greenhouse: Design, Construction, Operation*, 1980, John Muir, Santa Fe, NM. dceg

ARTICLES

Some very useful one-page nontechnical summaries of tests of pertinent materials are included in the articles at the beginning of this list.

"Comparing Window Thermal Barriers," *Solar Age*, Aug 1984. Wide variety.

"Fabrics and the Sun," *Solar Age*, May 1986. Effects on color, strength, etc.

"Floor Coverings and Heat Storage," *Solar Age*, Sep 1984. Vinyls and carpet.

"A House for All Seasons," *New Shelter*, Feb 1986. Guide to the PBS TV series plus directory of information sources, books, schools, manufacturers of windows, doors, sunspaces, and insulating shades.

"Sizzling Slabs," *Progressive Builder*, Dec 1986. Coloring and stamping concrete floors, with sources.

"Sunspace Heat-Blockers," *Solar Age*, May 1985. Shading, shades, ventilation.

"Test Results on Window Insulators," *Solar Age*, Oct 1984. Curtains, quilts.

"Which Way Is True South?" *Solar Age*, Jul 1983. Compass correction.

Bliss, Steve. "Warm Wraps for Cold Windows," *Solar Age*, Jun 1983. Many types of window insulation, with directory of manufacturers.

Bregman, Lillian. "Pools for Fitness," *New Shelter*, Aug 1985. Lap pools.

Canine, Craig. "Summer in the Sunspace," *New Shelter*, Aug 1985. Keeping a sunspace cool in summer in the south—eight strategies.

Carter, Joe. "Traditional and Thoroughly Modern," *New Shelter*, Mar 1985. Large sunspace on Pam Dawber's house.

Cooper, Nancy. "Sunlight in a Package," *Home Mechanix*, Nov 1986. 10 sunspace manufacturers described.

Cox, Jeff. "A House of Light," *New Shelter*, Mar 1986. Example of house with interesting sunspace.

Crosbie, Michael J. "Let the Sun Shine In," *New Shelter*, Aug 1986. Screened porch converted to sunspace.

Germer, Jerry. "The Sunspace Guide," *Solar Age*, May 1985. Includes descriptions of 29 manufacturers of sunspaces.

____. "Sunspace Planning Basics," *Progressive Builder*, Aug 1986. Short.

____. "What's New in Sunspaces," *Progressive Builder*, Aug 1986. Hints and a directory of manufacturers.

Haupert, David, and CarolAnn Shindelar. "Add a Solar Greenhouse," *Better Homes and Gardens*, May 1980. Examples of sunspaces in color.

Ingersoll, John. "America's Favorite Addition: Where People, Plants, Heat, and Light Come Together," *Home Mechanix*, Nov 1986. On sunspaces.

Jones, Robert, and Robert, McFarland. "The Last Word in Sunspaces," *Solar Age*, Jun 1984. Well, almost the last word; general summary of practical design points.

Kihlstedt, Folke. "Crystal Palace," *Scientific American*, Oct 1984. 1850 London glass building.

Lafavore, Michael. "Dining in the Sun," *New Shelter*, Aug 1985. Sunspace as dining room.

Lau, Andrew. "How to Design Fixed Overhangs," *Solar Age*, Feb 1983. For shading.

Lunde, Peter J. "Realistic Overhangs," *Solar Age*, Nov 1985. For shading.

____. "Sizing Overhangs," *Solar Age*, Oct 1985. For shading.

Poole, Catherine M. "Subtly Solar," *New Shelter*, Feb 1986. House with sunspace.

Reed, John. "Timber Framing," *Home Resource*, Apr/May 1986. See also other related articles on this method adaptable to sunspace construction.

Sands, Jon. "The Meaning of Percent Sunshine," *Solar Age*, May 1983. Review of insolation measuring.

Silverstein, S.D. "Effect of Infrared Transparency on the Heat Transfer through Windows: A Clarification of the Greenhouse Effect," *Science*, 16 Jul 1976. Semitechnical.

Smith, Rich. "Sun Blockers," *New Shelter*, Aug 1985. Awnings on sunspace.

Spears, John W. "A New Slant in Sunspace Design," *Solar Age*, Sep 1983. Identifies problems with sloped glazing.

Stong, C.L. "Among Other Things a Greenhouse Shade that Recreates the Lighting of the Tropics," *Scientific American*, Jul 1975. dc

TenWolde, Anton, and Jane Suleski. "Controlling Moisture in Houses," *Solar Age*,

Jan 1984. Broad, including sunspaces.

Trombe, F., et al. "Concrete Walls to Collect and Hold Heat," *Solar Age*, Aug 1977. Original, somewhat technical report on the Trombe wall.

Wilson, Alex. "A Buyer's Guide to Prefab Sunspaces," *Practical Homeowner*, Oct 1986. Summary of many considerations and list of manufacturers.

MANUALS

All-Weather Wood Foundation: APA Design/Construction Guide, 1984, American Plywood Association, Tacoma, WA. For greenwood. tdc

All-Weather Wood Foundation System: Design, Fabrication, Installation, 1982, National Forest Products Assn, Washington, DC. For greenwood. tdc

Dwelling Construction under the Uniform Building Code, 1979, ICBO, Whittier, CA. Partly technical. dc

Finishing Concrete Slabs, Exposed Aggregate, Patterns, and Colors, Portland Cement Association, Skokie, IL.

House Beautiful's Building Manual, Spring 1986, Hearst Corp. Many sunspaces. ce

Wood Frame Design, 1985, Western Wood Products Assn., Portland, OR. Free. Partly technical. dc

CATALOGS

For sources of products, see also books and articles that list sources.

Energy Products Specifications Guide, SolarVision, Inc., Harrisville, NH, 03450. Detailed and exhaustive; with sources; no pictures.

Grainger's catalog. Every blower, fan, vent, and control imaginable; about 200 locations—see your local telephone book.

Solar Components Catalog, Solar Components Corp., Manchester, NH, 03105.

RESOURCE

National Appropriate Technology Assistance Service
A telephone hotline for help with greenhouses, sunspaces, and other small-scale conservation and renewable energy applications.
Highly technical help as well as help with the basics.
1-800-428-2525.
NATAS, P.O. Box 2525, Butte, MT 59702

Index

Other Bestsellers From TAB

☐ **MAJOR HOME APPLIANCES: A Common Sense Repair Manual—Rains**

Prolong the life and efficiency of your major appliances . . . save hundreds of dollars in appliance servicing and repair costs . . . eliminate the inconvenience of having an appliance quit just when you need it most *and* the frustration of having to wait days, even weeks, until you can get a serviceman in to repair it! With the help and advice of service professional Darell L. Rains, even the most inexperienced home handyman can easily keep any major appliances working at top efficiency year after year. 160 pp., 387 illus., Large Format (7″ × 10″).

Paper $14.95   **Hard $21.95**
Book No. 2747

☐ **THE COMPLETE BOOK OF BATHROOMS—Ramsey and Self**

Simple redecorating tricks . . . remodeling advice . . . plumbing techniques . . . it's all here. Find literally hundreds of photographs, drawings, and floorplans to help you decide exactly what kind of remodeling project you'd like to undertake; plus, step-by-step directions for accomplishing your remodeling goals. It's all designed to save you time and money on your bathroom renovations! 368 pp., 474 illus. 7″ × 10″.

Paper $15.95   **Book No. 2708**

☐ **ROOFING THE RIGHT WAY—A Step-By-Step Guide for the Homeowner—Steve Bolt**

If you're faced with having to replace your roof because of hidden leaks, torn or missing shingles, or simply worn roofing that makes your whole house look shabby and run down . . . don't assume that you'll have to take out another mortgage to pay for the project. The fact is, *almost anyone can install a new or replacement roof easily and at amazingly low cost compared with professional contractor prices!* All the professional techniques and step-by-step guidance you'll need is here in this complete new roofing manual written by an experienced roofing contractor. 192 pp., 217 illus. Large Format (7″ × 10″).

Paper $11.95   **Hard $19.95**
Book No. 2667

☐ **PLANNING AND BUILDING FENCES AND GATES**

This colorfully illustrated guide gives you all the expert, step-by-step guidelines and instructions you need to plan and build durable, cost-effective fences and gates. You will be able to design and construct just about any kind of fence you can think of—barbed wire, woven wire, cable wire, mesh wire, board fences, electric fences, gates, and much more! 192 pp., 356 illus. 8 1/2″ × 11″. 2-Color Throughout.

Paper $14.95   **Book No. 2643**

☐ **THE BUILDING PLAN BOOK: Complete Plans for 21 Affordable Homes—Ernie Bryant**

Here, in one impressive, well-illustrated volume, are complete building plans for a total of 21 custom-designed homes offering a full range of styles and features—efficiency dwellings, ranches, capes, two-story homes, split-levels, even duplexes. It's a collection of practical, good looking home designs that not only offer comfort, convenience, and charm but can also be built at a reasonable cost. 352 pp., 316 illus., 8 1/2″ × 11″

Paper $14.95   **Hard $24.95**
Book No. 2714

☐ **THE GARDENING IDEA BOOK**

Whether you have space for a full-space garden or only a pocket size back yard, this exciting collection of articles from *Farmstead Magazine* shows how you can grow all kinds of delicious, healthful fruits and vegetables. Here's expert advice and guidance that's guaranteed to make your garden more productive, easier to take care of, and less expensive! 208 pp., illustrated.

Paper $10.95   **Book No. 2684**

☐ **ALL ABOUT LAMPS; CONSTRUCTION, REPAIR AND RESTORATION—Coggins**

You'll find step-by-step directions for making a wall lamp or a hanging lamp from wood, novelty lamps from PVC plumbing pipe, and designer lamps from acrylic or polyester resins. Shade projects range from needlepoint and fabric models to globes, balls, and tubular forms. There are suggestions for advanced projects, using salvaged and low-cost materials, and more! 192 pp., 196 illus. 7″ × 10″.

Paper $16.95   **Hard $24.95**
Book No. 2658

☐ **101 PROJECTS, PLANS AND IDEAS FOR THE HIGH-TECH HOUSEHOLD**

If you're looking for decorative effects, you'll be impressed with the number of projects that have been included. And electronics hobbyists will be amazed at the array of projects—all of them with clear building instructions, schematics, and construction drawings. You'll also find exciting ways to use your microcomputer as a key decorative element in your high-tech atmosphere. 352 pp., 176 illus. 7″ × 10″.

Paper $16.95   **Book No. 2642**

Other Bestsellers From TAB